HC

30

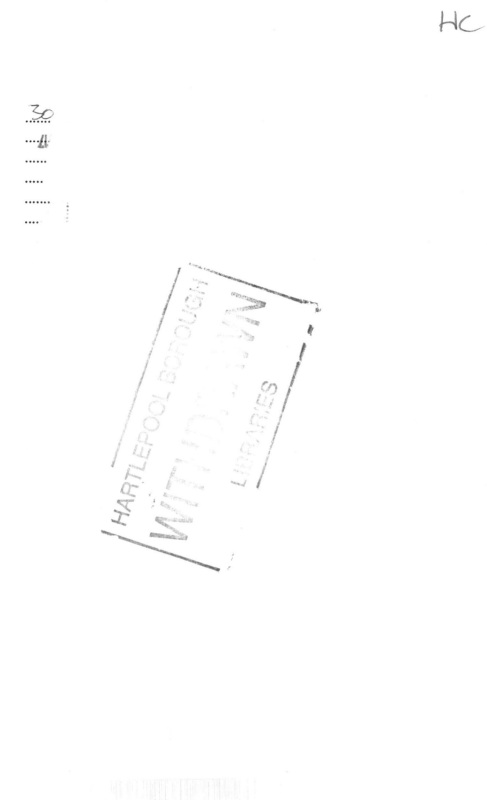

D0418883

TOMORROW YOU DIE

TOMORROW YOU DIE

The Astonishing Survival Story of a Second World War Prisoner of the Japanese

ANDY COOGAN

ISIS

LARGE PRINT

Oxford

Copyright © Andy Coogan and Graham Ogilvy, 2012

First published in Great Britain 2012
by
Mainstream Publishing Company (Edinburgh) Ltd.

Published in Large Print 2013 by ISIS Publishing Ltd.,
7 Centremead, Osney Mead, Oxford OX2 0ES
by arrangement with
Mainstream Publishing Company (Edinburgh) Ltd.

All rights reserved

The moral right of the author has been asserted

CIP data is available for this title from the British Library

ISBN 978–0–7531–5336–9 (hb)
ISBN 978–0–7531–5337–6 (pb)

Printed and bound in Great Britain by
T. J. International Ltd., Padstow, Cornwall

To the fine people of the Gorbals and my comrades who never made it home.

And to my dear wife Myra, who helped me learn to forgive, even though I'll never forget.

ACKNOWLEDGEMENTS

I am grateful to the many people who encouraged me to write the truth of what happened in the Far East. Thanks to Graham Ogilvy, senior writer at Scottish News Agency, our agent Stan at Jenny Brown Associates and Bill Campbell at Mainstream, who worked together to make this book happen.

Neil Mudie has spent many hours patiently recording my memories, Lesley Wilson transcribed notes and Dave Martin assisted with photographs.

Thanks to Agnes Dougan and Campbell Thomson, who have worked tirelessly to reunite veterans and ensure that the proud name of the Lanarkshire Yeomanry is not forgotten. Michael Hurst, who has spent many years researching the history of the POW camps in Taiwan, has helped answer many queries about the war. Thanks to Anne Wheeler for photographs of her father Major Ben Wheeler and to Jim Gilchrist and Billy Kay, who have recorded interviews and shown so much interest.

Thanks to Eric Martindale, who helped with the family history, and Reverend Paul Grant for his wonderful address.

I would like to say a special thanks to my dear wife Myra, my son Andy and daughter Jean and every one of my seven wonderful grandchildren for their love and support. Last, but not least, I would like to thank my daughter Christine, whose encouragement and support at every stage of this book has made it possible.

CONTENTS

INTRODUCTION

I gave a lot of thought to writing this book, wondering if it was the right thing to do. I do not want to upset my family, or the families of other veterans. Like so many of my comrades who made it back, I kept quiet about what really happened in the Far East during the bloody Battle of Malaya and the Fall of Singapore. As we sailed home over the Atlantic Ocean, we spoke about our experiences and thought people would just never believe us, and, like many captured British servicemen, I was ordered to sign an undertaking to the British government that I would never talk about my time as a prisoner or describe the awful atomic wasteland of Nagasaki. Anyway, everyone had a war story to tell, folk had had enough and wanted to get on with their lives. But as time passed by, so many things came back to me, as clear as anything, and would stay with me all day and all night. When I was in the camps, I would dream of home, wake up and still be in the camp. When I got home, I would dream I was in the camp, then wake up and find myself in the Gorbals. This happened for many years.

My own experiences of working as a slave in the Kinkaseki copper mine even when I had gone blind, of twice being forced to dig my own grave, being subjected to a mock execution, endless beatings and two hell-ship voyages, have been painful to recall. It's hard to believe that human beings could do what they did to young, decent, fit men in their prime. Japan did not recognise the Geneva Convention, and as prisoners, then slaves, we had no human rights or protection from our brutal jailers. Three per cent of prisoners died in the stalags of Germany but over thirty per cent of prisoners died in the camps run by the Japanese. We lived in a constant state of terror. There were no Red Cross parcels and very, very few messages from the outside world. Our captors despised us for having surrendered. Under the bushido code, Japanese warriors were supposed to commit suicide, though many of our jailers did ultimately surrender and then face war-crimes trials.

When we returned to Britain in 1945, the prisoners from the Far East served as an embarrassing reminder of Britain's biggest-ever military disaster — the Fall of Singapore. The war in the Far East was a sideshow to the battles in Europe. In 1942, we were a forgotten army, and if it had not been for the efforts of the Far East Prisoners of War Association our sufferings as prisoners may have been forgotten too.

I heard that many men felt ashamed for having been part of a surrender. But my comrades in the Lanarkshire Yeomanry fought to the bitter end. We always believed that we had "ceased fire" and not surrendered. We were let down by our leaders, who made such a mess of it, and let down again when we returned home with broken bodies and broken minds.

Looking back, most returning prisoners had a bad time. There was no understanding of combat stress and little awareness of the extreme nature of our ordeal. Some men committed suicide on their return and others tried to drown their sorrows with alcohol. All of us suffered from nightmares — I still do.

I was Called to Colours in May 1940 and formally released six years later, in June 1946, but I was one of the lucky ones. I was raised the right way, brought up with stories, music and humour in a loving family and among the good people of the Gorbals. My mates at the Maryhill Harriers instilled a love of running and helped me rebuild my life. I was fortunate to meet my wife Myra and have a family of my own. But above all it was the closeknit camaraderie and support of my fellow prisoners — Father Richard Kennedy, Dr Peter Seed and the men of the Lanarkshire Yeomanry — that saved my life. We cared for each other with a devotion and tenderness that belied our tough backgrounds as working-class Glaswegians and Lanarkshire lads.

A few years ago, I was privileged to attend a reunion of the Lanarkshire Yeomanry organised by Agnes Dougan and Campbell Thomson of the Lanarkshire Yeomanry Group. Agnes's father, John McEwan, also survived the Kinkaseki mine. What a day that was, meeting my old comrades Benny Gough, Tarn Hannah, Tarn Laird, John Marshall, David Paton and Pat Campbell for the first time in nearly 70 years. Some of them I hadn't seen since we were separated in India. We got answers to questions that had been troubling us for years — who got back, what became of everyone. Tarn Hannah had been puzzling for 70 years about how Bella Divers got his name — well, I was able to tell him! I could never work out where the small pieces of rice bread in Changi came from, and 70 years later I found out. Benny Gough, a baker to trade, described how he hammered out an oven from an oil drum and baked a form of bread using rice water. David Paton, who grew up in Hamilton and who said he was "a gey raw lad at that", was just 20 years old when he was captured and ended up in Burma. One man remembered how he was starving and stole two sweet potatoes, one for him and one for his mate: "For 65 years, I've lived with the guilt of taking the biggest potato. I should've halved them both and taken half each." We were citizen soldiers, ordinary men leading ordinary lives, until we found ourselves fighting in the jungle and learning Japanese at the end of a bayonet.

But we had plenty laughs that day, too. When one of us shouted, "Ah'm Sergeant Major Flaherty . . ." there was a roar from the rest, "and Ah'm Mrs Flaherty's son!" We remembered the kindnesses from Japanese civilians, the Gurkhas who were very clever soldiers — you always felt safe if they were about — and the poor Indians who had a terrible time. I'll never forget the friendly Americans in Okinawa, who would not allow us to carry our bags.

As we exchanged stories, the memories came flooding back, and I could see that it was important to tell my story. It would be a testament to the loyalty and

4

bravery of the men of the Lanarkshire Yeomanry, who stuck together in the most terrible circumstances.

To begin with, I did not want my grandchildren to read this book. But now I believe it is important that their generation should learn from the mistakes of mine. Many of my good friends endured terrible deaths. I could never let my family go through that, never.

I have gone on to live a long and fulfilled life. Competing as a runner has given me great pleasure, but passing on my love for the sport through coaching young athletes, sometimes generations of the same family, has been just as rewarding. Carrying the Olympic Torch at the age of 95 in the run-up to the 2012 Olympics was a very special day. I was fortunate to have my wife Myra, my family and so many friends beside me to enjoy it. As I check this manuscript one last time, I can't believe the man in this book is me. But it is me. And this is my story.

CHAPTER ONE

Gorbals Boy

"On your knees!" Lieutenant Koji Tamaki's broad features creased into a twisted sneer of hatred and contempt as his black moustache drew back in a vicious snarl.

"Oh, Christ! This is it," I thought. I had survived a *banzai* charge, bombs and flying bullets during the bloody Battle of Malaya and the fall of Singapore. I had come through a hell-ship voyage and the forced march to the Kinkaseki death mine, where we slaved and starved and withered and died. Now my luck had run out, and as I sank to the parched Formosan soil I felt warm water run down the inside of my legs.

I looked up at Tamaki in mute appeal. He was short and squat but towered above me now as he drew his samurai sword and held the glinting steel aloft in the tropical sun.

"Say . . . goodbye . . . to . . . your . . . friends," he drawled.

As the ragged skeletons behind me found their voices, I was suddenly transported out of that terrible camp. They say a man's life flashes before him as he faces death and, as my comrades shouted out for mercy in accents honed in Australia, America, England, Scotland and Holland, my mind raced back in time. I saw again the kindly faces of my mother and father and the smiles of my brothers and sister. At last I

7

had escaped the Japanese Imperial Army. I was back in the streets of my beloved Glasgow.

I was sitting up on the cart beside my dad. Just Dad, myself and Paddy the horse — the three of us travelling slowly out of Glasgow, on our way to sell coal to people in Bishopbriggs. Dad would hum Irish tunes to the rhythm of Paddy's clip-clopping and tell me thrilling tales about being a boy in the little Irish fishing village of Annagassan and yarns of how he went to sea with his father and brothers.

My mother Agnes and father Andrew met on the Marquis of Bute's estate at Mount Stuart on the lovely Isle of Bute where Mum worked as a dairymaid and Dad was an agricultural worker. They married in 1916, the year of the Battle of the Somme and the Easter Rising. Conscription had begun that year, and not long after they married my father was ordered into the Dublin Fusiliers. Later, he was posted to the Merchant Navy, which was running the U-boat blockade. My mother returned to Glasgow to be near her family and to give birth to their first child. I was born on April Fool's Day 1917 in a soot-stained Victorian tenement on the very fringes of Glasgow where fresh farmland fields met the sprawling slums of the second city of the Empire.

The crumbling tenement was the last building on the road to Bishopbriggs, and, as home to the Donnellys and the Connollys, the Dougans and the Coogans, 799 Springburn Road rejoiced in the nickname of "Paddy's Mansions". It had been home to Irish immigrants for decades. Even the Post Office recognised the name and postcards arrived from distant lands addressed simply to "Paddy's Mansions", Glasgow. We children felt we were at the centre of the world.

I can only just remember my father coming back from the First World War — "the war to end all wars". He had twice been torpedoed but he never spoke about what had happened to him.

My mother was hard-working and very enterprising. She was about 5 ft 8 in. and was lightly built with light-brown hair. Her often-repeated advice to us kids was: "Always be humble. You never know what is ahead of you." After I was born, she worked as a milkmaid on the farm next to our house and I would have a seed-sowing basket lined with straw as a cradle. She did the same thing with my sister when she came along.

My early childhood was spent in a strange mixture of town and country. The farm was only 40 yards or so from the tenement and there were around a dozen cows in the byre. We loved it when we supped the creamy milk still warm from the cow and we would run around laughing at our frothy white moustaches. As I got older, Mum would say, "Go down and get some buttermilk for making scones, Andrew." I would return in triumph with a big can of buttermilk. I used to help Mum make butter too in a big glass bottle. She would put the milk in the bottle and I used to shake it and shake it for about half an hour until it thickened and the butter started to form. Then we would spread it on the warm thick scones she baked on the range. They were wonderful and I can taste them still.

Dad was at sea and earning very little. It was no life for a young couple. My mother wanted more children and longed for her husband to be at home with her to help bring them up. Dad would always tell Mum, "Our ship will be in soon, Aggie!"

To help make ends meet, Mum started taking in lodgers. Usually, they were young Irish lads who had come over to work in Springburn's vast locomotive works, where a quarter of the world's railway engines were produced. They were very nice lads and they were never a problem with too much drink or wild behaviour. They used to amuse themselves by playing a kind of handball, with around half a dozen of them in two teams endlessly hitting the ball off the gable end of the tenement.

We lived in two rooms with an outside toilet shared with other families and no scullery, just a sink in the room that served as kitchen, bedroom and living room. There was a recess for a hole-in-the-wall bed in the kitchen, where my mother and I slept, and there would be two, sometimes three, of the young Irish lads sleeping in the other room. We washed in the kitchen sink and called it the "jaw box", because that was where we washed our faces and "topped and tailed". I never knew the sink as anything other than the jaw box and was later surprised to learn that not everybody called it that.

We never had much in the way of furniture. There was linoleum on the floor but the walls always boasted a holy picture of Christ and a simple crucifix. We had a wee sign hanging on the door, which was very typical. It read simply: "Bless This House". The rent was not cheap at around ten shillings a week and it was always a struggle for my mother. But Paddy's Mansions was a world of wonder to me. On Sunday nights, some of the Irish boys would produce fiddles and there would be a sing-song. The kitchen floor would be cleared and there would be Irish dancing. My mother's friends Mrs Harrigan and Mrs Connolly would come up to our flat. The women, who were older than the young Irish labourers, would do all the singing, and they all had great repertoires of songs and poetry. My mother had a hearty laugh and a lovely voice, and I inherited my love of singing from her. She would always sing her favourite song, "The Soor Milk Cairt". To this day, I can hear her soft voice accompanied by one of the lodgers on the fiddle.

Oh I am a country chappie and I'm serving at
    Polnoon,
On a fairm near to Eaglesham, that fine auld-
    fashioned toon,
Whaur, wi' the milk each mornin', a little after three,
We tak the road richt merrily, my auld black horse
    and me.
Wi' her cheeks sae red and rosie, and e'en sae bonnie
    blue,
Dancin' and glancin' she pierced me through and
    through,
She fairly won ma fancy, and stole awa' ma hert,
Drivin' into Glesga on a soor milk cairt.

When I was three, Mum and Dad had an unimaginable stroke of good luck and it was a story that Mum told to her dying day. The local policeman was a chap called Martin Watters, who, like Dad, came from County Louth, the smallest county in Ireland. One day he told my dad, who was home between voyages, that he had a hot tip and said that Dad should back two horses, Polmarch and Moneyglass, as they were "dead certs". Off-course gambling was strictly illegal then but it flourished across industrial Scotland, with bookies organising an army of clandestine "runners" to collect bets from every street. They frequently paid off the local bobbies, who knew perfectly well what was going on and liked to gamble too. A couple of days later, my father was walking back from nearby Robroyston. He had been at the railway line that ran from the colliery, picking up wee bits of fallen coal for our fire — it was against the bye-laws but a lot of the poor folk did it. He was halfway home with his bag of coal when he met Martin Watters.

"Andra, did ye back these two horses I told ye about?"

"Aye, I did that."

"Well, the two of them has won. How much did ye put on them?"

"A sixpenny double!"

It was a sensational windfall and at last my mother's dreams were realised — Dad could come home from the sea. Mum bought a horse and cart for Dad. Horses were cheap because so many had come back from the war. Paddy was an Irish gyp and cost five pounds. The cart was the same price and Dad went into business as a coal merchant. Paddy was stabled in the field behind Mr McIntyre's smiddy at the end of our tenement building, and they kept the cart there too. Mum helped Dad when she could. In the mornings, she would tell him, "You just have your breakfast, Andy, and I'll go down and get Paddy into the harness."

Often, Dad would sit me up on a bag of coal and take me out on the cart as he went on his rounds. I would sit hypnotised at first by the clip-clop of Paddy's hooves. Then I would ask, "Tell me a story about Ireland, Dad, when you were a wee boy. Tell me a story, Dad."

He had been known as "the Owl" to the villagers because of his nocturnal poaching activities, and the lush green countryside of County Louth would unfold as Dad recounted in his soft rolling accent breathtaking tales of outwitting gamekeepers with his loyal greyhounds and whippets to poach rabbits and hares for the family cooking pot.

It was marvellous to have Dad home. He was very gentle and soft-hearted — Mum was the disciplinarian of the family — and he would sit by the fire and pick up a piece of firewood to carve me a wee boat or a whistle. My father was about 5 ft 8 in. and was a well-built, physically fit man. He had a shock of black curly hair — Irish black. He was a wonder with animals, and people would often bring their sick dogs and horses to him to see if he could help. He liked a flutter on the horses and would ask Mum for a shilling to put on a "sure thing". Often, he won and then he would always hand the winnings back to Mum. He was not a big drinker but would sometimes go across the road for a few pints to the Boundary Bar, so named to mark Glasgow's northeastern city limits. On one occasion, he had one too many and fell asleep in the pub toilet. The staff never noticed and he was locked in the pub when it closed for the night. Mum was wondering where he had got to when one of the neighbours heard him shouting that he was trapped inside and came to tell her. She was furious and they had to fetch Martin Watters, the bobby, with the keys to get him out.

Dad was very passionate about greyhounds, and on the nights when he did have a few drinks he would enjoy reciting "Master McGraw", the story of a famous Irish greyhound. It became his party piece. Over the years, I memorised it too:

> Eighteen sixty-nine being the date of the year
> The Waterloo sportsmen they all did appear
> To win the great prize and to bear it away
> Never counting on Ireland and Master McGraw.
> And when they arrived there in big London town
> The great English sportsmen they all gathered round
> One of the gentlemen gave a haw-haw
> Is this the great dog you call Master McGraw?
> "I know," said McGraw, "we have wild heather bogs
> But you'll find in old Ireland we have good men and
>   dogs.
> Lead on, bold Britannia! Give none of your jaw.
> Stuff that up your nostrils," said Master McGraw.

14

I've known many greyhounds that filled me with pride
In the days that are gone and it can't be denied,
But the greatest and bravest the world ever saw
Was our champion of champions, brave Master McGraw.

Dad would always finish by shouting "Hooray for Old Ireland!" and jump up to punch the air. On more than one occasion, he broke the glass over the gas mantle that lit the house, much to Mum's annoyance.

Soon after Dad's return, my sister Betty was born, and, two years later, my wee brother Eddie made his appearance. When Betty was about one, I would go out with her tied on my back in a shawl and play with my friends — it was the usual practice for small children to take their baby brothers or sisters with them this way. Betty was a good baby and never cried much. She inherited my father's dark hair and his warm good nature. We grew very close over the years and she became my greatest pal.

I used to take her on my back too when I went to Mr McIntyre's smiddy. Mr McIntyre was a big strong man, with a small beard and a white moustache. He was a typical countryman and worked with a big leather apron over his black waistcoat. I loved watching him working his magic. I loved everything about it — the smell of the place, the huge Clydesdale horses and the ringing of the hammer on the anvil as Mr McIntyre fashioned horseshoes out of glowing red-hot iron. I was mesmerised as the sizzling shoes were hammered onto the feet of the imperturbable gentle giants who barely blinked amid a cloud of smoke and steam. I loved those horses and sometimes Mr McIntyre would lift me onto their broad backs — they were so broad it was like sitting on a table. I was never afraid of falling off.

Gradually, I was allowed to help at the smiddy. That was a real thrill. The carters would bring in the Clydesdales for shoeing and I would hold the reins of these mighty beasts that seemed ten times my height. Sometimes they would raise their heads and nearly lift me off my feet. The horses were kept in a field behind the smiddy and they were a magnificent sight when they galloped around, enjoying their brief taste of freedom. I was allowed to help with the bellows too and as I squeezed them up and down I would watch in fascination as Mr McIntyre would produce a gleamingly spotless shovel, place it over the grate and cook his breakfast of bacon and eggs on it. He would give me a tasty snack and wash down his breakfast with a wee dram of whisky purchased from the nearby licensed grocer.

Mr McIntyre was a very kind old man. I had a toy that was my pride and joy at the time. It wasn't a real cleek and gird but an old spokeless bicycle wheel that I could push along the traffic-free streets with a short stick. I never went anywhere without pushing my self-styled hoop in front of me. It was as if I was welded to it and I felt that it pulled me along, going faster and faster. When I ran errands with my gird, I always seemed to get there quicker. One day, I ran along the road and left my wheel outside a shop. When I came out, it was gone. I was heartbroken.

The woman in the shop came out. "What's wrong, son?" she asked.

I replied tearfully, "Someone's taken my gird, missus. How will I get hame?"

As I dejectedly wandered home, Mr McIntyre saw me and asked me why I was crying. When I told him, he took me back to the smiddy, where we got the bellows going and then he hammered out a brand-new gird with an iron cleek attached. It was a real cracker, big and black. I could race the older boys now. It was just amazing and as I took off along Springburn Road I felt I was the luckiest boy in Glasgow.

My mother and father tried hard, but things were bad. People couldn't afford to pay for their coal, and Dad often gave folk coal on tick — he felt sorry for the poor people and could never refuse anyone. Mum was always going round the doors trying to get people to pay for their coal. Eventually, we had to sell Paddy and the cart, and Dad was forced back to sea, joining the other seafarers thronging the quays of the Clyde hoping to "get a jump" and be hired for a voyage to Spain or Sweden.

Times were hard, unemployment was on the rise and then, to cap it all, the landlords put the rents up. It was 1922 and a Labour woman called Agnes Dollan stood in Springburn for election to the council. She had been one of the leaders of the great Glasgow Rent Strike of 1915. The men were away fighting in the trenches at that time and the landlords thought they could get away with sticking up the rents. But they underestimated the Glasgow women and a rent strike spread like wildfire. Huge crowds marched through the city with placards exhorting Glaswegians to "Fight the Hun at Home" and branding landlords "The Prussians of Partick". Thirty thousand tenants joined the strike and, fearing trouble in the munitions factories, the government intervened to protect the workers.

Agnes Dollan was an inspirational figure and now a new rent strike broke out in Springburn. My mother, who held strong left-wing opinions, was in the thick of it. She was a strong woman and said, "We'll pay our rent fair and square but we're not paying the extra."

The women hatched their plans in the wash houses we called steamies and went around the back courts of the tenements calling up to other families to join them. They held protest meetings and organised a march with posters calling on tenants to "PAY NO RENT!" Soon it seemed every window in Springburn sprouted signs declaring "No To Rent Rises!" To begin with, everybody was solid behind the strike, but gradually support began to crumble, as the people were frightened of losing their homes. But my mother was a fighter. She held out — until the landlord got an eviction notice and we were out on the streets.

Mum had no choice but to go back to live with her mother in Balgrayhill Road, the nearest thing Springburn had to a posh area. But they never got on. My granny, who was better off than us, had always been very hard on Mum and had put her out to work on the farms when she was just 14. Mum's sister Lizzie was my granny's favourite. (Lizzie would later meet a tragic end. She emigrated to Australia, and, after losing her husband and two sons in a bush fire, she became a nurse. During the war, her ship was torpedoed. She was captured by the Japanese and died as a prisoner in one of their camps in Hong Kong.)

Granny Devlin didn't get on with my father, maybe because he knew of the bad time she had given my mother growing up and always took her part. My granny was also of Irish stock. Her father Frank McNulty, who trained boxers in Lanarkshire, had come over from the old country to work in the pits, and she had married an Irishman. My grandfather was called Ned Devlin and his family arrived from County Cavan after the famine of 1848 to work in the Lanarkshire mines.

While we were living there, one day, for whatever reason, Mum and my granny had a terrible row and Mum left the house, taking us with her. We didn't know where to go. The only place we could turn for help was the chapel and we went to see Father McBertie, who was the priest at St Aloysius in Springburn. He told my mother, "I will get a place for the children and I'll find a place for you and the baby."

The place he found for me and Betty was a convent. We were to be put in a home run by the nuns. It was a dark, blustery March morning and we seemed to travel for a long time. Finally we got to a place to the south of Glasgow called Rutherglen and we went into a huge building, but I didn't really know what was happening. We were met by two or three nuns, who looked quite scary in their austere black-and-white habits. Mum told us we were to be good, that we would be staying with

19

the sisters for a wee while and they would look after us. As she turned to go out the door, Betty was clinging to me and howling inconsolably. I stood with my arms around Betty and watched Mum walk away with great big tears rolling down my cheeks. Then just before she reached the door, Mum turned around and said, "Don't worry, don't worry, Andrew. Don't cry, Betty. I'll be back for youse. I'll be back for youse."

It must have broken her heart as she pulled that heavy oak door behind her. It certainly broke ours.

We were then taken upstairs to a dormitory and I gazed out of the window watching dozens of rooks circling around tall leafless trees repairing their nests against a darkening sky. I had never seen anything like it before and I couldn't take my eyes off them. The circling black birds were an eerie spectacle as they crawed and fluttered into the trees but I somehow knew then that Mum would come back — that she was building a nest for us.

That night, we said our prayers and went to bed. In the morning, the nuns gave us porridge and we could see that there were around 20 children in the convent. They were all poor like us but the nuns were very nice. They took us on walks up the Cathkin Braes into the countryside, and one of the young nuns played the piano beautifully, albeit the same tune over and over again.

After about two weeks, the Mother Superior came up to me and said, "Come on, Andrew. Your mother is here. She has come to take you back."

It was great to see Mum's smiling face again. She had got a job as a cleaner for a house factor and had managed to rent a "single end" — a one-roomed tenement dwelling with a shared outside toilet. It was in Stevenson Street in a place called Calton — a terrible slum area to the east of Glasgow city centre with a largely Catholic Irish population. Ninety years later, it has the lowest life expectancy in Britain. Calton folk in the twenty-first century can expect to live just 54 years. I hate to think what it was in 1922.

We were so glad to be with Mum and excited about our new home. It was tucked away in a back close in a warren of tumbledown condemned tenements. We went up a wooden stair right to the top of the building. In the garret, we had a room with no stove, no fire grate, no bed, no furniture — nothing. But Mum said, "We'll soon get it fixed up. Don't worry." The important thing to her was that she had her children back.

We went along to the famous Barras market and Mum bought a second-hand bed. We were struggling down the road with it when an old man took pity on us, and said, "You're having a struggle there, son. I'll get youse a barra."

It was much easier pushing the bed along on the barra. In the corner of the back court, there was a ramshackle wee house where an old Highland woman lived. She was a poor old soul but she came out when she saw us. "How are you getting on? You've no fire grate? I'll put the kettle on for you." She was the poorest of the poor but she helped her new neighbours.

Next we went down to the grocer's shop and my mother asked if he had any old orange boxes. He said, "Aye, I've got two."

So we took them up and used one as a cupboard for the jam jars we used for cups and turned the other one over to use as a table. My mother cut up flour sacks, sewed them together and filled them with straw from the huge egg boxes that were used to deliver eggs to the grocers — now we had a mattress.

That night, we were all in the one bed, a happy family again. But that longed-for feeling of warmth and security didn't last for long. During that first night we heard strange scratching and scuffling noises from within the walls, then high-pitched squealing and squeaking. The place was infested with rats. Mum was scared; she hated rats and we cuddled into each other for comfort.

The next day, the old Highland lady put her cat Tibby in to chase the rats. She also cooked for us on her fire until we got some bricks and my uncle Frank, Mum's brother, built a fireplace for us in the hearth.

While we stayed in the Calton, I went to school for the first time, to St Luke's across the river in the Gorbals. I also took my First Communion and was given a gift of a small piece of cake.

Mum was desperate to get out of the Calton. Even by the standards of the time, it was grim and she feared for the safety of baby Eddie with the rats around. Within a few weeks, Mum had impressed the factor with her honesty and hard work, and he agreed to find us a new home. We were going up in the world. We were moving to the Gorbals. The factor offered us a house at 212 Thistle Street, and Mum jumped at the chance to get out of the Calton. Uncle Frank came to help us move, and I went with him to Hyslop's in Gorbals Street where he hired a barra for a shilling. Hyslop's hired barras for everything — for folk to flit their houses, or to sell things, like whelks, mussels or puff candy. We went back to the Calton, put the stuff on the barra and shoved it all the way to 212 Thistle Street, with my sister sitting on top. I was at the back helping young Frank, and I looked up at him as we pushed the barra along. He was a handsome man and my favourite uncle, and it felt good to be helping him. My very first memory was of going down the Clyde on the boat to Rothesay with Mum to see Frank. He met us coming off the boat and put me on the handlebars of his bike to take me to the farm where he was working. He was on the run from the army. He had been called up just before the end of the war but he had gone absent without leave. The war had ceased to be so popular; too many young men had died or been maimed and wounded. He didn't want to fight and he went to work at the farm where Mum had worked when she met Dad. The war had finished but he was still lying low there. I was about two and when we got to the farm they had a sing-song, a wee ceilidh. The women were all dressed in blouses and long skirts, and they made a great fuss of me.

During the flitting, Mum followed us in a tram car with Eddie, and when we got to the house in Thistle

Street a woman came out. "Hello, son. Can I help you?"

"We have got the house upstairs, missus."

"Oh, you're the ones that are getting the house upstairs. That's fine and what's your name?"

"Andrew Coogan."

"I'm Mrs McEwan. Have you been upstairs yet? Hold on a wee minute."

Then she shouted to her husband, "Hey, Jim! Come here a minute. Give them a hand up these stairs with their things."

When we got up the stairs, Mr McEwan unlocked the door and went in and looked around. "Christ," he said. "They've taken the range away and you've not even got a gas stove."

The previous tenants had removed the black range, our only means of cooking and our only source of heat, from the fireplace.

Mrs McEwan came up, shook her head and said, "What a shame. I'll put the kettle on and make you something to eat."

Then Mum turned up with Eddie in her arms. When she saw that the range had gone, there were tears in her eyes, but Mrs McEwan said, "Don't worry. We'll cook up your food until you get sorted out."

Mum thanked Jean McEwan for her kindness and then said that she wanted to register us for school right away. We went along to St Francis and Mum saw Father Leonard. Then I met Mr McCartney, the assistant headmaster.

When I told him my name, he said, "Oh, you're Irish."

I replied, "No. My father is Irish."

"Well, that's good enough for us!" he said, and after that I became a Gorbals boy.

We didn't know it at the time, but Jim McEwan, a man in his thirties and unemployed as so many were during that awful period, was a member of the Beehive Boys — one of the most feared gangs in Glasgow. But we could not have asked for a nicer neighbour. Jim got some of his pals to put a fireplace in and took me along to a place in Main Street and we got a big bag of wooden blocks, off-cuts for the fire. When Mum came home with Eddie from her work that night, she was greeted by a roaring fire and a boiling kettle. This time it was tears of gratitude and not despair that came to her eyes. The Friday night after we moved in all the neighbours came round for a "ter" and Alice McCartney sang "Teddy O'Neill".

I've seen the mud cabin he danced his wild jigs in
As neat a mud palace as ever was seen
And considering it served to keep poultry and pigs in
I'm sure it was always most elegant and clean
But now all about it seems lonely and dreary
All sad and all silent, no piper, no reel
Not even the sun thro' the casement is cheery
Since I miss the dear darling boy, Teddy O'Neill.

Thistle Street was so much better than the Calton. There was no bathroom or inside toilet, though, and four large families shared the candlelit toilet on the landing downstairs from us. We just had to form an orderly queue but sometimes wee Eddie couldn't wait for his turn. He would rush up to Mum and cry out, "There's someone in there and I can't use the toilet." And she would say, "Right, jump up on the jaw box."

It was pretty primitive. But the house and close were clean and to Mum's relief there were no rats.

Our neighbours were fantastic. The Gorbals was a rough place all right. It is true there was terrible drunkenness, violence, domestic abuse, child neglect, vermin, rickets, diphtheria and all the other deadly and crippling diseases that resulted from the slum housing and grinding poverty that were prevalent. I do not look back at the Gorbals through rose-tinted glasses. However, after the publication of *No Mean City*, the 1930s novel about gangs and drink, the Gorbals quickly acquired the reputation of being the "most notorious slum in Britain", and I have always felt that the tremendous spirit of the Gorbals people who struggled to retain their dignity, improve their lot and help each other was unfairly overshadowed and ignored.

A good example of that spirit came shortly after we moved to Thistle Street and Mum found herself penniless with a family to feed. Dad had got a job as a donkeyman with the Glen shipping line, working as a greaser in the engine room. He got a "jump" after another casual sailor failed to turn up. The shipping company had given Mum a cheque but she couldn't cash it until a week after the boat left the harbour and was well under way — this was to prevent the men from getting their cheques, drinking the money and never returning to the boat. Mum mentioned her plight to our neighbour Alice McCartney. Alice was very sympathetic but she couldn't help either. Then about an hour later, Alice reappeared with five shillings. She had gone to see her sister-in-law Beeney. The pair of them argued like cat and dog but they were united by our situation and it turned out that Beeney had pawned her shawl to get five bob to see us through. These were the kinds of neighbours we had. We all helped each other and it didn't matter to us if they were Catholics, Protestants or Jews. They were all working-class people facing the same hardships.

Mum used to send me downstairs to Sammy Munn, the coalman who lived with his family on the ground floor of our tenement. He had a bad throat and Mum would get me to take a jug of water from boiling our vegetables or some potted hough, saying, "Take that doon to Sammy for his throat. He's got a bad throat and it will maybe help."

I liked going down to Sammy's house. Sammy's horse, Hector, was in a stable down Cumberland Lane, and he gave me sixpence to look after Hector on Sundays, his day off. I would feed him and brush him down, and let him walk over to the water trough in the street, although I got a fright the first time I did it. When Hector finished lapping up the water, he turned and made his way at a pretty smart lick along Cumberland Street to Thistle Street. When he got to Sammy's house, he stood outside the kitchen window and tapped on the glass with his nose until the window was lifted and a piece of bread and jam was handed out. I found out he did this every Sunday. After a while, Sammy would just tap him on his backside and say, "Away hame, Hector," and he'd set off by himself back to his stable.

Dad helped our neighbours too. When he was unemployed and couldn't get a jump, Dad would go out to Stewart's farm to get some casual work. He would come back with a bag of cabbages and we had the job of taking them round the doors selling them for tuppence or threepence. One of our neighbours was Mrs Reynolds, who had 11 children. As we set off to sell the cabbage, Dad would say, "Give a couple to Mrs Reynolds and, remember, don't accept any money from Mrs Reynolds. She has 11 of a family."

With the arrival of my younger brothers Pat and Frank, there were five of us siblings living in 212 Thistle Street. In 1924, not long after we moved to 212 Thistle Street, I had another wee brother. James wasn't well when he was born and died when he was just eight weeks old in Yorkhill Children's Hospital just at a time when my dad was away at sea. Mum was so broken-hearted, she was crying all the time. She was ill herself. Uncle John, my dad's brother, came with me to Yorkhill to see about James. I was seven years old, the eldest in the family. The man at the hospital passed us a wee white coffin and said to me, "Here's your wee brother."

The funeral people saw to it that we had a horse and carriage. I sat with the white coffin across my knees as we made our way to Dalbeath cemetery where the

28

priest was waiting for us, and we buried James. I didn't cry until I got home and saw Mum, who was so sad, crying for James. The terrible thing was that it happened to us again. In 1930, Kathleen was the last of the Coogans to be born and she died when she was only eight months old.

It was a common thing to hear about babies dying. Babies were six times more likely to die in the Gorbals than in the well-off parts of Glasgow. In 1934, infant mortality in London and Birmingham was 67 per 1,000. In the Gorbals, it was closer to 200 per 1,000. Eight decades later, I still remember James and Kathleen in my prayers.

For us children, the Gorbals was so exciting. It was full of strange and exotic sights, sounds and smells. I marvelled at the sheepdogs that drove great flocks of sheep through the streets of the Gorbals to the market. It was amazing to watch them at work. They would jump on the backs of the sheep and run across them to get ahead of the flock. It sounds odd now but there would be hundreds of sheep in these giant flocks being driven through the slums, and the shepherds actually lived in the heart of Glasgow. Cattle were driven through the streets too, and every now and then there would be a panic when a cow bolted. Sometimes, they would run up a close, which was a worry because often the women left babies sleeping in the prams at the foot of the stairs.

The Gorbals was Scotland's melting pot. Living cheek by jowl with the Catholic Irish who made it the second most Catholic constituency in Britain was a huge Jewish population. Of the 12,000 Jews living in Scotland, 9,000 lived with us in the Gorbals. Most of them had fled the violent pogroms and repression in Tsarist Russia, with large numbers from Lithuania and Latvia as well as Poland. Later, yet more Jewish families would arrive from Germany as refugees from Hitler, and one of them, a German-speaking teenager called Karl, used to visit our house and taught me to play several new tunes on the mouth organ.

All around the Gorbals there were posters in Yiddish and shop signs in Hebrew. There was a Jewish daily newspaper, a Jewish theatre, Zionist reading rooms, Jewish restaurants, Jewish tailors and kosher butchers and bakers. There were Jewish grocers like Mrs Goldberg, with bulging barrels of salted herrings on the pavements outside their shops. There were synagogues, and rabbis were a common sight. We even had the world's only Jewish boys' pipe band! Yiddish was spoken in the street. The Gorbals Cross was nicknamed "Little Jerusalem". Our neighbours were the Goldbergs, the Isaacs and the Cohens. Some of them could only speak broken English and some could speak none at all. They were good people and never bothered anybody, ever. At Passover, I would light the candles for Mrs Goldberg and Mrs Cohen. The Jewish boys played football with us and I had two Jewish friends, Isaac and Sarah. When my brother Pat became ill as an infant and was taken to hospital, I remember all the Jewish women in their shawls came into the house and were weeping and wailing.

As well as Jewish people, we had plenty of Protestants in the Gorbals, including Gaelic speakers from the Hebrides. Every day we heard voices in the street speaking Yiddish, Polish, Italian, Russian, the Gaelic of the Western Isles and the Gaelic of West Donegal. In Thistle Street, we even had a Japanese family. They worked for the Japanese consulate but they were working-class people like us. The Japanese laddies played football with us. Jews, Irish, Poles, Catholics and Protestants — we were all one crowd in the same boat. The only difference was that the Jews went to the synagogue, the Protestants went to the kirk and we went to the chapel — my mother made sure of that. We attended Mass every week, and we often had to take our white shirts and good boots out of the pawn shop on the Saturday and return them on the Monday. A lot of folk did that in the Gorbals; we found it quite comical and we used to talk about "resurrecting" our boots and shirts for the chapel.

Mum was very strict about how we conducted ourselves. I was only tempted into dishonesty once. Mum saw to that. One day I was sent to fetch the milk and, when I discovered the price had dropped from threepence to tuppence ha'penny, I pocketed the ha'penny change and made a beeline for Mrs Bailey's sweetie shop.

When I got home with the milk, Mum asked, "How much was it?"

"Threepence."

"Are you sure?"

"Yes."

"Right, come with me."

"Where are we going?"

"Up to see that dairyman. To ask the price."

Oh, God! My heart sank into the depths of my stomach and my face reddened. We went down the stairs and walked along the street for about five minutes. My mind was going through the torments of hell. Eventually, I meekly owned up. "Mum, the milk was just tuppence ha'penny."

Wallop! A deafening blow to the ear sent me reeling. Then another and another. I got the hiding of my life and luckily Betty was on hand to jump in and calm Mum down.

Betty and I always looked out for each other. Most of our teachers at St Francis were nice, but one was a real bully. Mr Hare always wore spats and was a heavy drinker. If you were late for school, you had to stand outside until Mr Hare came out, and we all dreaded being disciplined by him.

One cold winter's morning, I was going to school with Betty, who was only about six years old. We were frightened we would be late, so we ran all the way along Cumberland Street to the school. The school gates were still open but all of the children had already formed into lines and were going into school, and we were too late to get into line. There were three other boys, myself and Betty, and we were told to wait outside for Mr Hare. When he appeared, he told us boys to pull our sleeves up and put our hands out. Then he strapped us with his thick leather tawse, hitting us up the wrists and forearm. It was very painful and the red marks on our arms didn't take long to turn black and blue. Then he turned to Betty, who was shaking with nerves. People sometimes thought she had St Vitus's Dance but she was a nervous child, and now she was trembling, frightened of this big bully. When he told Betty to put her hand out, a red mist of rage descended on me. I pushed him back, grabbed the belt off him and threatened to hit him with it. There was a bit of a commotion and the headmaster came out. As luck would have it, the local policeman Jack Scott came along. He was from Dundee and ended up marrying a Gorbals girl. He would be a great influence on me later on when I took up running. He knew everybody in his beat. Like everybody else, he always called me "Jackie" after the child star Jackie Coogan, not that I looked like the cute curly-haired American. I had a mop of dark hair and suffered from a squint that I developed at around the age of three after a bout of German measles.

"What's going on here?" demanded Jack Scott.

The headmaster replied, "We're charging this boy."

"What for?"

"He lifted the belt to Mr Hare."

The other boys were all standing there but someone had gone and fetched my mother.

I was fighting back the tears.

"Jackie, why did you lift the belt to Mr Hare?" Jack asked. "You're not supposed to hit your master. What have you got to say for yourself?"

"I never hit him. He was going to hit Betty."

My mother piped up, "Look at his hands, Mr Scott. Roll up your sleeve, son."

My arms were horrible, all black and blue. The rest of the boys rolled their sleeves up too.

I said, "That's what he was going to do to my sister."

Jack Scott turned to my mother and said, "Mrs Coogan, do you want to charge this man? He had no right to do this to your son. That's not punishment."

Then he smelled drink on Mr Hare's breath. "Have you been drinking? Do you do this to these boys every day? I am going to take a note of this." Then he turned to the headmaster, saying, "I don't think you have control over your staff."

The headmaster asked my mother, "What do you want to do about a charge, Mrs Coogan?"

"Well," she said, "I just don't want it to happen again." But she was angry and she told Mr Hare, "If ever I hear of you doing this to any children, I'll be putting you on a charge."

I was never very interested in school, except when we got history from Mr Hainey. He was a great teacher and brought everything to life. He would get down on his knees, doing all the actions for the tales of Arthur and the Round Table, and tell us stories about Mary Queen of Scots.

I could never concentrate and was always dreaming of getting out and playing football. I always wanted to be a jockey. Two of Dad's brothers were jockeys. Dad's father was a fisherman in Annagassan. Tragically, he drowned along with seven others in a disaster that devastated the tight-knit community. My granny was left with eight children, and, overwhelmed, she developed a fondness for brandy. She died prematurely and the children were orphaned. As a result, two of the young boys, my uncles Patrick and Harry, were sent to the racing stables to become jockeys.

I inherited my father's passion for horses. I would go out on a Sunday to feed the horses belonging to the carters and earn a penny. At lunchtimes, I would run around with Betty to Annie Knott's working-men's restaurant where all the carters would go for their threepenny dinners and tether their horses outside. When the horses threw their nosebags off, I would put them on again and keep them calm. Mrs Knott was famous for her mouth-watering "clootie dumpling", which always sat gleaming on the counter, richly studded with sultanas and currants. Sometimes, the carters would give us a piece or they would say, "Here, I've had enough of this," and push a half-eaten plate of mince and tatties across to us. It was great.

The carters could easily tell that we were hard up, as I was usually clad in the clothes handed out to needy kids by the Glasgow School Board. At the start of each school year, we would go along to a big hall where there were hundreds of kids queuing up. There was a huge pile of boots and you would get a dark-grey jumper and a pair of woolly rough drawers that made you itch and scratch like mad. They also gave you a pair of trousers and sometimes a jacket. But, to get this, your family had to be means tested. It was a humiliating experience for my parents, and it was meant to be.

I remember the dark-suited means-test man arriving in Thistle Street with his clipboard. He would arrogantly poke about the house and speak down to Mum and Dad. Loftily pointing to an old chair or some wee ornament, he would demand, "You can sell that, can't you?"

Everybody hated the means test, and the inspectors were horrible men, cruel and heartless. They treated us like dirt.

Sometimes, the school and various charities like St Vincent de Paul and the Glasgow Poor Children's Fresh Air Fortnight committee would organise trips to get us out of the smoke-bound slums. These Fresh Air Days were a big event in the Gorbals. We would be seated on carts and given Union Jack flags to wave. The St Francis pipe band would lead the procession and large crowds gathered to wave us off.

On one trip organised by St Vincent de Paul, we went to a convent near Kilbarchan. When I was older, we had another outing and were taken to Dunoon Grammar School and slept in the school classrooms. The train going down to Dunoon was freezing but I looked out the window and was able to see the boats going up and down the Firth of Clyde — it was a wonderful sight.

Our trip to Dunoon was great fun. We were given palliasses that we had to fill with straw to sleep on, and I helped with the cooking and washing the dishes. We went on walks into the countryside and for the first time I saw wild roses. They were beautiful and we picked big bunches of them to take home to our mothers, but sadly the petals fell off and they never made it back to Glasgow.

Two of my friends on that trip were brothers Tim and John McGrory. They were always fighting each other, so it was no surprise that they both became boxers. John McGrory became a British Empire champion in the featherweight class. In the Gorbals, a boy had to be a good fighter or a good runner — preferably both. The schools all had boxing clubs and I went to the St Francis club. I liked it, and all my pals went, but my mother stopped me going because she was worried about my poor eyesight.

Getting out of Glasgow on the Fresh Air Days was a big thing for us, and on one of them we were marched into a photographer's studio one by one and I had my picture taken with a brightly painted rocking horse — a toy that we could never have afforded in a million years.

We enjoyed the streets too, though — they were our playground. We were not supposed to play football in the streets but it never stopped us. We played every night using lamp posts for goalposts. To begin with, we made a ball out of paper and string. Mrs Bailey, who had a small grocer's shop, was always worried about her windows and would come out and warn us, "Watch my windaes, watch my windaes." She was a good old soul, though, and once gave us a sixpence to buy a tanner ball. After that, we always seemed to have a tanner ball. Quite often, we would get chased by the police and if they caught you they would give you a rattle across the back of the neck with their gloves or a belt round the ear with the back of their hand.

All our games were running games, chasing, football, tearing up and down the closes. We didn't have bikes, but you could hire a bike for threepence an hour. It had no brakes on it, but then there was very little traffic.

All of our entertainment was in the street because there was no place else to go. The girls played hopscotch (peevers) and rounders. We would climb lamp posts, dykes and wash houses. We used to dare each other to jump from one to another, and if you didn't do it, you were chicken.

Sometimes we got up to mischief but it was always harmless. One night, we decided to play a joke on Mr Lebiski. He was a Polish Jew with a big family, and as a result he slept in the wash house out the back with his eldest son. One of his younger sons was with us and we got a long piece of knotted string and pinned it onto the window frame. When Mr Lebiski, wearing his nightshirt, went to bed, we were on top of the dyke pulling up the string and tap-tapping on the window. Of course, when he got up to investigate the noise, we would stop and then start again when he went back to bed. We thought it was hilarious until all of a sudden a window in the tenement behind shot up and a big pail of freezing cold water was thrown over us all.

Tying door handles together was another prank and we would also take delight in going into the butcher's shop and giggling as we asked the man if he had a sheep's head. If he said, "Yes", we would cry back, "Looks normal to us!" before running out the shop in fits of laughter.

At 11, I applied to the school for a permit to deliver milk — you had to get permission — then I started with Isedale's dairy, where I got three shillings and sixpence for delivering the milk and gave every penny to my mother. I had to go up to the dairy every morning at six o'clock. There were two customers that were miles away from the rest up in Carfin Street and Allison Street — they'd been customers for years and I had to deliver two pints of milk to them every day, summer and winter. They could have got their milk from another dairy but stuck with Isedale's. In the end, I used to run up to their houses with the milk and run back every morning; they sometimes gave me a twopenny tip, which was enough to get into the pictures.

Around the same time, I also got my first dog, Pim, who was an old black whippet and a friendly dog. He had raced under the name "Wee Pim" but his racing days were well over and my dad said we could keep him for a pet. I didn't have Pim long before he died of old age; I missed him and was determined to have another dog. Within a year or two, I got Beever — a fawn brindle lurcher, half greyhound, half whippet; she was a very fast dog who was a great wee companion and came with me everywhere. We even entered her in a race at Clydebank. She was going great until my brother Pat shouted out, "C'mon, Beever!" — then she stopped and came racing over to lick Pat, who was standing in the crowd!

A few years later, Beever had pups in my mother's bed. She was mad and that was the end of ever being allowed to have dogs in the house again. Not long after this, Beever died and I thought I'd never get a dog again.

Much of our spare time was spent trying to earn a few pennies to take home to Mum. We would rake the middens — the rubbish dumps and bin recesses out the back of the tenements — looking for empty lemonade or beer bottles. We always had great success at Govanhill and dubbed them "the lucky middens". There was one particular shop in the Gorbals, Meiklejohn's, that would take our bottles. He would take any bottle you brought along but he would only give you a ha'penny, while all the other shops would give you a penny. So we would walk all round Glasgow for miles with our bottles to avoid going to Meiklejohn's because he was such an old robber.

Then we made a barra using the wheels off my wee brother's pram and went around the wash houses offering to take the women's washing home for them and maybe get a penny for that. I would to go to the market, anywhere, to get sticks and break them up. Then we would bundle them up and go round the doors in Govanhill — that was where the toffs stayed — selling the kindling for tuppence a bundle. We used the money from the sticks to buy briquettes at the coal yard for ninepence a dozen, which we sold on for a shilling a dozen. We were real wee capitalists and it was a joy to see Mum's face when I came back with a couple of shillings for her. We used the barra for everything, and when disaster struck and one of the wheels came off we replaced it with a great big wheel. It looked odd but it didn't bother us — the barra was back on the road and we were back in business, dashing up to the gasworks to buy bags of coke for Mum and the neighbours.

We were always running about everywhere and as a natural consequence were extremely fit, which led to another source of revenue. Sometimes, after we had finished playing football in the street, drunk men would tumble out of the Cosy Bar and bet on us running around the block. It was always a source of great hilarity to them but we took it all very seriously as the winner would get pennies. They would line us all up outside the pub and the men, some of them Irishmen with fiddles under their arms, would shout, "Ready, steady, go!" Then we were off, tearing up Cumberland Street, down Thistle Street and Hospital Street and back to the Cosy Bar. There were times when it was a bit rough and the drunks would start knocking lumps out of each other, but they never troubled us, and more often than not I was able to claim the pennies.

My biggest commercial break came when I was about 11. It was winter and I made an old sledge to go down the steep brae at Queen's Park. It wasn't very good and some of the toffs were there with proper sledges that went much further than mine. This time, I went well, well back with my brother Eddie and we took a real run at the brow of the hill. We flew down the brae and went for miles. A man at the bottom of the hill was impressed. "Look, son, would you like to sell me that sledge," he said. "I'll give you half a crown for it."

He gave me a shiny half-crown and I turned to Eddie, "Let's go! Quick! They will need a horse to haul that sledge back up the hill!"

Sometimes, Mr Goldberg would give me a job as a "soap-boy" in his barber's shop and I would get a couple of coppers for lathering up the customers before Mr Goldberg scraped away at them with his cut-throat razor. When I delivered the milk in Govanhill, I sometimes got a penny tip. It was quite a journey pushing my barra up there and I would stop at the top of Thistle Street where I would get a roll with butter and a glass of tea at the baker's shop. It was a treat and I was always fascinated by all the cockroaches scurrying across the floor. I had to be quick on my rounds, though — Mum was always waiting to get the wheels back on the pram again!

I also delivered newspapers for Miss Campbell, a wee spinster who had a newsagent's in the Gorbals. She paid me one shilling and sixpence. My father was at sea during that period and my mother got a job cleaning houses. One day, she came home and said, "I've got you a job, Andrew. It's with Mr Gillespie, who has boot shops." He sold boots and shoes in Buchanan Street. I went to see him at his head-office shop in Crown Street in the Gorbals. He explained that after school I would deliver boots to his shops across the Clyde in Cowcaddens and Bridgeton. On a Saturday, I would have to go further afield to Ballieston. I was to be paid four shillings a week. Usually, I would have a bag over my shoulder but the Bridgeton shop had an old-fashioned three-wheeled basket barra.

I was a bit wary of going to Bridgeton. It was a predominantly Protestant area in Glasgow's east end and home to the Billy Boys — a vicious street gang led by the fearsome Billy Fullerton. They were anti-Catholic and referred to all Catholics as "Fenians". Fullerton was a fascist who later became a leader of Sir Oswald Mosley's blackshirts. He had won a medal for strike-breaking during the General Strike of 1926 and was never happier than when he was inciting sectarian strife. In the Gorbals, we looked on the Beehive Boys as our protectors and there were frequent pitched battles between the two gangs. Mum and Dad warned me to stay well away from gangs of all kinds and to avoid the criminal element.

One day, I was coming back to the Bridgeton shop with the barra when three lads stopped me.

"Where are you from?" one of them asked.

I was a bit naive and replied, "Thistle Street in the Gorbals."

That was it. They started pushing me and hitting me, trying to take the barra off me. I was struggling with them when luckily enough an old man came along.

"Leave the laddie alane!" he shouted.

I gave one of my attackers a well-aimed punch and they ran off.

The old man turned to me and said, "Good for you, son. But, if I was you, I wouldnae come back around here."

Glasgow could be a frightening place. So often a group of boys would menacingly issue the challenge: "Are you a Billy [Protestant] or a Dan [Catholic] or an Old Tin Can?" Woe betide you if you gave the wrong religion.

You had to keep your wits about you. I was always on the lookout for potential trouble, but gangs like the Beehive Boys, who were named after a draper's shop in Thistle Street, never bothered the local folk. They were tough, though, and when they clashed with the Billy Boys, razors and knives were used by both sides.

Sometimes, the Beehive Boys kept order in the Gorbals. I remember an episode one day when they heard that a newly arrived lodger in the street had been bullying the old people. The Beehive Boys got a hold of him and, by God, they nearly finished him. They gave him a hell of a beating.

On another occasion, I was walking my sister back from the Palais cinema where she had got a job as an usherette. We were coming along Cumberland Street into Thistle Street and had just got to the corner, with our house only about 60 yards away, when two young lads, teenagers but older than me, appeared.

"Have you got a match?" they demanded.

That was the usual way trouble started. I said, "No, I don't smoke."

So they started to pick on me and made remarks about Betty. I said, "That's enough." Two against one — I was heading for a thumping.

Just then Mr McEwan came along. "Hello, Jackie," he said. "Are you all right?"

I replied, "Mr McEwan, these two lads are annoying us. They want matches off me for smokes. They are saying things about Betty and they are not very nice."

Jim McEwan turned to them, asking, "Who are you?"

The oldest of the pair squared up to Mr McEwan. "We are the 'Wee Hives'!"

"Oh aye," said Mr McEwan. "Well, meet the Beehives." In a flash, Jim McEwan grabbed the pair of them and knocked their heads together. They were completely stunned and left holding their heads.

Then he turned to me. "Away you go hame now, Jackie. I'll fix this pair."

I was on the go all the time, running between my jobs, running to school and playing football with my pals. I was very physically fit but I think it may have been a family trait too, because one day Dad mistakenly thought I had been bad to my sister and chased me up Thistle Street to give me a clip round the ear. It was the only time he ever hit me. I never thought he would catch me. But he did!

I used to take the tram up to Cowcaddens to deliver Mr Gillespie's boots but I always ran back to the Gorbals to save the penny fare. One day, I was in Cowcaddens and I bumped into my uncle Pat, Mum's brother. He stayed up in Port Dundas and was on his way to the Gorbals to visit Mum. He got on the tram and I got on behind him, hoping he would pay my fare. But he was a real skinflint and chucked me off, telling me to walk.

What a miserable old bugger. We joked that he was so mean that, if he was a ghost, he wouldn't give you a fright.

So I decided to race the tram. I ran right down West Nile Street and across George Square, keeping pace with the car and irritating Uncle Pat by constantly

45

knocking at the window to shame him. He tried so hard to ignore me but you could see he was embarrassed. I kept it up right through Glasgow city centre before I took off to be ahead of the tram when it arrived in the Gorbals. I was 12 years of age when I beat that tram and I was still too quick for Uncle Pat when he tried to give me a smack around the head for being cheeky.

Dad's return from a voyage was another big highlight in my childhood. We all looked forward to it with mounting anticipation and often he would bring us little gifts from far-flung places. We would know when the boat was due in and sometimes I would go down to the docks to greet him. On one occasion I ran down to the quayside and saw his ship, the SS *Jura*, coming in from Valencia. It was so exciting. The dockers had just started unloading big cases of oranges when one of them fell off the pallet and crashed onto the dockside, scattering fruit everywhere. I eagerly started picking them up, stuffing them down my jumper to take a rare treat home for my sister and brothers. Then I quickly tore the peel off one of the oranges and sank my teeth in. Grooch! It was bitter beyond belief and the sailors who had been hanging over the handrail started laughing and shouted down to me, "They're marmalade, son."

Then they chucked down some of the eating oranges and told me to come on board to see my dad.

I scrambled up the gangplank, munching on oranges that had never tasted so good. When I went downstairs on the boat, another treat awaited me. One of the sailors produced a basket of emerald-green grapes. I

46

had never tasted grapes and they were even nicer than the oranges. I was greedily devouring the grapes when I heard a bird singing and whistling like there was no tomorrow. I looked around the crew's quarters and saw a beautiful little bird, green, gold and red, chirruping its heart out. I was gazing, transfixed by it, when Dad came in. "Hello, Andrew, let's go home and see how your mother's getting on."

As we went up the metal stairs to the deck, Dad turned round and asked, "Are you not bringing your bird with you?"

I couldn't believe it. "Oh, is that mine, Dad? Is it for me?"

I was thrilled, and as we walked home I clutched the birdcage to my chest and juggled a jumper full of oranges. I was the happiest wee boy in the world.

On the way home, we had to make a detour. Dad had promised to buy Mum a pair of gold earrings from Spain, and, as we entered Woolworth's store, where every item was priced at sixpence or less, Dad said to me, "Now, Andy, this is our wee secret, OK?"

"Yes. OK, Dad."

Dad forked out a tanner for the earrings and Mum was delighted with them. She would show them off to the neighbours, who were all mightily impressed. "Oh, they're lovely, Aggie."

"Aye," she would proudly reply. "Andy brought them back all the way from Spain."

Life was hard at times but we never went hungry. I would go to the Co-op bakery and get cheap day-old bread, which suited us fine. We would go along to

Salisbury Street and maybe the lads coming in from the farms would bring in tatties or carrots, cabbage or whatever. The women would say, "What are you wanting, son? Enough for a pot of soup?"

They would give us carrot, turnips, all that was going, to make a pot of soup. Then we would run down the road and go into the butcher's and get a ham bone, and there was our pot of soup straight away. We would ask for liver for the cat too. But we didn't have a bloody cat. We ate the stuff ourselves! Mum would send us along to the butcher to buy a cheap sheep's head and always joke, "Remember and ask him to cut it as near the tail as possible!"

Our luxury was to take a plate and go to the Jewish kippering store at the bottom of Thistle Street. We would get maybe three or four kippers for a shilling. They were lovely big kippers and sometimes the man would say, "There's another one, son. There you go."

Another special treat was to wait until late on a Saturday afternoon and run around the fishmongers' shops just before they closed. They didn't have fridges and couldn't keep the fish until Monday. So we might get a big fish for just a few pennies.

My parents never had much but they shared what little they did have. Mum came in one night with a young woman called Mrs Callaghan and her two wee boys. The woman had come over from Ireland with two small children, looking for work, and met Mum in the street. Mum offered to put her up until she got settled and we were all put in one room. Through time, she got her own place and got a nice wee house where she took in lodgers and did well. More than 40 years later, Eddie and I were at a car auction in Glasgow called Callaghan's car auction, run by two brothers. Eddie asked their first names, and, sure enough, it was the two boys. They said they would never forget Mrs Coogan as long as they lived.

On another occasion, there was a knock at the door from a man looking for a drink of water. He had walked all the way from Dundee to Glasgow, looking for work. Dad answered the door and brought him in, gave him a cup of tea and half of his tobacco. The man sat by the fire and Dad said he could stay with us and have the chair by the fire, and that's where he stayed until he got work and on his feet. Years later, he came back with his wife and a young child to thank us.

On Saturday nights, when my mother had folk round to the house, we would be sent for a "pail of ale". A lot of the pubs had a "family department" attached to them and children could go in with a billy can or bucket and buy stout that cost fourpence a pint. We would come back with the stout and Mum would heat up a poker in the fire until it was white hot then plunge it into the beer to improve the taste. There was no radio at the time and, as children, we used to like sitting by the fireside listening to the craic of these people in our home.

Dad had travelled to Europe and America and always had wondrous tales to tell. Once he told how he and a shipmate won a guinea in Liverpool. They went to a famous ironmonger's and ship's chandlers that boasted it stocked everything from a needle to an anchor. If they didn't have the item requested, they would pay a guinea. Dad had just come back from Spain and the trip had given him an idea. The two of them went in and asked the shop for a ring for a bull's nose — and, as the shop didn't have one, they got a guinea.

Families made their own entertainment — they had to. We would often meet up with the Reynolds family and have little dances. The Reynolds family were great people. There was Frank, Angus, Mary, Jenny and Willie and they were all into cycling. They started up the Regent Cycling Club. Whenever I went into their house, there was always a load of bikes hanging up from a pulley in the ceiling of their lobby. You couldn't move in their house for bikes. I think Mr Reynolds was maybe ahead of his time in realising the importance of exercise and fresh air. He used to take us out to the countryside for walks on a Sunday. Sometimes, we walked to Newtonmearns and sometimes to Clarkston. He did it to get us out of the Gorbals, and on these walks I learned about wee birds and developed a love of the countryside.

Our other big entertainment was the picture house. With the Electric Theatre in Sauchiehall Street, Glasgow boasted the first purpose-built cinema in Scotland. Throughout the 1920s and '30s, cinema soared in popularity. By 1939, Glasgow had 114 cinemas with over 175,000 seats — more cinema seats per head of population than any other city in the world. It was so popular that the powers-that-be began to talk of restricting cinemas to protect our morals.

I was firmly part of the craze. Mr Gillespie closed his shops on a Tuesday, so I had no deliveries that day and after school I would rush around to the Paragon in Cumberland Street, where it cost a penny to get in. The villain of the time was Fu Manchu, who was thoroughly evil, cruel and cunning with dastardly ways of killing his victims. When our heroes were in mortal danger, we would be on the edge of our seats, shouting out, "Watch your back! Watch your back!" Fu Manchu was part of the so-called Yellow Peril scare that predicted a threat emerging in the Far East from the huge Chinese population. However, our leaders didn't seem to realise that there was indeed a threat looming in the Far East, not from China but from Britain's former ally Japan.

My favourite film star was Eddie Cantor and I followed him throughout my teenage years. He had hits with songs like "Makin' Whoopee", "Ma, He's Making Eyes at Me", "If You Knew Susie" and "The Kid from Spain", and I sang them all at our get-togethers at home. The picture house was a magical place for us. After watching a western, we would tumble out onto the streets, pretend we were on a horse and gallop home. Those were happy days.

Some picture houses were better than others. We could get into the "Crownie" on Crown Street for a couple of old jam jars, sometimes even one. If you went to the cheap seats up in "the gods", there was always a danger that you would pick up fleas or head lice. Some of these cinemas really lived down to their nicknames — they were indeed "fleapits". I would go home and Mum would shout, "Have you been to the Crownie?

Get that shirt off!" and fling it in the jaw box to be scrubbed.

When you picked up fleas, we called it "Love from a Stranger". There was terrible overcrowding in the Gorbals. The classrooms at St Francis were jam-packed and it was not unusual for families of ten and twelve to sleep in one room. There were no bathrooms and so infestations of fleas, head lice and bedbugs flourished. When we got bugs in our first home in Thistle Street, we were all covered in angry bites that itched like crazy. Dad wasted no time in distempering the walls and he borrowed a blowtorch to burn them out of room corners; most importantly, he took the blowtorch to the bedsprings, where the foul-smelling bedbugs lurked, waiting to come out at night and suck our blood while we slept. I never realised it at the time but my fleeting encounters with bugs in the Gorbals were to be a useful preparation for my three and a half years as a prisoner of the Japanese, when bedbugs and body lice would be my constant and maddening companions.

At around this time, my old grandfather Ned Devlin came to live with us. He loved the cinema too and they used to let him in to the matinees at the Crownie for nothing because he would keep the rough kids in line by banging the floor with his walking stick when they made too much noise. Granddad's favourite films were westerns and his all-time favourite was *The Last of the Mohicans*.

I loved my granddad. He was a kindly old man and good to us. We were lucky to have him. On 22 October 1877, when Granddad was a young miner, he was too ill to go down the pit. That illness saved his life. A terrible explosion ripped through the pit at Blantyre. It was Scotland's worst-ever mining disaster; 207 men were killed — the youngest a boy of 11 — creating 92 widows, 34 of whom were later evicted by the coal company from the tied houses.

As his health began to fail, Granddad spent more and more time in his bed. I would go and see if he was all right and give him a miniature of whisky, which he would tuck inside his pillow. He would have around half a dozen squirrelled away in there.

Eventually, Mum and Dad managed to get a bigger house. We moved across the road to 223 Thistle Street and instead of one room and a kitchen, we had two rooms with a kitchen — and an inside toilet. But our good luck was not to last. I turned 14 in 1931, right in the middle of the Great Depression. The Gorbals became even more depressed, with groups of dejected men hanging around the street corners. Some with their sleeves or trouser legs pinned up were disabled veterans of the First World War — their sacrifice had long been forgotten by a government that branded proud men who had the misfortune to be unemployed as "idle". To add insult to injury, already meagre benefits were cut. Huge crowds gathered to send off Hunger Marchers from Glasgow to London as part of the campaign organised by the National Unemployed Workers Movement. You could tell by their bearing that a lot of the marchers were ex-military. The men who had marched on the Kaiser were marching on London now.

There was trouble in Glasgow with riots and free-speech fights. Shop windows were smashed and looted. The streets and walls were chalked and whitewashed with the hammer and sickle and slogans like "No Means Test" and "Fight or Starve!" The shipyards were closed and fleets of ships were tied up and mothballed due to the trade depression. Times were bad and Dad joined the growing ranks of the unemployed. Mum's cleaning job brought in only nine shillings a week. My part-time jobs now brought in ten shillings — which made a big difference to Mum.

CHAPTER
TWO

The Man of the House

I left school at 14 to work more hours and when I was 15 I landed a job with Cohen's Trongate Clothing Company delivering clothes at ten shillings a week. I still had my milk round in the morning and I rushed back at night-time for the paper round, but I had to give up the shoe deliveries.

It was a good job and I soon discovered ways of making additional cash. The cloth used to arrive in bales wrapped in large sheets of brown paper and I would take these along to the Barras and sell them for a penny each. I was making money all the time.

One day, Mr Cohen took me to the back of the warehouse and pointed to a mountainous pile of ropes in the corner. "Jackie, these ropes are taking up too much space," he said. "Can you get rid of them for me?"

"Aye, sir. I'll do that."

Mr Cohen wanted me to bin the ropes that had tied up the bales but my mind was always working. I took a few of the ropes down the Saltmarket to where they had the coal carts and I jumped up on one of them.

I asked the carter, "Hey, mister, are these ropes any good for reins for your horses?"

"Aye, sure, sure. How much do you want for them?"

"How much will you gi'e me for them?"

"I'll give you a shilling a pair."

God, there were hundreds of these ropes! I was sitting on a gold mine. Soon, I was taking the ropes all over Glasgow, sometimes getting a shilling, sometimes sixpence a pair. When I took the money home to Mum, she was suspicious at first and gave me the third degree about how I came by the money. I reassured her and she knew me well enough to know that I wouldn't steal stuff so the ropes provided a welcome addition to the family budget for a few weeks.

The money-spinner I most enjoyed was helping Willie McLaughlin, the bookie, run his greyhound kennels. I loved working with the dogs, as I was mad about greyhounds. Their elegance, their grace and their speed appealed to me. I had been brought up with tales of greyhounds and in the early '30s Britain was gripped by a greyhound mania. Dog tracks sprang up everywhere and the sport was popular with women too. One of the tracks in Glasgow even had a crèche. I used to walk the greyhounds and prepare their feed. Willie would give me five shillings a week but I enjoyed it so much I would have done it for nothing. He had two dogs that were my favourites. They were called Laurel and Hardy and I would take them to tracks all over Lanarkshire.

One day, I was at Willie's place cooking up feed for the dogs. We had a big boiler, the kind that women had in the wash houses, and had filled it with vegetables, sheep heads and old bread. It was just like the soup we ate at home and I was giving it a stir when Mickey Cassidy, a well-known boxer, came in with a pal. Willie was looking after their dogs for them. Mickey's pal was a new face but he seemed a nice lad and was about four years older than me.

"That smells good. What's in it?" he asked as he sniffed the boiler.

"A bit of everything. It's just like soup. It's good enough to eat. Would you like a taste?"

"Aye. I'll try it."

I passed over a ladle and he sipped at the steaming liquid. "Mmm. Aye. You're right. It's braw."

When the stranger walked away to clap his dog, I turned to Mickey. "Hey, Mickey, is your pal a boxer?"

"Aye."

"What's his name?"

"Benny Lynch."

"Any good?"

"Are you kidding me? He beat Jim Campbell, the Scottish flyweight champion, last month. He could be a world champion one day."

Over the next few months, I would regularly walk with Benny and Mickey. Benny gave me half a crown a week to walk his dog. He was good to me and I used to follow his career in the papers.

One day, they came to the kennels and Mickey said, "Hey, Jackie, Benny's fighting Jackie Brown, the world champion, in Manchester next week."

I looked at Benny with undisguised admiration. "Oh, Benny. That's great. Good luck."

The following week, on the evening of Benny's fight in Manchester, I was sitting in the Paragon Picture House, looking forward to watching Eleanor Powell and Robert Taylor in *Broadway Melody*. The newsreel had just started and up came Benny on the big screen. It proclaimed in huge letters: "Benny Lynch — The Champion of the World". The place erupted and everyone jumped to their feet. We were cheering and cheering to the rafters. Then highlights of the fight showed Benny in his silver shorts going at Jackie Brown like a terrier. Every time Benny knocked him down, the audience was roaring. I was so proud to know Benny. A Gorbals boy, one of us, a boy from Glasgow, was champion of the world. It was amazing.

A couple of days later, Benny returned to Glasgow victorious. When he came back to Thistle Street, everybody was shaking his hand and waving to him. He was like royalty to us. Benny showed us that even a boy from the slums could become a world-class athlete. It was a lesson that stayed with me.

I always dreamed of owning my own greyhound but they were expensive. And then one day Willie asked me to meet the Sunday boat from Belfast and collect two dogs for Monkey Reilly, a well-known Gorbals bookie and local hard man.

I went down to collect the dogs but there were three dogs instead of two. Two were lovely dogs and Monkey had reputedly paid 100 pounds each for them but there was another one that was in a terrible state. It was very thin and it had big bald patches with mange. I doubted that Willie would let it into the kennel, and, sure enough, when I got the dogs back, he took one look at the dejected-looking animal and said, "That thing is not coming in here. He's got the mange and he's just skin and bone."

I took the dog along to show him to Dad. After a brief examination, Dad said, "This dog has been abused and he has worms."

The poor dog's eyes looked horrible, they had a greyish film over them and there was a discharge of pus at the corners. Dad chewed on a bit of tobacco and asked me to hold the dog's eyes open. As I held the dog, he spat in the dog's eye and did this over and over again. After a while, the rheum lifted from the dog's eyes and he washed them with water till they were clear.

The next day, we took the dog up to Pomadie. Dad gave him a piece of sausage meat and he jumped for it and then another piece. Then Dad put a Mayfairn worming capsule in the third piece. We let him off the leash, and after a while the poor dog was passing a mass of worms; it was horrible, I'd never seen the like, and the dog was exhausted. Then Dad gave him a drink of warm milk from a flask.

Mum was emphatic that the dog, which we called Jerry, would not be allowed in the house so I kept him at Mr Campbell's stable where I watered the horses. Dad got sulphur and lard and he made up an ointment, which he smeared on Jerry's face and bald patches. Then he told me, "Take him out walks, son, but don't overdo it. Forget about the rest of those dogs. They can look after their own dogs. Just concentrate on this one."

I started walking Jerry religiously and scrounged the best of food for him. Dad prescribed a spoonful of olive oil every day too. Gradually, Jerry began to get better and you could see the glow returning to him. He was a bonny dog and he was affectionate too. Eventually, Dad and I persuaded Mum that I should be allowed to bring the dog up to the house just so she could see him. She was amazed.

"That's no' the dog you brought here before," she declared.

"I'm telling you, Aggie," Dad replied. "It's the same dog."

I chipped in, "Clap him, Maw, clap him. His skin is really silky now."

"I can't believe it," Mum said. "What did you do with him?"

"We just treated him as best we could," I replied proudly. "He's a bonny dog, Maw. Can we keep him in the house?"

She finally relented. "Oh, all right then. If you must."

As Jerry got stronger, we decided to see if he could run. Willie McLaughlin came along with us and we took him up to a field above Hoggansfield Loch.

Willie said, "There's a hare at the back of this field and nobody has managed to catch it. Look, there he is, there in the corner."

I took Jerry into the field and watched his reactions. Suddenly, the hare jumped up and Jerry got all excited. He was only a young dog but my father said, "That dog has chased a hare, he's done this before. Let him off."

As I let Jerry off, the hare jumped and started to run and he chased it around the field.

Willie was surprised. "That's the first time I've seen any dog turning that hare."

The hare made for the end of the field and bolted under the gate. Jerry was going so fast that he flew over the gate and narrowly avoided a truck coming down the road. It was so exciting to watch the sheer speed and beauty of the dog's graceful movement.

I remembered Dad's tales of poaching as a boy in Ireland and took Jerry out into the countryside to catch rabbits. He was pretty good, sleek and fast. One of my poaching expeditions ended in disaster, however. I was hunting in fields above Carmunnock and Jerry was doing great. I was too engrossed in working with the dog and never noticed the mist coming down on the moor. I was walking among cattle and they started chasing me. I was hopelessly lost and couldn't see the road so I bedded down for the night in a hay shed. It was quite cosy in the straw and I fell soundly asleep with Jerry resting his head on me. When I woke up in the morning I heard a hen clucking and found a clutch of half a dozen eggs. I helped myself to three or four of them and set off for Thistle Street. I felt quite the hero bringing home a couple of rabbits and some fresh eggs. Whenever I got a spare rabbit, I would hand it in to Mrs Goldberg or Mrs Cohen.

However, my illusions of glory were soon shattered. As I approached our tenement, the first person I met was Mrs Goldberg.

"Hello, Mrs Goldberg," I said breezily.

Smack! She landed a stinging blow on the back of my neck. "Never mind 'Hello, Mrs Goldberg'. Your poor mama is worried all night. Your poor mama."

Then she landed me another stinger almost as an afterthought and added, "You selfish boy. Everybody is out looking all night for you. Your poor mama."

Jerry was looking good and had made a full recovery. He was a lovely dog and always eagerly waited for me to come home to make a fuss of him. He was so fast that Willie suggested that we try him at an unlicensed "flapping track" near Blantyre.

It cost half a crown to enter Jerry in the trials to get a racing card. I put him in the traps but he had never been in the traps before and he wasn't used to it. All the other dogs left Jerry standing and I was so disappointed. Then Willie asked the organisers to give us another chance and to let me slip Jerry with just my hand. I took Jerry to the side of the track about three or four yards from the other dogs. When he caught sight of the hare, Jerry took off and came in 10 to 15 yards ahead of the rest of the dogs. The man at the track said, "OK we'll put him in for the ten-pound handicap next week."

Ten pounds was a lot of money in the '30s and we were so excited.

We changed Jerry's name to Ready Money and took him back to Blantyre the following Tuesday. The bookies gave odds of 2-1 in the qualifying race and Ready Money won by five yards. We came back on the Thursday for the next heat and I asked if I could put the dog in the traps myself instead of the local lads.

They said it was OK and I put Ready Money into the trap but all the time I was whispering in his ear, "Rabbits, rabbits, rabbits!"

The traps went up and he took off and won easily again. That was us through to the Saturday-night final.

I could hardly sleep on the Friday night for thinking about it. All of the neighbours got behind us and were putting on a shilling here and a shilling there. Everybody's hopes were pinned on Ready Money.

Dad went up with me on the Saturday night. I nervously watched the first few races, and then they announced the ten-pound handicap. I put the dog in the traps and held my breath. Then they were off and I could hear Dad shouting, "Come on! Come on! Come on, Ready Money!"

I could hardly bear to watch but Ready Money sailed into the lead and never gave it up. He crossed the line a good ten yards ahead of the others and we were in the money! Jerry had lived up to his new name. It was brilliant. Everybody was cheering and shouting. We collected the prize money. Ten pounds — I had never seen so much money. Next Dad went to the bookie and collected his winnings and all the winnings for the neighbours. Everyone was waiting for us when we got back to Thistle Street. It felt so good going around the doors, giving people their winnings. People said things like, "Did he win? Did he win? That's great. Let's get fish suppers with the winnings."

Our luck had changed, and, a couple of weeks later, Dad, who had been unemployed for so long, got a job cleaning out boilers at the City Sawmills. However, it was not to last. A month into the new job, he came out of the boiler room to cool off one night and caught a chill. He fell ill and was eventually hospitalised with pneumonia. I would go and visit him every night after work.

One night, I came home expecting Jerry to jump up on me as usual, but he was not there.

"Maw, where's Jerry?" I asked.

"A man came this afternoon and took him away. He said Jerry belonged to him. I'm sorry, Andrew."

There was no mistake. The man she described was Monkey Reilly.

I went round and saw him. "Monkey, please could I get the dog back?" I pleaded. "He was at death's door. I nursed him back to health and trained him up. He's a pet to us too. Please, Monkey, could I have him back?"

He looked at me with his dead eyes and showed no expression when he replied, "Naw. Get lost. He's mine."

I was shattered at losing Jerry, and maybe I didn't disguise it too well when I went to see Dad the next morning. Dad's condition had deteriorated, and he was lying quite ill with a tube into his nose but still conscious.

"How are you, Andrew?" he asked softly. "How's the dog?"

"The dog's gone, Dad. Monkey Reilly came round to the house and took him away."

I could see that Dad was pained to hear the news. He was such a kind man but his features hardened and he lifted his head from the pillow as he rasped out an old

64

Irish curse on Monkey Reilly: "May the curse of Cromwell be upon him. That man will have no luck."

I sat with Dad from ten in the morning until half past midnight that day. They wanted me to go at ten o'clock but I wouldn't leave Dad. Finally, I fell asleep in the chair and a nurse came and said, "Come on, Andrew. It's time for you to go home. It's late and your mother will be worried about you. We'll look after your dad."

Eventually, they got me to go home and I walked along Duke Street and, as I came down High Street into Glasgow Cross, I had tears in my eyes thinking about Dad, who had always been so kind to me.

Then a big policeman stopped me, "Where are you going? What are you doing out at this time of night?" He started bawling and shouting. "You get up that road or I'll kick your bloody arse!" He never gave me a chance to tell him where I had been. I fought back tears of injustice.

When I got to the Saltmarket, another policeman stopped me. "You're out late, son. Where do you stay?"

"Thistle Street."

"What are you doing out at this time?"

I started to cry.

"What is it, son? What's happened?"

"I've been sitting with my father since ten o'clock this morning and they told me to go home. He's very seriously ill."

"I'll get you along the road, son, to the corner of Adelphi Street. I hope you get good news."

Mum was still up waiting for me when I got home.

The next morning, before I went to work, a policeman came to the door. My father had died at the age of 52. Officially, it was pneumonia that killed my father but maybe the truth was that he was worn out. He had been orphaned, torpedoed, unemployed and struggled so hard to bring up his family.

Dad's death was terrible for us all, but Mum was brokenhearted. Once again, our Gorbals neighbours rallied round to help us. With their help and some assistance from the Salvation Army, we buried my dad. I was 16 and on the day of the funeral the parish priest said, "You're the man of the house now, Andrew."

I didn't cry then but all these years later I shed a tear when I think of how those good Gorbals people, people with nothing, helped us to bury my poor father.

CHAPTER
THREE

On the Right Track

A couple of months after Dad died, a group of us were playing football in Thistle Street. It was a Sunday and the police were quite strict about enforcing the law against playing football on Sundays. The previous month, I had been caught playing football on a Sunday up at St Leonard's Park and was fined half a crown at Queen's Park police station. Luckily for me, I had some money that Benny Lynch had paid me for walking his dog — if Mum had found out that I had been fined she would have murdered me.

We were having a good kick about in the afternoon when a woman suddenly pushed up a window in one of the tenements and shouted down, "Hey, the polis are coming over the back dyke from Hospital Street! The Hurdler's comin' over!"

The Hurdler was a big, athletic cop of about 30 years of age. He would climb the walls that separated the parallel streets, come through the tenement closes and suddenly appear in the middle of the street. He was famous for catching people. The only thing that separated Hospital Street and Thistle Street was this back dyke so he climbed over the dyke from one street to another. I was in the middle of the street when one of the lads shouted out, "There he is!"

I was about 40 yards away from him, and there were other lads closer to him, but he seemed to fix his eye on me for some reason. Then he made for me. So I turned and started to run up Thistle Street towards Caledonia Road. When I looked back, he was about ten yards behind me. "Bloody hell," I thought, "I had better get going here." So I got to Caledonia Road and ran towards Crown Street as fast as I could. When I got to Crown Street, the Hurdler stopped and was all out of puff. I kept running down Crown Street and I climbed over the dyke into Thistle Street and up to the house.

I was breathless when I got indoors and Mum asked suspiciously, "What's the matter with you?"

"Nothing! I just came up for a drink of water."

Soon after, there was a sharp knock at the door. It was firm and loud and I knew straight away it was the police. We were scared of the police in those days so I was shaking a bit when I opened the door and there stood Jack Scott.

"Is your father in?"

"No. He died two months ago."

"Sorry to hear that. Is your mother in?"

"Aye, come in."

Mum was surprised to see Jack. "Hello, Mr Scott. What's he done? What has he been up to?"

"Nothing, Mrs Coogan. The lad's not done anything. No harm done. Can I have a seat? Do you mind if I have a smoke?"

"No. Carry on. Would you like a cup of tea?"

Jack took off his tall helmet, put it on the table and sat down. He lit up his pipe as Mum got the tea ready.

"I'm sorry to hear about your man, Mrs Coogan. I would like to take young Jackie here to the Maryhill Harriers and see if they can make a runner out of him. I have a friend who is a runner with the Harriers and I'm going to have a word with him to see if they will take Jackie."

Mum was delighted. "Oh, Mr Scott, that would be great. Thank you."

I was sweating and shaking and couldn't believe my ears. I said, "They'll never let me in at Maryhill, Mr Scott. Not a boy from the Gorbals."

The Maryhill Harriers were quite famous and they had a lot of world-class runners, but I was under the impression it was posh and full of doctors' sons and university blokes.

Jack finished his tea and said, "Don't worry. Leave it to me. I'll see what I can do. I had better get away now."

As he got up from the table, he put his hand in his pocket, pulled out a ten-shilling note and placed it on the table. "That's for you, Mrs Coogan," he said. "I had a bet on with the Hurdler that he would never catch young Jackie here."

Mum was amazed and grateful for his generosity. Ten shillings meant a lot to us and Jack Scott knew it.

A couple of days later, Jack got word to us that I had to meet him the following Tuesday night outside the police station in Cumberland Street. When I went round, Jack came out in civilian dress. He was doing this in his own time and not just for me. Jack was a boxer in the southern division and would take young lads to boxing clubs too and get them in. It was his way of getting kids off the street and into positive pastimes that would absorb and channel their energies. He was a very decent man. He was a self-appointed community policeman and social worker all rolled into one — long before such posts were even invented.

We took a tram up to Maryhill and Jack paid the penny fares, then we went round to the baths. There was a gym inside with around 40 to 50 young men going through their exercise routines with a punch ball, speed balls, skipping ropes and everything. Jack went up to the oldest of the group and said, "Hello, Dunky. I've got a young lad here. Maybe you could do something with him."

Duncan Wright was a British Empire champion who represented Scotland as a cross-country runner every year from 1920 to 1930. He was a famous marathon runner, and in 1932 he had come fourth at the Olympics in Los Angeles. Now he was training future Olympic athletes with the Maryhill Harriers.

Duncan looked me up and down. "OK, we'll give him a go. Where are you from, son?"

"The Gorbals."

He turned to the rest of the lads and said jokingly, "The Gorbals! Oh, Jesus Christ! Lock everything up, guys!"

Then he asked me, "What's your name?"

"Andy Coogan."

70

"Well, from now on you're Jackie Coogan." He shouted to the others, "Hey, lads, we've got Jackie Coogan here tonight."

"Don't worry, Dunky," Jack said. "He'll not give you any trouble. Young Jackie is a good lad. I'll leave him in your hands."

Then he said to me, "Right, I'm away home. I'll leave you here. Do you have enough money for the tram to get home? OK, see you later, Jackie."

As Jack left, I surveyed my new surroundings and new friends. I was thrilled to be in the company of these runners. I used to read about the Maryhill Harriers virtually every day in the paper. It was a wee bit daunting, as the club was very prestigious. It had been founded in 1888 and had a great track record. As well as Dunky Wright, their ranks included famous runners and national champions like Donald Macnab Robertson, Walter Calderwood, David Muir, Tom Blakely, John Emmet Farrel and Donald Mclean.

As I was standing there, a tall chap with spectacles came over to me, shook my hand and said, "I'm Andy Blair. Are you gonna train here? What kind of racing do you do, son?"

"I've never raced before."

"Well, I've been looking at you. I think you'll be a half-miler. We're going down to the Maryhill Barracks now. We train at the barracks. Have you any running gear with you?"

"No, I don't have anything."

He took me over to a big wicker basket propped against the wall. He started rummaging among all this

71

stuff, and finally selected a pair of shorts and a vest that had been left by other runners. "Here, try this and this," he said.

In no time, I had a vest and shorts. Everyone made me so welcome. Andy told me that my sandshoes would do for now but that we would see about proper running shoes later.

When we got to the barracks, a small chap, one of the sprinters, came up to me and introduced himself. "I'm Bob Bell — just call me Bob. Can you sprint? I want you to line up there with these three lads and give it your best when I say, 'Get set, on your marks, go!'"

Everyone took up their positions, but I didn't know what to do and, when they took off, they raced ahead of me. And I thought I could run too — it was a bit of a wake-up call. But they were older men and Bob said, "Not bad, son, we'll give you another go."

I was pretty slow in getting off my mark but when we got to the finish line I was up beside them. Big Andy Blair was watching and said, "You're a half-miler all right. You finished level with them and they've been at it for months and months — and they've got spiked shoes on. You leave it to me. Just you do what you're told."

Andy introduced me to Gordon Porteous.

"Oh," I said, "I played with a lad called Gordon Porteous. My mother cleaned his house in Queen's Park."

"Well, that was me you were playing with," he said.

I remembered my mother taking me with her to clean Mrs Porteous's house and I played with the son at the pond where we sailed his toy boat.

We went back up to the baths and they introduced me to the training regime. Bob gave me a skipping rope and showed me how to skip. Then I was instructed in push-ups and how to train with the speed ball. I was soon worn out but they kept me going at it. They had a big ball that you punched and it came back to you. Then Andy Blair got to the other side of the ball and as I punched it to him he punched it back, faster. He got me going all the time and before I knew where I was he said, "Right, into the showers now."

I got a shower for a penny. They had put up showers in the women's wash house, the steamie, for us, using the water the women had boiled up for washing their clothes. There were just three showers and all the lads crowded under them. There was nothing fancy about the place but it never did us any harm.

I was on top of the world as I walked back to Thistle Street that night. My head was buzzing with the possibilities and, although I was sore the next day, I was hooked and pitched into the sport with a passion. I was getting better and better all the time and my confidence was growing. However, I lacked confidence to start with, and to train as an athlete you've got to have confidence.

That year, the club decided to enter me in a two-mile Christmas handicap run. I was shocked to win it because a lot of the runners were a year or so older than me.

I finished up running the mile and the half-mile, which was part of my training for the mile. Soon I was running competitively every week. Athletics were really big in Glasgow in the '30s. We ran against clubs from Bellahouston, Springburn, Shettleston and Monklands, and a lot of supporters would come along to watch. These clubs really built up the sport. Athletics were hugely popular with working-class lads, because apart from football it was the only sport that we could take part in that were not expensive. Rangers and Celtic ran sports days in which top teams played five-a-side and then during the intervals there was cycling and running races. The Ibrox sports day was the biggest of its type in Scotland and athletes came from all over the world to compete in it. Celtic had a sports day at Parkhead and then there were the Hampden races. We had a sports meeting every week. At a smallish event, there might be 30,000–40,000 spectators and at a big event the crowd could be upwards of 60,000.

We had wonderful competition all the time, and instead of two clubs running against each other there would be three clubs in a triangular contest, and it was all the year round. Then we went to run in Edinburgh against Edinburgh Northern, who were a very strong club. We used to go through to run against them on Saturdays. It cost us a couple of bob on the train from Queen Street station, but I used to think it was great. We always ended the day with a visit to a nice restaurant and a big plate of fish and chips. We would go for our run from Portobello Baths out into the country and come back again. When we reached the Portobello promenade at the Musselburgh end, with around three-quarters of a mile to go back to the baths, the best runners in each club would race to the finish. It was a brilliant day out and a lot of fun.

When we ran inter-track contests, we were learning all the time — it was part of our education. Big Andy would come up and say, "Now, look, don't take the lead. I want you to hold back. I know these lads are better than you and I want you to just learn as much as you can. Get as close to them as you can and maybe 100 yards from the end you can start using your arms like I've been teaching you."

I would listen to Andy's advice and let rip with 100 yards to go, leaving the others in my wake. At one half-mile race in Carntyne, I raced on grass and cinders and won my first prize — a little canteen of cutlery to take home to Mum.

Then the Harriers entered me in the St Mirren Mile, which was run at Paisley. I got a 20-yard start from the back marker. He passed me and then I came up and passed him. When it came up to the finish, there was only one lad to catch, but, somehow, I made a mistake. I thought I was on the last lap but there was still a lap to go when I eased up a bit and ended up being beaten by about ten yards. I was given a Westminster chiming clock as second prize.

Big Andy was so proud. "That was great," he said, "but you threw it away. What made you stop?"

I was frightened to tell him that I had been concentrating on the lad in front and not heard the bell.

I was 18 and my abiding memory of the journey home on the bus clutching the clock was a drunk

75

woman who drove me mad by repeating over and over, "Your mother will be very proud, son. Your mother will be proud."

The funny thing was that the clock never went and Mum put it under her bed. The following summer, I went over to Annagassan to visit Dad's sister, Aunt Rosie. I took her the clock, which she put on her mantelpiece — right away, it started ticking!

Soon, I began to win a lot of races over cross-country in my age group. I was coming on, building up my stamina, my confidence and my ability to do things. And I was getting keener and keener all the time. On Andy's advice, I started jogging from the house at night-time. I would see Jack Scott out on his beat and he would give me a cheery wave. Jogging was not that unusual in the Gorbals, as a lot of the boxers jogged and I would sometimes go running with them.

As I got more and more wrapped up in athletics, my involvement with looking after greyhounds started to wane. Mum was pleased that I was getting away from the greyhound crowd. They were all very kind and gave me cakes and food, but they were a lot of rogues and vagabonds too. If Jack Scott hadn't got me into the Maryhill Harriers, I could easily have been sucked into their activities or joined up with one of the street gangs.

I was pleased to start afresh too, as one particular incident with the greyhounds had set the alarm bells ringing for me. I used to walk a dog called Tim for a well-known former footballer. He was an affectionate wee thing but not very fast — I could walk faster than he could run. Whenever he saw me, he would jump up and lick me. One day, I went to collect Tim, and his owner asked me to take him to the dog track at the Nelson Athletic grounds in the Gallowgate. But he added, "Don't clap him today, son. He's in a very bad mood. I've got a muzzle on him."

So I took Tim to the track, and just before his race was due to start a man whom I had never seen before came up to me and said, "Look, son, I've got to run out with Tim today. I'll put him in the traps."

As soon as Tim saw him, he was all over him. The dog obviously knew him and started licking him. The stranger asked me if I had any money. I said no but he put two shillings on Tim, saying slyly, "He'll win, all right."

Well, he certainly did. He left the other five dogs trailing and won the handicap easily. I was chuffed that Tim had won, but, as I walked home, the whippet men at the bird market said, "That wasn't Tim. It's a ringer!"

Sure enough, this dog was the spitting image of Tim but it had been brought up from Greenock to fleece the Glasgow bookies. I took the dog back to his owner but I had a very uncomfortable feeling as I returned him.

As well as developing into an athlete, I was busy learning a trade that would get me through life. Just before Dad died, Cohen's clothing firm had packed up and I was reduced to just having my part-time jobs again. Then, one day, my mother came home and announced, "I've got you a job as an apprentice

77

painter. You've to go down to Pollock and Traill in Hospital Street and see the gentleman in charge."

I went round to the shop straight away and went up to a man wearing a bowler hat. "Mister, I'm here about the job as an apprentice," I said.

"What's your name?"

"Andrew Coogan."

"Oh, aye, your mother was in here. So you would like to be a painter?"

"Oh, aye, sir, I would."

"I'm Mr Pollock. Well, it's not easy now. You'll need to pay close attention."

"I will, sir. When can I start?"

"Monday morning."

I was nervous when I turned up on my first day. There were three journeymen painters and another two apprentices. I was standing outside the shop for a little before I went in and met the other two apprentices. I was pleased to recognise one of the journeymen, Mr Cuthbertson, who I remembered had done a job for my mother when I was a boy. It was a big event to get a painter into your house then and Mr Cuthbertson whitewashed our ceiling.

Mr Pollock told me my wages. "Ten shillings a week less your insurance stamp."

It wasn't too bad, I thought. I was still delivering the milk in the morning and the papers at night, as well as helping out with the dogs occasionally too.

I was given a set of white bib-and-brace trousers, which I would have to pay for, and Mr Pollock had a

78

good look at me. "Now, son, you don't stay far from here, do you?" he asked.

"No, Mr Pollock. We stay in Thistle Street."

"Well, run along to your house and get a tie. All our painters wear ties," he explained. "When you go into a house with a tie on, folk know you are a tidy person. We are very strict about wearing ties."

I noticed the journeymen were all wearing white collars with ties and ran home to get one. That was me started.

I was sent out on my first job with a painter called Willie Morrison. He was a man in his fifties and his son-in-law, Alec Elliot, was a well-known footballer with Partick Thistle. Lo and behold, our first job was at Mrs Knott's restaurant, and I was pleased it was somewhere I knew. We went along with instructions to paint the outside. I carried the steps and Willie had the scrubbing brushes and the rest of the stuff.

My climbing career in the Gorbals meant I had no fear of heights so I was sent up the ladder to wash down the sign and the frontage. Mrs Knott's restaurant was so well known. All the tables were scrubbed white and everyone went there. Benny Lynch was a regular. Mrs Knott knew my mother and they sometimes had a wee dram together. After we had washed down the front, she came out and said, "I know your face, son."

"Aye. Me and my wee sister used to come in here from the school for a threepenny dinner. The carters used to come in and leave their horses outside and I used to look after them."

"Ah, you're the wee lad that used to put the choke bag back on them. Come away in and have your dinner, lads."

What a start to my working life. I was pleased to be recognised but was a bit embarrassed after lunch when Mrs Knott insisted that I wear a pinny to keep the paint off my clothes. Willie had me up the ladder painting the high bits that he couldn't reach and I felt very useful. Willie was a patient and caring tutor, and he taught me a lot, not just about painting but also about life.

Most of my time at Pollock and Traill was spent working with Archie Patterson. One day, we were going to a job at Glasgow University and I was pushing all our gear on a barra up Woodlands Road. Archie suggested that we have a break and then reminded me that it was the day of the Grand National. I told Archie that my dad had picked the winner the previous year and put my hand into my pocket and fingered his wallet that I always carried with me. I took it out and found a piece of paper folded inside with the word "Reynoldstown" written in my father's curly script. It was a year to the day that the Irish-bred horse had romped home three lengths ahead of the course.

"Oh, Andy, Reynoldstown is running again today," Archie said. "You'd better put something on it."

We went along to the bookie's at lunchtime and backed the horse, each of us putting a shilling on it to win. Later that afternoon, we were jubilant when Reynoldstown became only the third horse ever to win the Grand National two years in a row. As I stood in front of the bookie's counter and collected my winnings, I felt my father smiling down at me.

I enjoyed learning my trade. Pollock and Traill had their own colourman to make up different paint colours, as sometimes you had to match the shade of a curtain or a carpet. The paint was made up in a big barrel of white lead — thick stuff with linseed oil and driers. Then it was thinned out with turps, before colours like Burnt Sienna, Umber and Yellow Ochre were added. The paint was then strained through a lady's stocking into a pail.

I took pride in a job well done and we saw a lot of life going to different places and parts of Glasgow. We painted offices, shops and factories as well as the homes of well-off families. Sometimes, the factors would send us in to distemper and paint vacant flats that were bug-ridden. You could always tell where there were bugs. We could smell them immediately we went in the door. When Mum knew I was working in the slums, she always used to shout after me as I went off to work, "Remember to tuck your trousers into your socks, Andrew — we don't want you bringing bugs home with you."

My workmates were great guys too. Archie Patterson was my boss and was a terrific teacher. I got on very well with Archie. His big weakness was for drink but he was a fantastic tradesman and I learned a lot from him. One day, we were decorating a shopfront and the manager gave Archie money to buy gold leaf. Archie went off to buy the gold leaf and I got on with washing down the woodwork of the shop. However, when Archie eventually came back, he was very much the worse for wear; even worse, he had spent the gold-leaf money on whisky.

"Oh, God, Archie, what will we do? We're in trouble now," I said, trying not to panic.

"Don't worry, don't worry. Here, take these coppers and go and get some mustard powder."

"Mustard powder?"

"Aye, mustard powder. They'll never know."

When I got back, Archie set about mixing the mustard powder with varnish. Despite having had a drink, he did a great job. But he was not pleased with it at first and ordered me to clean it off with white spirit. Then he started again and made the most fantastic job of graining the front of the shop, and then used the mustard-and-varnish mix for the gold-leaf effect on the signage. When Archie finished, it looked absolutely marvellous.

He was a real character. On one occasion, we were working in the YMCA in Glasgow and I went to wash out a brand new pail, but Archie shouted not to use the new pail. It was being kept back for their beer on a Saturday when the painters would club together to buy a bucket of beer after they got their wages. When Saturday came, I was sent to get the beer.

"How will I get back into the YMCA with beer?" I protested. "There's a big commissionaire at the door in a fancy uniform. What if he stops me?"

"Just tell him it's for washing down the mahogany."

I went off to the pub and got the pail of ale. Sure enough, on the way back the doorman stopped me.

"What's that?" he asked.

"Beer, sir."

"What are you doing with that at your age? You can't come in here with that. The YMCA is teetotal."

"But I'm a painter, sir. We use beer for washing down the mahogany."

"Oh," he said, "I never knew you could use it for that. You're always learning, aren't you?"

Archie had a beautiful set of brand-new brushes, but I was under strict instructions that they were never to be used. I couldn't understand why — until one day, he said, "Andy, I could fairly go a good dram. Could you take the good brushes down to the pawn shop and get a couple of bob for them?"

Those brushes were in and out of that pawn shop like a yo-yo.

One day, Archie got dead drunk and I had to get him and all our tools and ladders home. I managed to get him into the barra and then covered him up with dust covers and painting sheets. I placed the tins of paint and varnish around him and pushed the barra about four miles through the streets of Glasgow to Archie's house. Nobody seemed to notice, although there were one or two funny looks when Archie started to snore. He had four daughters and he was always trying to marry them off. When I got him home, he came to his senses and said, "For God's sake, Andy, will you not take one of these women away with you?"

We worked long hours at Pollock and Traill, and on a Saturday morning too, but we had a lot of laughs. On one occasion, while painting the exterior windows at a big convalescent home outside Glasgow, I peered in and saw a piano in one of the large sitting rooms. I asked the nurse in charge if I could have a go on it at lunchtime, but, when I went in, I discovered it was a pianola complete with punched cards to churn out all sorts of beautiful classical music. I decided to play a joke on the lads and got the nurse in on it.

When we were all outside having our sandwiches, the nurse duly appeared and said, "You can come in now, Andrew, and do your practice."

"Oh, that's great. I won't be long, lads. I'd better keep my practice up."

I went inside and made sure the window was left wide open. Then I selected a few cards — piano concertos by Chopin, Tchaikovsky and Beethoven. I settled down in front of the piano and started moving my hands over the keys as the glorious music echoed around the room. I soon gathered an audience and the lads were hanging over the window watching in awe. When I came out, they were full of praise. "Here, Andy, you're wasted at the painting. You should be on the stage. You could turn professional."

The next day, Mr Pollock turned up to check on our progress and the same thing happened. The nurse called me in and my hands were flying up and down the keyboard. I was doing all the passionate body actions too, hunched over the piano. Soon Mr Pollock and the others stuck their heads in the windows. When I finished the first tune, they all applauded. Then, in the middle of the second one, I got up and took a bow as the pianola continued to play on. There was great hilarity and plenty of laughter.

When I turned 21, my apprenticeship was over and I began earning the full journeyman's wage of three pounds twelve shillings a week. The day I got my first full wage packet, we were working in the big offices of the American Oil Company in Argyll Street. We went up to the Horseshoe Bar to celebrate and I ordered up a drink for Archie and wee Sammy, my fellow apprentice, but they insisted on paying for it. Archie said, "No, no. You won't open that bloody pay packet. We'll buy the drinks and you'll take that pay back to your mother unopened."

I had enjoyed learning all the tricks of the trade and the more complex jobs that included gold-leaf work. But my overwhelming passion was for running. I couldn't afford proper running shoes, but about a year after I joined the Maryhill Harriers I was walking through the Barras market when I spied a pair of spiked shoes in among the jumble on an old man's barra. I couldn't take my eyes off them, sitting there like treasure trove among all the junk. I knew if I showed too much interest the price would go up. So I asked, "Mister, what are these shoes with the nails in them for?"

The old man looked at me pityingly and shook his head. "You must be really ignorant. They are for climbing mountains," he said. "Are ye interested in them?"

"Well, I might be."

"How much have you got?"

"Two bob."

"I'll take one shilling and sixpence."

I was buoyed up with my purchase and took the shoes round to Mr Miller, who was a cobbler to trade. He lived in Waddell Street in the Gorbals. He was stone deaf and worked from his bedroom but he was a gifted cobbler and made the running shoes for all of the athletes in Glasgow. He put new soles on my shoes and sorted them up for five shillings.

I made some good friends in the Harriers too. A couple of the lads came from Hamilton and Larkhall — quite a distance outside Glasgow — and they would come and stay with my mother at the weekends. But it was a little bit of a worry for me. Mum was lonely after Dad died and she sometimes took a good dram, which I hated. I see now that it was fairly harmless and that she just enjoyed a sing-song in the pub for the company. But, at the time, the Gorbals had about 170 pubs for its 40,000 inhabitants — some of which sold cheap red wine, red biddy — and I worried too much that Mum might go down that slippery slope.

I was still too young to get into the Scottish international team, but it was my dream to run for my country and be like Andy Blair, Dunky Wright and Bob Bell, who were all Maryhill Harriers that had made it into the international team. After a while, Dunky Wright decided I was to be a miler. I was to get strengthened up over the winter by running cross-country, and the following season Dunky thought I could be entered for the Hampden Mile. Well, that was a surprise. The annual Hampden Mile had entries from all over, including some Yanks from the Ivy League universities of Harvard and Yale. They came over for the sport, and had a season of running at all the big events in Britain.

It was a real honour to be entered because a member of the Maryhill Harriers had often won the event. The previous year, it had been Ossie Osbourne and the year before that it was big Andy. I was beginning to get my distances and learn a lot about how to run this race. I was really enjoying it and thinking about it all the time.

One day, I beat Ossie in a training run and he gave me his tracksuit. He had been running in America and he had brought the tracksuit home with him. As he gave me it, Ossie told me that he thought I could win the Hampden Mile. The tracksuit had a Maryhill Harriers badge and some other fancy badges on it. It looked fantastic, but I felt it was too fancy and never wore it. I felt that I hadn't earned it. Only the top athletes had tracksuits; the rest of us wore our flannels and that sort of thing.

Finally, the great day dawned and Jack Scott drove me up in the car to compete in the 1938 Police Mile at Hampden. The police races were great events. The Royal Ulster Constabulary and the Glasgow and Edinburgh police forces all entered their best runners, and there were plenty of guest runners too. Glasgow's chief constable, Sir Percy Sillitoe, the man credited with smashing the Glasgow gangs, was sitting beside a big table loaded with prizes and trophies.

I psyched myself up and didn't feel nervous about the huge crowd. I was telling myself to focus, "Come on, Coogan, you can do it, you can do it." I thought it was funny that I had got into running because I was chased by the polis and here I was racing them. I knew I could do it.

The race started and I gave it all I had. I was determined not to let the Harriers down and flew past big Hare of the Ulster Constabulary and won the race. I went up to receive my prize and Lady Sillitoe presented me with a massive canteen of cutlery, saying, "Well, you'll be all right for your dinner with this."

Sir Percy said he was really pleased I'd beaten big Hare, who was the favourite. He even suggested that I should join the police.

Jack Scott was as proud as punch. He came forward and said, "He might have won that race. But he can't beat me, sir."

I explained to Sir Percy that Jack was the constable who had got me into the Maryhill Harriers in the first place. Sir Percy nodded and told Jack, "Well, you've done a bloody good job."

As I walked back home clutching the huge canteen of cutlery, Mr Fox the local newsagent had an *Evening Times* bill stuck up outside his shop. It read: "Coogan Goes His Mile!" and all the neighbours congratulated me. It was a great feeling but I always remembered Mum's advice to "stay humble". She was over the moon and so pleased for me when I got home.

There were no money prizes because we were amateurs. My canteen of cutlery contained fish knives, fruit knives, tea knives and all sorts of eating irons that were a complete mystery to us. It was said to be worth ten pounds, but the canteen was not much use to us — we were living on tatties and cabbage, and Mum said it was too good to use anyway.

A fortnight later I was competing in the Empire Exhibition Mile at Ibrox Park. Earlier, the King and Queen had opened the exhibition in front of a vast 100,000-strong crowd. It was estimated that there were 70,000 spectators standing in the ground for our race. I had never seen a crowd like it. I was confident because I had won the Hampden Mile against a field that included international competition, and, because of my victory at Hampden, I had a lot of support from the home crowd at Ibrox. As soon as we were off, they were right behind me, yelling, "Come on, Coogan! Come on! Come on, Coogan!"

When I won, there was a deafening roar. Sir Paddy Dolan, Lord Provost of Glasgow, presented me with the prize that day. It turned out to be another ten-pound cutlery canteen — exactly the same as the last one! We were broke but now we had enough cutlery to host a royal banquet.

Eventually, I plucked up the courage to approach Dunky Wright. "Dunky, do you think I could exchange this canteen for the ten pounds in cash? I could rig myself out. I could buy a suit for two pounds and a good pair of shoes for ten shillings. I could give my mum the rest."

Dunky fixed me with a serious look and told me earnestly, "Jackie, when you start getting paid money for what you've done today, this sport will be finished."

★ ★ ★

I was a happy-go-lucky 21 year old. Betty had taught me to dance and I had mastered the foxtrot. I was enjoying myself. I would go to the Dixon Dance Halls in Cathcart Street where we would have the choice of two different dance halls — an upstairs and a downstairs — with two different bands and they were both very good. Betty was working in Macfarlane's shirt factory and she would bring all her pals from work. I was in demand for my dancing skills — it was great.

Things at home were a little easier economically too. We had moved to a nice house in Hospital Street but still in the Gorbals, where we had so many friends. I was still the main breadwinner, bringing in three pounds and twelve shillings, but now Betty was working too, and Eddie was an apprentice bricklayer. It meant that Mum didn't have to do so much cleaning.

I was enjoying life to the full and things were getting better for us at home. However, on the international scene, dark clouds were gathering. Glasgow was a great place for politics and Clydeside had been "Red" since the disaster of the First World War. Although I was not interested in politics, I could feel that there was more tension in the air. Now the whitewashed slogans in the slums were all about "Arms for Spain" and lads from the Gorbals and the Calton were volunteering to fight in Spain against Franco, who was backed by Hitler and Mussolini. Jewish refugees were arriving in the Gorbals from Nazi Germany and blackshirt meetings in Glasgow were broken up by communists and anti-fascists. Few of us knew, though, that on the other side of the world Japan was on the march, conquering large parts of China and committing terrible atrocities like the Rape of Nanking, where over 300,000 innocent Chinese were tortured, raped and slaughtered in the most bestial way.

I never imagined that there would be another war. The last one had been so awful that we just never thought that there would ever be another one. So the news when it came on Sunday, 3 September 1939 was a great shock to me. We were working on the Capital picture house in Cowcaddens, and when I went to work on the Monday the declaration of war was the big topic of conversation. The consensus was that it would not last as long as the First World War and that, of course, Britain would win.

A few days later, I got a letter to go and register for the armed forces at a recruiting centre in Partick. When I arrived, there were a few hundred lads all the same age as me. We were given medicals and had our details taken. Then I was told, "You'll be hearing from us."

For a couple of weeks, I never heard anything and I began to hope that they had forgotten all about me. It was an anxious time, and every night when I came home, I would ask if there was a letter for me. Whenever Mum said, "No," I heaved a sigh of relief and went out dancing or training. Then, one Friday night, I was all ready and dressed up to go dancing when Mum said, "Oh, Andy I forgot to tell you. There's a letter for you up on the mantelpiece."

My heart sank. It sank even further when I picked up the envelope and read the dread words printed on the front: "On His Majesty's Service".

I was going to war.

CHAPTER
FOUR

The Fireside Soldiers

I was to report to Queen Street station the following week with a small kit. Mum had memories of the last war, of all the lads who had died and been maimed, and of how she had lived with worry after Dad was drafted into the Merchant Navy and spent two years running the U-boat blockade. She started to cry and was quite inconsolable. No matter what anybody said, it was the mothers who always sensed the true dangers that faced us.

"Don't worry, Maw. Don't worry. It'll be all right. It won't last long. I'll be OK," I said.

"Oh, Andrew, I'll pray for you. For God's sake, take care of yourself. I'll pray for you every day."

When I went to work on the Monday, Mr Pollock was furious that I had been called up. He was losing a skilled man. He was angry too that his own son had been called up. My workmates were sorry for me. Everybody was sympathetic.

The call-up was devastating for our family. It was not just the worry for Mum; it was also a terrible economic blow. Instead of the three pounds and twelve shillings a week I had been earning, I was to be paid just fourteen shillings. Seven shillings would be sent home to my mother and I would be given the remaining seven shillings minus two shillings for breakages. We were to fight the Nazis for five bob a week. It meant that Mum would have to get more cleaning jobs. For working-class people, the war meant even more hardship and poverty. Throughout my army service, I would worry constantly about how Mum was managing.

When the day finally came and I had to report to Queen Street, I didn't tell Mum. I was worried that she would have a couple of drinks and get too emotional. Betty and her friend Muriel came along to see me off. She was crying, as a lot of the women were. There were around a hundred lads there — a mixed bunch from Partick, Bridgeton, Cowcaddens, Springburn, all over Glasgow. Two sergeants appeared and started shouting out our names, getting us into some kind of order. I recognised a couple of friends from the Gorbals, Willie Moffat and wee Hughie Clark, a boxer.

Quite a few of the boys had taken a drink, enjoying their last few hours of freedom in civvy street. We were sitting in a carriage when a small, skinny guy came in. He had clearly had a few and immediately started shouting, "Git the windae doon. Git the windae doon."

We pulled the window down and he stuck his head out.

"Bella! Bella! Oh, Bella, don't forget me. Bella, write to me. I'll write to you, Bella. I love you, Bella! Oh, Bella, I'll miss you! I love you, Bella! Don't forget me, Bella! Cheerio, Bella!"

We were all laughing and instantly dubbed him "Bella". The nickname stuck with "Bella" Divers for the rest of the war.

As soon as the train steamed out of Queen Street, we began to speculate on where we were headed. Most of us thought we were heading for France, maybe to fight the Germans. Even though we'd had no training, we really thought we would be pitched straight into battle. Britain was in a desperate situation at the time and the British Expeditionary Force had already been sent to France. The fathers of most of the guys in the carriage had fought in France in the last war. So we fully expected to be going back to the killing fields of Flanders.

After about an hour, we trundled into Edinburgh, and then half an hour or so later we reached the Borders town of Kelso and were ordered to disembark. What a relief.

We followed a couple of officers, who wore riding breeches and spoke in plummy accents, up to the marketplace where we had to collect a load of bags and take them to a stables where we filled them with hay and straw for mattresses. The sergeant told us this was to be our lodgings for the night. When one of the lads protested, the sergeant told him, "You'll have a lot bloody worse to sleep on than this before you're finished, son."

How right he was. But not even this grizzled veteran of the First World War could have imagined the horrors that awaited us.

I slept pretty soundly that first night in the horse stall. In the morning, we were marched down to a church hall in the town and given a breakfast consisting of a big mug of tea, some scrambled egg and bread and butter. When we got back to the stables, we spent the day getting to know each other, finding out about our new comrades, their jobs and what team they supported. Most of my fellow conscripts were little guys from Glasgow, but there were some strapping country lads too.

We stayed another night in the stables and then we were paraded in the morning. Two officers appeared and divided us into two groups by marching along behind the lines of men, tapping us on the shoulder with a swagger stick and shouting the instruction, "Step forward!"

One group was sent to the right and the other to the left. Then one of the officers announced, "You men on the right are now "A" battery of the Lanarkshire Yeomanry. Those on the left are "B" battery."

I was selected for "A" battery. Next, we were marched back to the station. Now we were convinced that France was the next stop, but after an hour the train stopped and we got out at the county town of Lanark — another relief and much laughter as we disembarked.

We were ordered to "fall in" and marched up to a former clothing factory in Lanark. It had bunk beds piled up one on top of the other and this was to be our new billet. The cooks were there getting ready for our arrival. The Yeomanry were already set up and we were being added into their regiment. They gave us a meal and told us that the next day we were to go the quartermasters to be issued with shoes, boots, uniforms and get kitted out. What a performance that was. The boots were huge. The trousers were made of denim and looked like they had been made for circus clowns. They were flapping about our legs, and we were laughing our heads off. They were too big, too wide and too long, and we had to tie them up with string. The sergeant told us he wanted to see our boots looking like his in two days' time, but his were like glass and ours were scraped and dried out! Then they took us to get inoculated, which was really painful.

That night, a few of the lads had been drinking and decided to have a farting competition, which was hilarious to them but not so funny for the rest of us. It seemed endless and if anyone had lit a match the whole place would have gone up.

The next morning, we were told to get up and get shaved. We were directed to a cold tap in the corner. As we shaved in the freezing water, with our arms sore from the inoculations, we felt pretty sorry for ourselves. It was so cold in that place.

Before we could dwell on our misery too much, we were assembled outside and told we would learn to march. It was the beginning of our six weeks of basic training. We were just young lads, really, who knew nothing about the army or soldiering and our first attempts were pitiful. Marching drill was done down the side streets of Lanark and the women would be standing outside their doors looking at us. They would shake their heads in sympathy and say, "Aw, look at them. What a shame — they're just poor souls."

We just could not get the steps right, and, to make matters worse, I was behind a big hulking ploughman from New Cumnock in Ayrshire called Tarn Laird. He had ruddy red cheeks, just the two teeth in the front and a big moustache, and he walked at the speed of the plough. It was as if he was hitched to two invisible Clydesdales and, with this great slow stride, he just couldn't get properly marching at all. Tarn was a great lad, and was very good with engines and mechanical things. At nights, I wondered why he was always putting his hand down the side of the bed until I discovered he had a half bottle of whisky to keep him company.

I had never heard of the Lanarkshire Yeomanry before. It was not a famous regiment like the Argyll and Sutherland Highlanders, the Cameron Highlanders, the Gordon Highlanders or the Black Watch. It had been established by wealthy landowners mainly to put down riots and rebellions by the growing working class who worked in mines and mills around Glasgow. When it was founded in 1820, there had been a great uprising of radical weavers and three of the ringleaders were beheaded, so initially the Lanarkshire Yeomanry was a territorial force designed to impose law and order. It served as a cavalry unit in the Boer War and then, during the First World War, the regiment fought dismounted as infantry in Gallipoli, Palestine and the Western Front, where Sergeant Thomas Caldwell won the Victoria Cross in 1918.

The total destruction of the Polish cavalry in 1939 when they charged with lances against invading Nazi tanks finally persuaded the top brass, however, that the cavalry's days were over. We were a regiment in transition when I joined, on the way to becoming part of the Royal Artillery. We still had horses, though, and I was pleased to be given one to look after.

Our commander, Colonel Augustus Murdoch, strode around everywhere wearing a monocle, in jodhpurs and wielding a riding crop. He was tall and walked with a slight stoop but looked very much the cavalry officer. He had been decorated in the First World War for bravery and was regarded by us as firm but fair. Colonel Murdoch called us the "Tally-Ho Boys", and he would later have the nickname painted on our trucks and guns, along with broken spurs to remind us of our cavalry past.

A lot of our officers were county-set types who regretted the demise of the cavalry. Major John Wilson was fairly typical of their wealthy background. His family were wealthy coal-owners, and his father Sir John Wilson had also served in the Lanarkshire Yeomanry during the First World War. When my friend Tarn Hannah drove Major Wilson home to his family seat in Perthshire, Sir John presented him with a Colt 45 pistol for his protection. A notable exception among the officers was Captain James Mackenzie, who came from a slightly humbler Highland background. He impressed his interview panel by announcing that he had attended Tain Public School. They thought he was a fellow toff and never realised Captain Mackenzie had gone to the local primary school — which was open to all of the public.

Some of the other regulars still had cavalry uniforms, which were much smarter than our baggy battledress, and later we would borrow these uniforms with their smart riding boots when we got leave to go to Glasgow. We looked quite dashing in them and they improved our chances with the girls.

Our time in Lanark was devoted to basic training — square-bashing, drilling and learning how to deploy the guns. The only trouble was we didn't have any guns. Under the orders of two bombardiers who had been brought up from Aldershot, we shoved a couple of two-wheeled barras around, pretending that they were 25-pound howitzers and getting them into position. The bombardiers seemed unimpressed by our efforts and constantly complained about their misfortune in having to train a "load of bloody cowboys".

Marching drill was a bit of an ordeal and I could never quite get the hang of it. Rifles were in short supply, and we never ever had any ammunition. Eventually, they managed to scrape a few old weapons together, but they dated from before the First World War and probably wouldn't have been much use for target practice even if we had been issued with ammunition. We were marched down to a school playground for rifle drill where we met our new drill sergeant, a hard man and a professional soldier with the Irish Guards. He was all spit and polish and introduced himself by roaring, "Do you know who Ah am? Ah'm Sergeant Major Flaherty and Ah'm Mrs Flaherty's son.

And you lot will do what Ah tell you or Ah'll get my mother on to you!"

Flaherty was putting us through our paces and we were standing easy when the children in the school started singing. It had been quite a while since I had heard music and it was a song that my mother used to sing. It was a song I liked too, and I drifted into a dream world, listening to the kids singing the old Burns song "Ye Banks and Braes o' Bonnie Doon". So I never heard the command to stand to attention and was still standing with my legs apart long after everyone else had snapped to attention.

Flaherty went berserk, "Coogan! Get out here now! Let's see if I can get your attention now! Run around the playground with your rifle above your head and don't stop until I tell you!"

I started running but it was not long before I got painful cramp in my arms. Flaherty kept yelling, "Keep going, Coogan! Keep going!"

On the fourth lap, I started to swing the rifle and didn't know whether to chuck the rifle over the playground fence or clobber Flaherty with it. He was a complete bully. There were some women watching and Flaherty was enjoying showing off his power.

I had tears in my eyes, and was just about to whack Flaherty when an imposing voice boomed out, "That's enough of that! That's enough of that! What's going on here?"

The voice came from a sturdy-looking man of about 5 ft 8 in. and in his fifties. It was the first time I had ever seen him but I soon learned it was Sergeant Major

Scullion, who had served in the First World War. Flaherty had come up from Aldershot to train us, but Scullion was his boss at the Lanarkshire Yeomanry. He told Flaherty, "You've no right to do that, Flaherty. You'll not treat this boy like that." He gave Flaherty a right telling off and after that Flaherty never liked me.

Scullion gave me a row too. "Coogan, never do that again. You'll get in big trouble if you throw rifles about. Bloody well behave yourself and settle down."

Sergeant Major Scullion was a very devout Roman Catholic and always insisted that we were immaculately turned out for Mass. He had been a bus driver in civvy street and had stayed in the territorials after his service in the First World War. In one famous episode, our regimental bugler Arthur "Trumpeter" Smith managed to get on his wrong side. Trumpeter was a real character who used to wake us in the morning by sitting up in bed and blowing an earsplitting reveille inside our barracks and then rolling over back in bed, as we hurled boots and insults at him. Trumpeter was a talented musician, who had played with a Salvation Army band. He had also played in a band of the Protestant Orange Order. One day, we were all on parade with Sergeant Major Scullion casting a critical eye over us when suddenly the bugle sounded and Trumpeter belted out a spirited version of the Protestant anthem "The Sash My Father Wore". The song is regarded as very anti-Catholic in Scotland, and we all laughed as Scullion went mad and marched a smirking Trumpeter off to the guardhouse.

Being stationed at Lanark was not so bad. We were about an hour from Glasgow and we could skip into the city. I would meet my mother and see my pals from the Maryhill Harriers. My sister came up to see us with her friends, and one day we had a picnic.

Mum came up to Lanark too. On one of her visits, the Lanark races were on and we were sitting in a little Italian cafe having our tea when two stable boys came in. Mum offered to pay for their tea and asked them, "Any tips, lads?"

"Aye, missus. There's a horse running tomorrow called Aranzis. Make sure you put a bet on it."

The next day, we went to the raceground. Aranzis looked awful; it had a head the size of a monument. I had seen a better-looking donkey. It was an ugly horse and I thought it would only do well if it had wheels stuck on it. But Mum said, "You don't go on appearances with human beings, so we'll just wait and see."

The horse's odds were 10-1 and I thought it had no chance. Mum put a pound on it, and she had little enough money. Well, it won out the park. It was amazing. Mum stayed at the Royal Oak Hotel for ten bob that night, and the next day we saw the stable lads again. "Did you back it?" they asked.

They were pleased when Mum replied, "Yes we did and we're better off for it."

We were quite happy in Lanark. It was close to home and the local people were very friendly. The area was famous for its greenhouses and soft fruit, and when we were on route marches the women would give us tomatoes and strawberries. I was able to keep up my running training too and would frequently run up to and around the racecourse.

It was the time of the so-called "Phoney War" and we were nicknamed the "fireside soldiers", but Britain was steadily moving onto a wartime footing. Gas masks were issued to the population, even for babies; tree trunks were painted white because of the blackout; railings were cut down for scrap metal and ration cards were issued. It was a worrying time. The Germans were blitzkrieging their way across Europe in armoured columns with ruthless lightning tactics. We were always wondering what would happen, anxious about where they would send us.

After about a month, the word came that we were moving on. Around the middle of the day, Flaherty turned up and said, "Get yourselves ready — we're moving out tomorrow."

We had never fired a rifle let alone a field gun but we thought, "Oh, God. This time this is it. We're off to France to fight the Germans."

We got our kit ready and started asking around where we might be going. There was some talk that we were going to a place called Port Seton. We had never heard of it, but Bella, Tam and the rest of them were all talking about Port Seton. I skipped home on the bus to say goodbye to Mum. It was about half a crown for the bus but Mum paid the fare back. She was surprised to see me. Then I broke the bad news. "Maw, we're moving tomorrow. We're being posted to Port Seton."

She promptly burst into tears and became very upset. In between heaving sobs, she said, "Oh, my God. You'll get malaria there. You'll get all sort of diseases over there. Port Seton — there's Arabs there, you'll get burned alive. There are elephants and lions and tigers over there too. I'll pray for you, Andrew, I'll pray for you."

We were worried to death. I got the bus from Waterloo Street back to Lanark at about nine o'clock and promptly told the other lads about the elephants and tigers. Some of them had been told the same sort of stuff. It was a restless night — we were off to the unknown.

The next day, we all lined up and got on the train. Soon, we were in Edinburgh and then we were on our way again. Then we stopped at a place called Longniddry, and the cry went up: "Everybody off."

We were flummoxed and didn't know what was happening. We marched along the road till we came to a sign that proudly proclaimed "Port Seton". The whole column erupted in laughter but we felt ashamed and right stupid too. We had alarmed our families over nothing. Maybe we had got confused with Port Said, the British base in Egypt that protected the Suez Canal. There was nothing very threatening about the peaceful little fishing village of Port Seton on the shores of the Firth of Forth — there was not an Arab, elephant or tiger in sight along the golden Seton Sands that fringed the Lothian shores.

We marched on for a bit until we reached Gosford House, a vast palace built in handsome blonde sandstone by the Earl of Wemyss, whose family were aristocratic coal-owners. It was a spectacular building and the officers were given lodgings inside, while we stayed in cold and draughty corrugated-iron Nissen huts in the grounds. It was a very cold and bitter winter. There were thirty of us to a hut with just one small stove in the middle. All we could get was one bucket of water in which every man had to wash and shave. If you were too late and came last in the line, it was like mud!

As a painter, I was lucky enough to get into the big house and work on some of the officers' rooms. It had a huge double staircase that was quite breathtaking. I was able to spin the job out quite a bit, which was great because I was excused from going on boring route marches, which often included a bracing dip in the Forth to toughen us up. I was about 10 st. 7 lb at this time and I was feeling really fit in any event.

We also managed to enjoy ourselves. Sometimes, we would get a lift into Edinburgh and I would get off at Portobello to go to the baths. Occasionally, there would be a run from the baths.

While I was stationed at Gosford House, I was selected to be a signaller. The first things they taught us were semaphore and Morse signalling with torches — neither of which would be much use in the dense Malayan jungle. We didn't have field radio communications then, let alone today's lasers, so the job ultimately became laying telephone cable to link the artillery-spotting officers in their forward observation posts with the battery so that they could relay their instructions and target coordinates to the sightsetters on the guns. There were four guns in each battery and each gun had two signallers.

One day, we were on manoeuvres laying cables through the fields from Port Seton up to Haddington when we noticed that there were land girls about in the fields too, picking potatoes. I was with two other signallers, Geordie Carson and Eddie Cunningham, and one of the girls shouted us over for a cup of tea. They had flasks with them, which was great because we were so cold. We eagerly ran over to the girls. They were wearing men's caps and were covered up in scarves and big heavy coats. They looked like refugees and we felt sorry for them. We had our tea and then one of the girls asked if we would like to come to a dance on Friday night. It was at the baths in Port Seton where they had put a floor over the water. Naturally, we told them we would be delighted and they promised to send a bus to pick us up at Gosford House.

Sure enough, on the Friday night, a bus arrived for us, and we had a great night. I was shy, though. Then a girl came over to me and asked, "Are you not going to give me a dance? You're a fine one. I got you sorted out and you're not even asking me to dance?"

It was the land girl from the field and I hadn't recognised her. She was all done up like a model and was nothing like the scarecrow I had seen in the field the day before. She was a beautiful dancer and we had a great time. Then she saw my terrible boots and said that if I wanted to come along the following week she would get some boots from her brother, who was a size eight-and-a-half. Sure enough, the next Friday, she and the other girls came along with shoes and boots. They left them lined up for us to pick a pair. They were so kind, really kind. Their parents came along too. There was a long table with coffee, tea, sandwiches and some of the lads did a turn, some singing and playing an instrument.

After six weeks or so training at Gosford, we returned to Lanark,

It was 1940, and it was a grim year. Britain stood alone. More than 350,000 British and French troops managed to get off the beaches at Dunkirk — thanks to the amazing bravery of the men in the little boats who sailed across the Channel to get them off — but nearly 10,000 men of the 51st Highland Division, the pride and joy of the Scottish army, had been captured fighting a doomed rear-guard action at St Valery. We had lost so much of our artillery and weaponry too — either destroyed or captured by the Germans. Nazi bombers were appearing ever more frequently over British cities and the Germans were planning Operation Sea Lion — the invasion of Britain.

CHAPTER
FIVE

The Mighty Atom

After Dunkirk, we really feared that German parachutists and saboteurs could land at any time. I was on guard duty with one of the few rifles we had on camp. We had done a little bit of target practice at Gosford House but never fired more than five bullets at a time. But now on those lonely nights on guard duty at Lanark, when it always seemed to rain and I was soaking wet, I had no bullets at all. I was tired in the mornings after night guard duty and it was a couple of days before I opened an envelope that had been dumped on my bunk.

When I did get round to opening the letter, I couldn't believe my eyes. Bill Struth, the manager of Rangers Football Club, had organised an international sports day at Ibrox. He was writing to invite me to race in the mile against Sydney Wooderson, the small bespectacled English lawyer known as "The Mighty Atom". Wooderson held the world record for the mile and was famous around the globe. I read the letter over and over until it fully sunk in. It was unbelievable. I told Sergeant Major Scullion, who was very pleased for me and said that I would get leave OK. Then, as word spread through the regiment that I was to be up against the fastest man in the world, lots of the guys came up to congratulate me and wish me well.

A couple of days later, I was sent on an advanced signals course to Redford Barracks in Edinburgh. There were four of us: Geordie Carson, Willie Moffat, Eddie Cunningham and myself. I would run around the barracks' football ground to keep fit and on Saturdays I would go down to Portobello for a run, but it was not proper training. There were twenty-eight lads on the course and only us four from the Lanarkshire Yeomanry were Scottish. The two instructors were English and for some reason took a dislike to us Scots. If there were any fatigues to be done, it was always one of us that was selected. They were bullies and enjoyed throwing their weight around. One day they came in and asked, "Any of you lads interested in music?" When Willie Moffat said, "Yes," he was told to go down to the canteen and help move a piano. They tried to make our life a misery.

The regiment in Lanark had said it was fine for me to attend the Ibrox event and the sergeant at Redford Barracks had promised me a pass but it never materialised. I fretted about what to do. There was no way I could miss my chance to run against the world's greatest runner. In the end, the temptation was just too much and I decided to go absent without leave. I dodged up the back way where we used to practise signalling, through the hedges and down the back roads. I made my way down to the main road at Corstorphine. Two or three of the lads were doing the same thing; they used to do it every week when we were there. You got away with it as long as you were back for first parade on Sunday morning, so some of the lads used to stay the night in Glasgow. Motorists were very helpful to servicemen in uniform during the war and we were never short of lifts.

The lads were getting lifts and one of them said that I should go first because I was going to Ibrox. A gentleman stopped and offered to take me to Glasgow. He was very friendly and asked all about what I was doing. Halfway to Glasgow, we stopped at a little cafe for a cup of tea. The man was well known in the place and he was going to have his usual order. Then a girl came along and gave me a pencil and paper.

"She wants you to write down what you want," the man told me.

I couldn't take my eyes off her. She was only about 18 or 19 and she was the most beautiful girl I had ever seen. I wrote down what I wanted — a cup of tea and a buttered roll. She never said a thing and took my order away.

"You need to understand, son, she's deaf and dumb," the man explained.

My heart went out to that girl; I couldn't believe it. She was so beautiful and so kind to us. It seemed so unfair. She was on my mind all the way to Glasgow so I never mentioned the reason for my trip.

As we approached the outskirts of the city, my benefactor asked me, "Where do you want off in Glasgow?"

I said, "Anywhere, sir, I can always get a tram car."

Then he replied, "I'm going to Ibrox."

"Ibrox, where about?"

"I'm going to Ibrox Park. Wooderson is running today and I wouldn't miss it for the world."

"Sir, do you mind taking me to Ibrox Park with you?"

"Are you interested in athletics?"

"Very much so."

"OK, son, I'll take you there. How long have you been interested in athletics? It will be some race. Wooderson is the fastest man alive."

"Yeah, I know — I'm running against him."

The man looked at me. "What?"

"I'm running against him. I'm in the same race as Sydney Wooderson."

He obviously thought I was nuts and never said anything to me for a quite long time and concentrated on his driving.

We got to near Bridge Street and he said, "Where do you want off, son?"

I said, "It would be fine if you took me to Ibrox Park, sir."

"Look, are you pulling my leg?"

I showed him the invitation.

"Jesus Christ, I'm sitting with the bloke who is going to be racing Sydney Wooderson!"

As we got to the main entrance of Ibrox Park, I was greeted by Dunky Wright and our team manager Freddie Graham. I asked Dunky to help the man who had given me a lift from Edinburgh and he was over the moon. He shook my hand and offered me a lift back to

Edinburgh, saying, "Oh, thanks. Wait until I tell my wife about this."

I went into the changing-rooms and started warming up. Wooderson came in and we sat down and talked to each other. I told him that I had seen him before, running with Jack Lovelock. Lovelock had won the Olympic Mile, but Wooderson went on to beat him in the race I watched. Wooderson was a legend, but he was a proper gentleman and he put me at ease as I chatted with him. There was a huge crowd of 90,000 gathered at Ibrox that day. It was the biggest crowd I had ever seen, and when I came out of the footballers' tunnel everybody started clapping. They thought I was Wooderson — I was very like him and we both wore specs. I was never so embarrassed in my life.

There were about eight of us in the race. Wooderson was obviously the big name, but there were also other international athletes in the race. It was a handicap race so I got an 80-yard start against the world champion. There were other lads in front of me with 100- and 120-yard starts. I was pretty apprehensive and not just because of the huge crowd; I hadn't been training properly. I had been running every day, but just to keep fit — not to compete in the mile. I'd been glad to get the invitation but mainly because it allowed me to go to Glasgow to see my mother, so I didn't have overly high expectations of the race.

Right from the start, there was a tremendous noise from the crowd. With a lap to go, there were three runners ahead of me. At about 150 yards, I overtook Stokoe, the British Universities mile champion. I was excited because I knew that Stokoe was very good. The other athletes were well behind us by this time. The atmosphere in the stadium was amazing. I wasn't sure where Wooderson was, but I knew he was coming up by the way the crowd were roaring. I wasn't racing using the head; I was just desperate to get to the finish. With about ten yards to go, Wooderson came level, then passed me. I was happy to be in second place and, to tell the truth, just happy to be in the race, as it was a great honour to run against Wooderson. He set the world record for the mile in 1937 at four minutes six seconds and that stood for five years. Later, Wooderson's amazing comeback in 1945 — when he ran at four minutes four seconds — would inspire Roger Bannister to go for the four-minute mile in 1954.

In the excitement after the race, Pat and Frank, my two wee brothers, jumped over the perimeter wall at Ibrox to give me a hug and I had to persuade the police to let them through. Then Mr Struth, the Rangers manager, was slapping me on the back.

Wooderson was three years older than me and in the changing-room afterwards he was very encouraging. He told me that I had a good future in athletics and gave me his pins, his numbers, as a souvenir. Albert Hill, Wooderson's manager, was there, and said that if I came through the war I should come down to England to see him.

I was elated after the run and, on my way home to the Gorbals to stay the night with Mum, I allowed myself to dream of running for Scotland and maybe ultimately the Olympics.

Two days later, on the Monday, the *Glasgow Herald* published a photograph of me leading the field in front of the huge crowd with Stokoe behind me and Wooderson coming up fast in third position. I carefully cut it out and placed it in my wallet to treasure. It was a photograph that would be my undoing in the army but years later in a Japanese slave camp it would be a lifesaver.

The lads had covered for me at the barracks by answering my name when the roll call was taken, but I was caught out by my newfound fame.

The duty sergeant sent for me. "Right, Coogan," he said. "You're on a charge — absent without leave. You were out of the barracks on Saturday."

"What, me? There must be a mistake, sergeant. I was here all the time. I wasn't out of bounds."

We argued for a bit then he produced a rolled-up copy of the *Glasgow Herald*. "Who's this then?" he asked, pointing to my photograph.

The paper had named me too and the story mentioned that I was in the Maryhill Harriers and was serving with the Lanarkshire Yeomanry. I was told I was to return to the regimental headquarters at Haddington to be court-martialled. I duly turned up to be met by Sergeant Major Scullion, who made it obvious that he thought the whole thing was bloody ridiculous. He and Major Wilson marched me up to the court as if I was going to be hanged. When we got into the room, Colonel Murdoch was sitting behind his big desk, looking very severe. I was flanked by Sergeant Major Scullion and Major Wilson.

Colonel Murdoch looked up and coughed. "Come forward, Coogan. You've been breaking the army rules. Absent without leave. And you denied it too?" He adjusted his monocle and squinted at the newspaper cutting.

"I'm sorry, sir. It's true, sir. I was promised leave but the office was closed."

"Well," he said, and started laughing, "that'll teach you not to get your picture in the paper. Will you accept my punishment?"

"Yes, sir."

"Very well. Ten days confined to barracks and no wages for two weeks. Right — dismissed."

Major Wilson came out laughing. What a way to get caught! It was up to Sergeant Major Scullion to decide what was to happen and I was sent off to do "fatigues". It was my cushiest job ever — looking after the canteen. The kitchen was cosy and I had home-baked scones and plenty of tea. On top of that, the rest of the lads had a whip-round for me not getting any wages! It was my best time in the army.

One day, Sergeant Major Scullion asked me, "Well, Coogan, how are you enjoying your jankers?"

"Oh, it's terrible, sergeant major."

"You're a bloody liar, Coogan! I can see you're having a great time."

During this period, a new contingent of men arrived to boost the regiment. My intake of conscripts had all been about 20 years old and fairly fit, whereas the new guys were all over 30 and totally out of condition. They looked like they had never done a day's exercise in their lives. A lot of them should never have been in the army. They were all from Glasgow and were great comedians. They were bookies' runners and the like. Wee Tubby Daly sold newspapers in the street and took a drink on the Paisley Road. There was "Doc" Sweeney and Tammy Donnelly — all great characters. They didn't take their new occupation very seriously. On their first parade, Sergeant Major Scullion looked them up and down, shaking his head in disbelief. His first enquiry — "Any of you men any good with horses?' — was met with stifled mirth and then open laughter when an anonymous voice piped up, "Aye, I've got a good tip for the 3.30 at Doncaster!"

The laughter didn't last, however. A couple of weeks later, there was snow and ice on the ground when three new officers turned up from the officers training corps. They were pretty toffee-nosed and posh-spoken, and they were determined to shake us up.

I had been on guard duty the night before and so was excused the day's exercise. My duty was to sweep out the officers' mess. It was a really cold day, so I was happy cleaning up inside and planned to toast some bread on the stove as soon as I had cleaned up the floor.

Suddenly, the peace of the barracks was shattered by the new officers, who announced, "Come on, come on! Everybody up! Everybody up! We're all going for a cross-country run."

The new lads were shouting, "You must be joking. We've never run in our lives and we're not starting now."

But the officers ordered them outside in their shorts, and off they went outside, shivering in the cold. I was feeling happy that I was excused, when one of the English officers came back in and asked me why I wasn't out with the rest of the men. I told him I was billet orderly and that I had been on guard the night before.

"No messing around — that's no excuse. Get out there at once!"

Sergeant Smithers, who was an older soldier, an old cavalryman of about 50 years of age, was lined up with the rest of them. He was freezing cold and angry; he thought horses were for running, not men!

I joined the group and we started up past Gosford House, then ran out of the grounds and down some paths towards the sea. It was very cold in the country roads. The lads began to fall back; they had no idea about running and many of them had never run before. I ran alongside Tubby Daly, who kept shouting out, "Ah'm deid, Ah'm deid, I cannae dae this. For God's sake."

We arrived at a stile where they all stopped. The officers came up and went mad. One of them shouted, "This is a disgraceful display. I've never seen such unfit men in my life!"

Sergeant Smithers stepped forward and said, "Sir, please understand, these men have only been in the army about three or four weeks. They've never done anything like this. But we will make sure we get them fit."

The officer grunted, "Take them back. What a bloody useless bunch!"

I was just heading back with the rest of them when the officer called me back. "How old are you?"

"Twenty-two years old, sir."

"Well, you don't have any bloody excuse, you'll come with us."

It turned out to be a great run, down into Longniddry. The three officers were racing each other. They were fairly striding out and I was just keeping up at their back.

When one of the officers started to fall back, I ran alongside him and enquired, "Are you all right, sir?"

"Of course," he replied tersely and he started off in front of me again.

Gradually, they all began to slow and were gasping for breath. I drew up to them and light-heartedly said to one of them, "Do you mind if I carry on, sir?"

They were annoyed but I carried on up to Gosford House along the coast road. When I got to the gate, the lads were standing outside, giving me a cheer and waving. For the best part of quarter of a mile up the drive, the lads were waving.

On parade the next day, Major Wilson and Captain Mackenzie were there along with Colonel Murdoch and Sergeant Major Scullion. We stood to attention as the colonel led the inspection. He paused and nodded as he passed me and smiled approvingly. Captain Mackenzie and Sergeant Major Scullion smiled at me too and nodded, "Aye, aye, Coogan," as they passed.

119

Then came the young officers, the newly made-up lieutenants. One of them stopped and whispered, "You should have your bloody arse kicked, Coogan."

Sergeant Major Scullion said to the officer, "What was that, sir? You owe every man a drink."

To give him his due, later that night after parade, the officer appeared and said, "Right, let's get the truck out. We'll get a barrel of beer. It's Port Seton for all the lads."

After that, I would quite often go running with the officers and we often had a nice wee two-mile run up the coast. Sometimes, Tarn Laird and Tarn Hannah joined me on a run, but they never lasted long and would stop at a small cafe near the camp.

Running was a great distraction for me because none of the war reports seemed to be good news. France had fallen and Britain stood alone. The Americans and Russians had stayed out of the war, and the fighting had spread to North Africa where Rommel's Afrika Korps had arrived with the aim of capturing Egypt and the Suez Canal. We knew that our departure was imminent.

Sure enough, in the middle of March 1941, we were kitted out with tropical gear — shorts and pith helmets we called "Bombay Bowlers". We were certain we were heading for the desert and there was much wisecracking about getting the hump at camels. On 21 March, we assembled and marched off through Lanark. It was a scene repeated throughout the country. While the Highland regiments had their pipe bands and stirring regimental tunes, we just had the old army songs. All the shop girls and folk in Lanark lined the streets to see us off. It was 1941 but it could have been 1918 as we sang the old drinking song that our fathers had sung before us — "The Carnwath Mill".

Oh, we're nae awa tae bide awa,
We're nae awa tae leave ye,
We're nae awa tae bide awa,
We'll aye come back and see ye.
As I was walkin' doon the street
I met wi' Johnnie Scobie.
Says he tae me, "Can ye go a glass?"
Says I, "Mon, that's my hobby."
Oh, we're nae awa tae bide awa,
We're nae awa tae leave ye.
We're nae awa tae bide awa,
We'll aye come back and see ye.

But we never, ever imagined that so many of us would be "awa tae bide awa", that so many young men would be killed in the jungles of Malaya or that many more would die a slow and terrible death in the prison camps of the Japanese army.

CHAPTER
SIX

Run for Your Life!

When we arrived at Gourock on the Clyde estuary, the SS *Strathmore* was waiting for us. Launched in 1935, it had once ferried wealthy passengers around the globe as a sleek P&O liner. Now it was a troopship and 4,000 of us piled aboard. Cramped and overcrowded, the voyage was a trial, but later, on a Japanese hell ship as my comrades died all around me, I would think back to our time on the SS *Strathmore* as a luxury cruise.

On 21 March 1941, we sailed out into the Clyde as part of a 36-strong convoy that was protected by the battleship HMS *Nelson* and her supporting warships. We were put down into the hold of the ship, well below the waterline with all the other cargo. Down in the bowels of the ship, we found cases and cases of tins of condensed milk and we soon got heartily sick of guzzling the sickly sweet concoction.

We were packed in like sardines. We often slept with our clothes on because there was no room to undress, and even washing was difficult. It was so crowded we could hardly move and we were issued with hammocks to sleep in. It was a complete pantomime; men were cursing and swearing as they birled around, fell out and hit the steel deck with a thump. I just couldn't get the knack of sleeping in my hammock, so I decided to spread it out down on the floor and slept on the deck, which was a great plan until some of the lads became terribly seasick and the deck was swimming in vomit.

Ironically, my friend Tam Hannah had a much easier voyage — and he was a prisoner! When we were told that we were leaving Scotland, Tam nipped home to say goodbye to his parents who lived just a couple of miles from our headquarters at Lanark. He was walking back to the regiment when he was picked up by the police. Colonel Murdoch gave him 28 days for going AWOL, which we all thought was ridiculous. It turned out to his advantage aboard the *Strathmore*, though. While we were cooped up down below, the officers occupied the top decks A, B, C and D. As a prisoner, Tam and about nine others were held in the former nursery on A deck. He was travelling in style and he even managed to persuade the officers that the doors should not be locked in case the vessel was torpedoed.

Conditions were so bad for the rest of us that one of our mates, whose father was a battery sergeant major of the regiment in Scotland, contracted TB during the voyage and subsequently died in India.

The canteen on the ship was always besieged by lengthy queues. It sold flat beer at fivepence a pint and, of course, tins of condensed milk — the very sight of which had us retching. The smokers were initially delighted to find out that they could buy duty-free cigarettes, but soon discovered that they were unsmokeable foreign brands.

We had constant lifeboat drills and had to learn the procedures in case of attack by prowling U-boats that were devastating British shipping. Down in the hold of the SS *Strathmore*, I tried not to think about getting torpedoed, as I doubted whether we would have much chance of survival down there.

There was a lot of grumbling among the troops. We had to take good care of our belongings, as things had an annoying habit of disappearing. Boredom soon set in, and men living on top of each other became quarrelsome and irritable. It was impossible to move when the hammocks were hung and chaos reigned as they were being put up. We were not allowed on deck after "blackout" and bedtime was 9.30p.m. Gambling was banned but some of the sailors taught a few of our lads Crown and Anchor, an old navy game that was illegal on the British mainland. It was played with three dice that had symbols on them instead of black dots — crown, anchor, hearts, spades, diamonds and clubs. Guys spent hours playing it, losing what little wages they had. I tried to keep fit by running around the deck and keeping myself occupied.

Eventually, the officers organised an inter-regimental boxing tournament to ease the boredom. Much to my dismay, Sergeant Major Flaherty told me I had to enter. I protested that I wasn't a boxer, but Flaherty, who hated my guts, was in his element and told me that because I was fit I had to enter. Luckily, I knew enough about boxing to hold my own and was quick enough to stay out of my opponent's reach, so, somehow, I managed to win two fights against pretty unfit

124

opponents to reach the semifinal. Then I was up against a monster from Manchester; he was a real boxer and knew what he was doing. He had fists like 14-pound hammers and one blow was enough to knock you out. He had already flattened all of his opponents, and I was frightened of getting in the ring with him, but there was nothing else for it. I knew if he landed one on me I had no chance, so I danced and dodged as fast as I could and he got exhausted chasing me round the ring. The lads were cheering and laughing when I eventually tired him out. Miraculously, the fight was declared a draw — and I had survived in one piece.

At long last, on 20 April, nearly a month after we had left the Clyde, we put in to Cape Town and marvelled at Table Mountain looming in the background. I had made a lot of close friends in the Lanarkshire Yeomanry and a group of us — Tubby Daly, Tammy Dodds, Hughie Carroll, Willie Moffat, Eddie Cunningham and a lad from Maryhill called Jimmy McGilvray — went ashore together. It felt strange at first as we wobbled down the gangplanks onto the dock, but it was such a relief to get off that ship and for the first time in a month there was no worry about U-boats at the back of our minds.

We decided to walk up to town and were standing at a station not far from the docks when Jimmy McGilvray announced, "I've got an aunt and uncle who stay here. I wonder if we could find them. They live in a suburb called Observatory."

We were wondering what to do when Jimmy saw a young mixed-race guy and asked him if he could help us. The chap was very kind and went to quite a lot of trouble. He eventually found a phone number and took Jimmy to a telephone. Jimmy's relatives were delighted to hear from him and told him that they would come and collect us. While we were waiting, a white man came up and started roaring and shouting at the young guy.

"What are you doing? What are you doing?" he screamed.

He looked apoplectic and our young helper was shaking with fear.

"Don't annoy these young men. Clear off!"

Then he turned to us. "You shouldn't be talking to this type of person. Don't speak to coloureds."

Jimmy, who was a bit of a tough guy, was raging with anger. He went right up close to the white guy, stared him in the face and said, "I asked this man to help us. If you don't bugger off right now, I'll put you through that bloody wall. Now bugger off!"

The guy got a fright and legged it pretty fast.

As we waited for our lift, I spotted a bazaar and we decided to buy a lovely fruit basket to take to Jimmy's relatives as a present. The basket was full of grapes, pears and all kinds of beautiful fruit. Our hosts thanked us profusely for our gift, but when we got out into the garden, where we were served cold lemonade and a beautiful meal by friendly black servants, all we could see were grape vines and fruit trees!

We had four wonderful days in Cape Town and we all had stories to swap. A lot of the lads were shocked at the way black people were treated and everyone had a tale to tell. Dave Paton also had a pal who had an aunt and uncle living in Cape Town and they loaned the lads their Rolls-Royce with a black chauffeur. When they stopped at a hotel for a drink and took the chauffeur in with them, the hotel refused to serve the driver, and Dave and his mates all walked out in protest. We all agreed it was a disgrace.

Before we set sail, we all had to parade on the docks for an identification parade. Some of the lads had intervened to stop two white blokes beating a young black man and a huge fight had broken out. Several of the South Africans ended up in hospital.

We set sail again, bound for India, to the port of Bombay. The ship, which had been freezing cold when we left Scotland, was now stiflingly hot. I was getting pretty tired and had rotten seasickness. I longed to get off that boat. After two weeks in our cramped accommodation, we were at the end of our tether when we finally docked in Bombay.

Once again, we were glad to get ashore, but we were instantly horrified at the stench of Bombay with its open sewers and also the terrible poverty of the people. It was searingly hot, and from the back of the open lorry that whisked us to the station we looked in horror at the shanty towns with people cooking, living and sleeping in the street. A lot of the adults seemed to have elephantiasis in their legs and the poor children were living in abject squalor. We could see that the coolies were being used as cheap labour and we were appalled. As Glaswegians, we knew a bit about being hard up, but we were shocked by what we saw in Bombay. It just didn't seem right.

At the railway station, British women volunteers were waiting for us with mugs of hot sweet tea, which tasted so much better than the stuff on the ship. We had a long journey inland on the train to Ahmednagar where the British had a big base. It was sweltering and we were relieved when we arrived at the barracks to find that we were to be housed in cool stone-built billets with fans in them. We had no beds, just mattresses with a big box at the bottom for our stuff.

We spent five or six weeks training with 4.5-inch howitzers. We were never given a hint about where we were going and simply assumed that we were being acclimatised for the deserts of North Africa where Rommel was pushing back the British.

We next moved to Kirkee Barracks in Poona for more training. The billets were better, and we were taking stock of our new surroundings when a regular soldier who had been there for years came in. He was something of a hard man and a bully too. He was letting us know who was boss and was forever telling us to keep the place tidy. He introduced a young Indian lad of about 18, who was obviously scared witless of him: "This is your punka wallah. He is responsible for you here. Anything you want, you tell him and he'll get it. He will organise your laundry and clean your boots. Don't take any nonsense from him."

The young lad was a nice guy and we felt a bit sorry for him. He did everything for us, tidied the place up and even shaved us as we slept — which felt really weird if you happened to wake up and he was hovering over you with an open razor. We weren't used to this. All of our washing was taken away and returned to us neatly ironed and folded. We were amazed. He was a very tidy person, always making sure the billet was spotless. We knew he didn't get much food, so some of us used to bring him back a plate of grub. He kept whatever we brought him and carefully put it in his bag to take home.

One day, the young lad was sitting on my box polishing my boots for me when the resident bully burst in.

He started shouting at the servant. "What are you doing sitting there? Get off your bloody arse!"

He aimed a vicious kick with his hobnailed boot at the lad and hurt him badly.

I stood up in amazement and angrily told him, "Don't you do that. We don't treat people like that."

Then he started shouting at me — he was really losing his rag. "You're in India now and you do as I bloody well say! These people only understand the boot."

I was getting angrier with him and began shouting back. Then a quiet voice said firmly, "Close that door!" It was big Willie Moffat. He grabbed the bully and punched him hard in the stomach. Then the rest of the lads joined in. We had had enough of this bloke and he was kicked up and down the billet and got to taste some of his own medicine. When the lads finished with him, they sat him down in a corner, got a bucket of water and threw it over him.

"You leave that Indian laddie alone!" Willie told him. "We don't want to hear another word from you or you'll get the same again. Bloody well stay away from us!"

The bully-boy groggily got to his feet and the lads opened the door and threw him down the stairs.

There was uproar about the incident and officers from the bully's unit came to investigate. But we all stuck together and maintained that the guy had tripped and fallen down the stairs. The next day, we were on parade and the bully wasn't there. His officers tried to make trouble but Captain Mackenzie said, "I know these men. If they say he fell down the stairs, he fell down the stairs."

We told Captain Mackenzie what had really happened and he said that the bloke had no right to lift his foot to the servant like that. It was a disgrace. The poor Indian lad was limping around for days.

I got back to running while I was in Poona. I was given permission to run in a nearby hockey park and started doing some training runs in the late afternoon, as we were relieved of duties between 12 and 4p.m. I was nowhere near my peak, but I felt pretty fit.

A big highlight was an inter-regimental athletics competition. Captain Mackenzie said, "Coogan, how would you like to go to a high-class sports meeting in Poona? All the colleges and other regiments are competing."

The lads got together and three of the Yeomanry entered a team.

I had done the mile in 4 minutes 14 seconds on a training run and was looking forward to having a race. There'd been plenty of talk about the athletics in the barracks, and I was hearing about how good the Indians were.

Captain Mackenzie and the rest of the officers loved sport and were in great spirits when we gathered at the cricket ground for the competition. I had never seen anything like it. It was like a billiard table; the bright-green grass was beautifully kept. There was a big crowd in attendance, and there was food laid out for us — juices, lovely bowls of fruit and teas and coffees. The Sikhs and other Indians working there were immaculately turned out; it was so bright and colourful.

Wee Johnny Guthrie was our driver, and we were standing together, enjoying the afternoon, when this colonial officer came over and demanded in a plummy accent, "What are you doing here?"

"We're here for the sports, sir."

"And who are you?"

"Andy Coogan. I'm running for the Lanarkshire Yeomanry, and this is John Guthrie, my trainer."

Johnny was a postman from Springburn who had never run in his life, but he kept a straight face.

"What are you standing there for? You go over there by those tents."

We were getting used to these posh colonials and knew there was no point arguing, so Johnny and I went off to the tents, away from the crowds. We were standing there when Captain Mackenzie came looking for us. "What the hell are you doing over here?" he asked.

We told him that we had been ordered away from the company.

"Bugger them!" he shouted. "Get back over to the track. I've entered you for the half-mile."

He took us over to a big tent to get changed into an army running outfit. It was typical nineteen-oatcake army stuff — a big, pure-white one-piece that came right down past my knees. I felt right out of place next to the Sikhs, who were very smart with proper tracksuits with badges all over them. I started jogging round to warm up, and Johnny started laughing his head off. "You want to see yourself," he said.

My outfit was so tight you could see right through it. I stopped jogging and ran off to hide. I was embarrassed, as it wasn't very modest, but there was nothing else to wear.

Captain Mackenzie shouted over that he didn't bloody care about my clothes. I had just ten minutes to get warmed up, then the races were starting.

"Very good, sir."

I started warming up round the track and, as I ran past the ladies in their beautiful dresses, I felt like I was in a pantomime. I tried to hide myself among the Gordons and the Manchesters.

First up was the half-mile, and I won that quite easily. I was getting ready for the next race, the mile, when Captain Mackenzie came over to have a word. Unknown to me, the officers had been placing bets on the races. Captain Mackenzie was pleased with his return for the first race, and he was looking cheery. He said, "I've put good money on you, Coogan. If you beat the big Sikh in the mile, you'll be in for a good few rupees yourself!"

As we warmed up for the mile, I cast my eye over the competition. There were representatives from the Borders Regiment, the Gordon Highlanders, a lad from the Manchesters and the Sikh I had been warned about. He was a tall, handsome bloke, and someone said he was the college champion.

There were five laps to the mile in the cricket ground. The Gordons went flying off, while the rest of us set off at a steady pace. With three laps to go, I started to move up. The Sikh and myself were running out in front and the race was on. When the bell went for a lap to go, the Sikh moved off and I went with him. The lads were shouting for me and there were roars of support for the Sikh.

With about 150 yards to go, I heard Captain Mackenzie shouting, "Go on, Coogan, let it go!"

I started to pull away and knew the Sikh was tiring. He didn't stay with me and I won the race by about 20 yards. Captain Mackenzie was so pleased. He must have done well because he gave me ten rupees and I got thirty rupees in prize money too, which wasn't bad as we only got paid five rupees a week. Later on, the colonial who had ordered us off the track came over and demanded, "What kind of outfit is that you're wearing? You're a bloody disgrace!"

Captain Mackenzie asked Johnny Guthrie and me to drive him to an officers' mess in Poona and return for him at 9p.m. It was great for us to get a night off, out of the barracks. In Poona, we met up with some Borders lads and had some bacon and eggs, then we went to watch *Bitter Sweet*, with Nelson Eddy and Jeanette MacDonald.

We discovered that the Sikh ran the canteen and also ran the betting on the base. There was betting on the running and billiards too; he was a good billiards player himself and a real wheeler and dealer, taking money off anyone who wanted a bet.

When we went to collect Captain Mackenzie and Major Wilson from the officers' mess, we found them both dead drunk and we had to shove them in the truck. When we got back, a batman helped us put them to bed.

The next day during parade, Captain Mackenzie looked a little rough but smiled and said, "That was a grand day, Coogan, wasn't it?"

Everyone seemed to be happy and enjoying themselves at the time, and dark thoughts about the war were very far from our minds.

It felt great to be running competitively again. I tried to keep fit during this period but none of the lads wanted to run with me, as it was too hot. I was still training at the nearby hockey park every day, and, one day, a young Indian boy turned up and asked me if I would mind if he ran with me. He ran round this makeshift track of cinders in his bare feet. He worked in the Kirkee arsenal. He was a nice person and really keen to learn about running. I was pleased, as he was good company for me and not a bad runner.

Then, one day while I was running, Sergeant McLaughlin came along and said, "The colonel wants to see you, Coogan."

I asked what I had done but he said nothing as we marched along to the colonel's office. When I got there, Major Wilson, Captain Mackenzie and Sergeant Major Scullion were in the office with Colonel Murdoch.

I was wondering what on earth was wrong when Colonel Murdoch looked up from behind his desk and said, "Now look here, Coogan, have you been running in the park with some Indian chap?"

I was completely shocked. "Yes, sir."

"Well, Coogan, ranks are not supposed to fraternise with the Indians and you should know that. Some of the local white people have complained."

I was stunned and didn't know what to say, when Captain Mackenzie chipped in, "Do you have any objection to him running with you, Coogan?"

"No, sir," I said. "In my club in Glasgow, I run against coloured people. I run against people from America. There are students from different parts of the world at the university and I train with them too."

"Well, good on you, Coogan," Captain Mackenzie replied.

Colonel Murdoch adjusted his monocle and harrumphed. "Very well, Coogan. Off you go and get on with your training."

The truth was that our officers had little time for the colonials who looked down their noses at us. Many of them were just ordinary people who had worked in jute mills in Dundee, but when they arrived in India to be waited on hand and foot by servants who were paid a pittance, they began to believe that they were superior beings. They lorded it over the Indians and enjoyed a life of luxury. At the weekend, a lot of the men dressed up in officers' uniforms and played at being soldiers in the Indian army. It was little wonder that Indian nationalist leaders like Mahatma Gandhi were attracting a huge following.

However, it wasn't just the rise of nationalist movements that presented a growing challenge to Britain's empire in the East. Japan's militarist leaders were bent on creating their own empire, under the guise of their so-called Greater East Asia Co-Prosperity Sphere. The Japanese had conquered Formosa and Korea in the late nineteenth century and now their hard-line fascist leaders were casting their eyes further afield. In 1931, they had invaded Manchuria, which was a prelude to the invasion of China. When the Japanese captured the old Chinese capital of Nanking in 1937, their brutality shocked even their Nazi allies. Chinese prisoners of war were massacred in their tens of thousands, and Japanese newspapers reported gleefully on how Japanese officers competed among themselves to see how many heads they cut off with their samurai swords. Innocent civilians were routinely massacred, while women and children were raped and murdered in the most sadistic way.

Japan was short of natural resources and, as American sanctions began to bite, it looked enviously at the Philippines, Indonesia, Burma, Malaya and India, where it could seize oilfields, vast rice-producing areas and most of the world's rubber and tin. Britain took the painful decision to divide its forces and send out some of the troops intended to fight the Germans to bolster our garrisons in the Far East, where the Japanese were increasingly emboldened by the success of the Nazis in Europe and North Africa.

In August 1941, I was assigned to "B" battery, who were short of signallers. I was now part of the 11th Indian Division. We went in lorries to the station to take the train to Bombay, and I was pleasantly surprised to find my Indian running partner waiting on the platform with his family. They put garlands of flowers around my neck and gave me a big box of candies. They spoke better English than any of us could speak. My friend's father was one of the head men in the arsenal at Kirkee, and he told our officers that they should be proud of us. I was sorry to leave Kirkee.

From Bombay, on 23 August, the men of "B" and "C" batteries sailed aboard a cockroach-infested old steamer called the *Ekma* to Malaya. Two weeks later, we arrived at Port Swettenham, a busy harbour near Kuala Lumpur built by the British to ship out rubber and tin. Australian troops were waiting for us with lorries and took us to a lovely town called Ipoh in the heart of tin-mining territory. On the journey, we soaked up all the sights. We saw Malays working in the paddy fields with water buffaloes and tapping the rubber trees for the sticky white sap that dripped into little cups attached to the tree trunks. For the first time, we saw great palm trees with coconuts on them. Ipoh was a beautiful place with impressive colonial buildings, and most of the population seemed to be Chinese. It all seemed so peaceful.

Our camp was in a rubber plantation and had already been set up for the army. The huts, each of which accommodated around 25 men, had beds with mosquito nets and windows with no shutters or curtains. They were built up on stilts with verandahs and showers. Again, we had servants, Malayan dhobi wallahs who did our washing for us.

A strange thing happened when we were in Ipoh. When we got up in the morning, we discovered that buttons were missing from some of the shirts. The lads were blaming each other, thinking someone was playing a daft trick. Then, as I was resting on my bed under the mosquito net, I saw a monkey climbing in through the open window. It looked around, then made straight for the shirts and started to pull off buttons one by one with its teeth. After a while, it skipped back out the window. I told the other lads, who didn't believe me until they saw it themselves. A few of us lay back under the nets to watch, and the next time there were two monkeys pinching the buttons. Someone thought that there might have been fish oil in the buttons, which the monkeys loved.

The plantations, which produced 40 per cent of the world's rubber, were gloomy and damp without much direct sunlight. I found them strange, eerie places and a little bit depressing. The silence seemed heavy and felt like it weighed down on us. We were warned sternly that the rubber trees were not to be damaged in any way.

We had been told not to leave the camp, but we quickly discovered that there was a path through the jungle to the nearby Australian camp and four of us made up our minds to pay them a visit. It was getting dark and we were a bit wary of snakes at first, fearful of encountering the venomous cobras, kraits and vipers that we had been warned about. As we moved through the rubber trees, we suddenly saw strange flashes of light and stopped in wonder to watch fireflies dancing in the air.

The Australians made us welcome, offering us cigarettes and lemonade. Then one of them suggested, "How do yon fancy going into Ipoh town tonight?"

We were reluctant because we were not supposed to go out of the camp, but the Aussies were no respecters of authority and they insisted that we should go with them. The Aussies knew their way about and took us to the Celestial Hotel and Dancehall. It was a wonderful place, built in modern art deco style above a bazaar on the ground floor, and was packed with well-off Malays and Eurasians. A Filipino band was playing and the women were beautifully dressed. We felt a bit out of it at first and stayed up near the back. If we had been down in Singapore city, we would never have been allowed in a place like this — it would have been declared out of bounds to ranks by the snooty locals. We didn't have any money but the Aussies bought us lemonade and we were content to watch the band, which was great.

One of my mates was a Londoner called Jim Brennan, who was a fantastic pianist. I approached the owner of the place, who was standing near us, and, pointing to Jim, I told him, "See this lad here — he's a top pianist from England. I'm quite sure he would entertain you if we could have our table looked after."

He took me up on the offer and I went back to tell Jim the good news. The owner went over and had a word with the lady pianist, then beckoned Jim across. In the middle of their big number, the lady got up and Jim took over with ease. He made that grand piano talk. The place was jumping, and people were dancing and clapping. We were so pleased that our friend was up there playing. We were asked what we would like to eat and drink and ordered a slap-up meal. The Aussies joined us and we all laughed as we tucked in while Jim was playing. Later, he played "Argentina Way" and all the modern dance stuff. As we were celebrating, in walked Captain Mackenzie and Major Wilson. They spotted us right away and smiled at seeing Jim up with the band. But they turned a blind eye and asked us not to say we had seen them — they were not meant to be out of the camp either.

We were in high spirits on our way back through the jungle to the camp. Then, for the first time since leaving Scotland, I heard the sound of bagpipes. The music tugged at my heartstrings, and it was strange to hear the pipes in the darkness of the jungle. I discovered that they were being played by Gurkhas, the legendary tough Nepalese hillmen who would later save my life.

A couple of days later, we were back at the Australian camp; we got on very well with them. As we were laughing and drinking lemonade, a buttoned-up British sergeant appeared from out of the blue. We froze as he started shouting, "What are you men doing here? This place is out of bounds to you men."

"Who the hell are you and what are you shouting about?" the Australians shouted back at him. "Who invited you anyway? These are our guests, so just bugger off. And bloody well don't come back — this place is out of bounds to you."

As the sergeant sloped off muttering, the Aussies said loud enough for him to hear, "If he gives you any trouble, just tell us. We'll bloody soon fix him!"

We had a great time at Ipoh. A lot of the planters were Scottish, and their wives and daughters organised a canteen for us. We were well looked after and the food was excellent. We felt that we were in the lap of luxury. One day, we went on an outing to Penang island where we swam in the wonderfully warm Indian Ocean.

However, the international situation was deteriorating, and, on 30 September 1941, we moved north to Sungai Petani to join the rest of the 11th Indian Division, which was guarding Malay's northern border with Thailand. The British feared — rightly, as it turned out — that the Japanese would invade through neutral Thailand, and we had a plan for a pre-emptive strike called Operation Matador that would have denied the Japanese the landing beaches. In October, the hard-line warmonger General Tojo was appointed Japanese Prime Minister, and it was obvious that war was imminent. Singapore, Britain's island fortress, lay at the foot of the 600-mile-long Malayan peninsula and was being frantically reinforced with tens of thousands of troops. It was constantly referred to as being impregnable and was described as the Gibraltar of the Far East.

However, the British always believed that any invasion of Singapore would come from the sea, and massive guns had been installed to deter any naval threat. The threat from the north was underestimated, and Operation Matador was never launched for fear of provoking war with the Japanese. Britain's best military commanders were kept in Europe, and our commanders in Malaya decided that we did not need tanks, as they would be ineffective in the Malayan jungle and mangrove swamps.

We were sent north to build a defensive line north of Jitra. Our defences were around 14 miles long and stretched from mangrove swamps on the coast across paddy fields and a rubber plantation to dense jungle in the interior. However, we never had enough time to prepare properly, and it rained constantly. We found it difficult to dig trenches and gun emplacements because the place was so waterlogged. The water table was only between 10 and 18 inches down, so when we took off the topsoil we were into water. The place was floating like a sponge. We laid cables from the guns up to the forward observation posts, where the officers were protected by detachments of Gurkhas. I laid a cable in half-mile sections up to the observation post manned by Captain Mackenzie, which overlooked the border and a bridge. All of our guns were targeted on an area a couple of hundred yards over the bridge and into Malaya. We had to wait until the Japanese had crossed over from neutral Thailand before we could hit them. It was hard, hot work with rolls of cable strapped to my back. As I waded through the paddy fields, streams and rivers, I was on the lookout for freshwater crocodiles and iguanas that could give you a nasty bite. I also attracted disgusting new companions; I was quickly covered in bloodsucking leeches, which seemed able to squeeze themselves even through the eyelets of my boots.

The water and damp played havoc with the field telephones, causing them to short and fail, so we were constantly checking the lines for problems. On one occasion, I went out to check the cable with a little English guy nicknamed Tich. He had a rifle with him, which was unusual as we were so short of personal weapons. We padded along a narrow path through the dripping jungle, keeping an eye out for snakes and the stinging red ants and huge centipedes that made our life a misery. Suddenly, about 50 feet in front of us, sitting bolt upright and silently staring at us was a Malayan tiger. Terrified, we stopped in our tracks and froze.

"Oh, Jesus," I whispered. "Don't move, don't move."

"I could try to shoot it, Andy," Tich whispered back.

I thought about our ancient rifles and doubted they could hit a barn door never mind a charging tiger. "Just stand still, stand still," I urged. "What if you miss?"

The tiger majestically surveyed the intruders into his domain for a few moments before blinking and slowly turning round to disappear into the dense vegetation. There was no doubting who was the king of the jungle. We heaved a sigh of relief and thanked the Lord for our good luck. As we pressed on, I thought back to poor old Mum's dire warnings about lions and tigers. "Bloody hell," I thought, "Maw was right enough!"

At the beginning of December, all leave was cancelled and two of our most famous warships, HMS *Prince of Wales* and HMS *Repulse*, arrived at Singapore to underline Britain's determination to protect our Far East empire. However, critically, the RAF was not sufficiently reinforced and, without proper air cover, it looked like we had returned to the Victorian days of gunboat diplomacy when the arrival of warships from Britain was enough to subdue rebellious natives.

Lying in our billets in Sungai Petani, we listened to radio reports of Japanese transports sailing towards Thailand. We knew there was a Japanese convoy heading to the northeast of our positions, but we were told that the *Prince of Wales* and the *Repulse* could do nothing because they were in neutral waters. We knew the enemy were coming and felt helpless.

On 6 December, we were ordered to "stand to" and be prepared. I began to think of all the stories we had been told about the Japanese. It was said that their planes were just like toys and that Japanese soldiers were all tiny and had bad eyesight. They couldn't shoot straight. They only had small bullets and couldn't fight at night. They were only fit to fight other Asiatics like the Chinese. We would soon learn just how much rubbish all that was.

Two days later, we heard aircraft over our heads at Sungai Petani. It was 8 December. Several time zones away, it was already 9 December and the Japanese air force was striking at Pearl Harbor, the giant American navy base on Hawaii. The Japanese had landed in Thailand and in Malaya at Kota Bharu where they took a British air base intact. We guessed — correctly, as it turned out — that the planes above us were heading south on their way to bomb Singapore. A couple of hours later, it was our turn. They knew where we were and bombs came whistling down on our heads. The earth shook and shuddered as high explosives detonated in deafening orange and purple fireballs all around us. This was my baptism of fire and it was absolutely terrifying. The air was filled with the debris of shattered huts, and fragments of hot metal were hurtling through the air. I dived under the nearest lorry to take cover from the lethal shrapnel. It was only when the air raid was well and truly over that I slowly emerged from under the truck and discovered that it was full of ammunition — I could not have picked a worse spot.

We scrambled into the trucks and headed north to our gun positions. The lorries were unable to leave the road because of the terrible mud and all of the guns had to be manhandled into position. The ammunition was laid out and we were all ready for action. Then we realised that there was a problem with the field telephone lines and I was sent out to check them. Wireless sets were virtually useless in Malaya, so these field telephones were extremely important and our only real means of communication. I walked for some distance from the battery and keyed into the line. I could speak to the battery but I couldn't hear from the observation post up ahead. I assumed it was yet another problem with the damp and wet, but, as I walked along running the line through my hand, my blood froze. The line had been neatly severed. "Jesus Christ," I thought, "the Japs are here already!" I quickly twisted the wire together again, then ran forward where I found a couple more instances of sabotage. I was breathing heavily and sweating. I had never felt so lonely as I did in that jungle where I feared a Japanese saboteur lurked behind every tree.

The Japanese were one of the many minorities in Malaya where Tamils, Indians, Chinese and Malayans lived as Muslims, Sikhs, Hindus, Buddhists, Taoists and Christians. For years, many of the Japanese, who worked as traders, managers, dentists and doctors, had been operating as intelligence officers sending information back to their motherland. Now they were an active fifth column, often assisting Japanese infiltrators disguised as native Malayans. I had personal experience of this. One day, two locals passed me wheeling bicycles and gave me a friendly wave. Then a couple of Argylls appeared. We never saw them very often as they were usually in the jungle.

"Seen any Japs?" one of them asked.

"Naw — thank God. Just a couple of Malayan lads pushing their bikes."

The Argylls took off and grabbed the two locals. They brought them back down the road and searched them. When their concealed wire-cutters were discovered, they tried to make a run for it. They were Japanese saboteurs. As they dashed for the jungle, the Argylls opened fire and shot both of them. It was terrible to see and the strange thing was that, even after they were hit, they managed to run for quite a few yards. The incident left me shaken. I had been innocently waving and saying hello to the very men who were out to kill us. It was the first time I had seen a Japanese. When the Argylls searched their bodies they found little packets of earth from the motherland.

The Japanese strategy was to strike with lightning speed, to constantly harass us and to leapfrog down the coast to land behind our defences or go through the jungle to encircle us. It was easy for them to do this because very early on — after our aircraft were bombed on the ground at their base at Alor Setar — the RAF was withdrawn south for the defence of Singapore and the Japanese became masters of the skies.

The British did send two battalions into Thailand to slow down the enemy advance but they were cut to ribbons. The sight of these defeated men streaming back to safety through our lines at Jitra was very demoralising for us. And they brought stunning news with them: the Japanese army had tanks — hundreds of them. We couldn't believe it. The heavy armour that our officers said could not operate in Malaya was carving through our lines like a hot knife through butter. When the Japanese crossed the bridge, we let them have it and killed a lot of them, but then they regrouped and attacked across a broad front. Our commanding officer, David Murray-Lyon, sought permission to fall back from Jitra to another position about 30 miles south at Gurun. Eventually, he was allowed to withdraw but the retreat was a terrible shambles. A lot of men never got the order to withdraw and were left behind to be captured and killed. Others made a run for it through the jungle. The chaotic withdrawal to Gurun was typical of the next few weeks of retreat down the Malayan peninsula. It was an awful mess.

The Japanese soldiers were tough and resourceful. If we blew up bridges, they quickly rebuilt them. They could also improvise. We had failed to destroy the railway, and they had specially adapted Nissan trucks that carried men and ammunition down the tracks. They had bicycle brigades, and commandeered local fishing boats to get around our defences. They were shock troops who had spent the last decade fighting nationalist armies and communist guerrillas in China, and these battle-hardened and ruthless fighters had specific orders not to take prisoners. Our intelligence officers found instructions on a dead Japanese soldier that could not have been clearer: "When you encounter the enemy, think of yourself as an avenger coming face to face at last with his father's murderer. Here is a man whose death will lighten your heart."

We were certainly not battle-hardened warriors. One morning, I returned to our emplacements exhausted after checking the lines in the jungle. I had to cover a lot of ground through dense jungle and the cables were being cut just as soon as we were mending them. I lay down about 30 yards from the guns and promptly fell sound asleep. My slumbers were sharply interrupted when the guns opened up in a terrific barrage. Our 16 guns were pretty old and would shortly be declared obsolete, but they were rapid-fire and each could send a salvo of four 35-pound shells flying every minute. I got such a shock that I was shaking badly and Sergeant Major Frank Billings, a kind-hearted English regular from the Royal Artillery, gave me a big mug of tea and a biscuit to calm me down.

The guns were firing at attacking waves of Japanese, who were launching themselves on troops from the Leicesters and the Surreys about three or four miles north. Along with Indian troops and Gurkhas, they were struggling valiantly to keep the Japanese out of Malaya. I was thankful I was not in one of those waterlogged trenches. It must have been terrible — visibility was poor and the enemy tanks came careering at them out of the mist and rain. Enemy snipers dressed as civilians infiltrated our lines and other infiltrators set off firecrackers behind our positions during the night to further undermine shattered nerves. We were firing continuously in support of the Jats of the Indian Division, who fought heroically. Incredibly, as the Japanese were pouring into Malaya, we had to argue with pompous quartermasters who queried why we needed more ammunition!

At some stage during the battle that raged from 11 to 13 December, we got the shocking news that both HMS *Prince of Wales* and HMS *Repulse* had been sunk with terrible loss of life. The outlook was decidedly bleak when we got the order to pull back. To make matters worse, the heavy rain that never seemed to stop had turned the place into a quagmire. Several guns, Bren-gun carriers and trucks were abandoned in the mud. The weather did us no favours and many of the demolition charges that were set to destroy roads, bridges and abandoned kit failed to go off because of the damp. It soon became clear that the Japanese were not just in front of us: they were also behind us. In fact, they were everywhere. It was very frightening and what made it more so was that so few of us in the artillery had any weapons to defend ourselves: there were just eight rifles for a hundred men in the artillery headquarters, and many of the men envied the assistant of our medical officer, Dr Peter Seed, when the doctor gave the grateful orderly his personal revolver. For the first time in my life, I knew real gut-wrenching fear and I would live in its shadow for another three and a half years.

On 14 December, the Japanese attacked in strength, supported by aircraft and led by tanks. The Surreys took heavy casualties and after 36 hours of fighting we were ordered to retreat once again. A lot of brave men — British and Indian — were fighting and dying. As we fell back, Indian troops would constantly ask us, "Where is the RAF, Johnny? Where is the RAF?" It was embarrassing and we felt that we had let them down.

150

The Indian soldiers could see — like the rest of us — that we could not win without air support.

On 15 December, the Japanese seized the air base at Alor Setar with its fuel dumps intact. The Japanese commander General Yamashita, who was to become known as the "Tiger of Malaya", set up his headquarters at the base and kept the pressure on, forcing us back down the west coast of the peninsula. Next they took Ipoh, and at the same time Japanese bombers raided the island of Penang, killing 2,000 civilians. On 17 December, the Japanese took Penang without a single further casualty and acquired even more boats with which to outflank us. They also took the radio station, which had been abandoned, and proceeded to broadcast demoralising propaganda.

On the way back to Gurun, we took the chance to swing by the base at Sungai Petani to retrieve our belongings. However, when we entered the billets, we found that they had been ransacked by looters. All my stuff had gone. The only things I had were the clothes I stood up in, the watch I had been presented with for winning the Partick Thistle Mile and my wallet, which contained the *Glasgow Herald* clipping with a photograph of my race against Sydney Wooderson and a picture of my mum with myself and my brothers and sister. There was no time to hang about. We jumped on the lorries and headed for Gurun.

It was bucketing rain all the time and, utterly exhausted, we had little time to prepare defences at the town of Gurun where the main road and railway line intersected. I was sent out on lookout duty and was constantly fearful of being shot by Japanese snipers, who were very active and skilfully camouflaged to blend into the tropical vegetation. I was scared being alone and unarmed out there and I was glad to be relieved.

Just as I returned to our camp we came under heavy Japanese mortar fire. I tried to jump into the first dugout I came to but it was full and one of the lads shouted out, "No room in here, mate, sorry."

I ran towards the next dugout as the mortars rained down and dived in. It was lucky for me that I had been chucked out of the first dugout, as just a few minutes later it took a direct hit — leaving a hole the size of a bus and killing everyone in it. The carnage was awful to see.

As we pulled back to Kampar to defend the city of Kuala Lumpur, we first heard the news that the Japanese had bombed Pearl Harbor. It was grim, but paradoxically for us it was good news and it cheered us a little. The fighting had scarcely begun but we already knew that we were doomed and that America joining the war was our only hope of salvation. The Japanese army had vowed to capture Kuala Lumpur as a New Year's gift to the emperor, but our commander Murray-Lyon had been sacked and now the British decided to stand and make a fight of it.

We dug in at Kampar on 22 December, and were behind the British and Indian defences when I was sent out with Tubby Daly to check the field telephone lines. We were worried sick as we went forward into the murkiness of the jungle — unarmed as usual. There was none of the normal banter; things were too serious and we thought it was better to stay silent out there. And we were right. We had only gone about three-quarters of a mile when in the rubber trees ahead of us we were startled to spot a Japanese patrol. We had just about walked right into them, and they saw us at around the same time that we saw them. It was a dreadful shock, and as we turned on our heels they raised their rifles. Bullets zipped over our heads and thudded into the rubber trees as we raced back into the jungle. We were running for our lives. Then the most astonishing thing happened. Tubby Daly, ten years older than me and certainly no athlete, pulled ahead of me. I'll never understand how he did that; even today, I think about Tubby sprinting past me and wonder.

When we got back to safety, it took us a while to recover and, with his breath back, Tubby weakly joked, "Do you think I have a future as a runner, Andy?"

It just showed what fear can do, I thought. But I replied tactfully, "Aye, a bookie's runner!"

We were pretty well surrounded and the Japanese were sending probing patrols to attack us.

Soon Sergeant Major Billings came around to warn us. "Right, lads," he said. "The bloody Japs are on the move and they are heading this way. So arm yourselves!"

"What with?" I asked.

"Anything you bloody well can. Make your own weapons," he replied.

We had some Gurkhas with us, who had rifles, but the rest of us started making our own weapons. We were too scared to reflect on how ridiculous this was or on how badly let down we had been by military planners. Men were frantically making clubs and tying knives to poles to act as staves to keep Japanese bayonets at bay. I found a trench spade and tried to sharpen it with a stone, while other soldiers picked up stones to throw at the enemy. It was beyond belief.

We lay down and waited and waited, but nothing seemed to happen. We were on edge and every screeching monkey or squawking bird had us worried. We peered at the impenetrable jungle ahead. Was it moving? Did I see something? What was that noise? Maybe it was a mistake. Maybe they weren't coming at all. Maybe it was a false alarm. My mouth dried and I began to wonder if I would ever get back home. I said my prayers, "Please, God, let me get home. Just let me get home." I thought of my family but forced myself to concentrate. There was no small talk just silence, as all eyes were glued to that dense wall of jungle. The tension was crackling in the air, but, when the attack came, it still came as a shock.

Dusk was falling when rifles suddenly started firing, forcing our heads down, and deafening firecrackers were set off. Then the sound of screaming tore through the humid gloominess of the jungle. About a dozen Japanese infantry dressed in greyish uniforms and covered in twigs and branches charged forward with rifles and lengthy bayonets that seemed far too long for their small frames. Their officer led from the front waving his samurai sword in the air, and they all took up his bloodcurdling cry.

"Banzai!"

It was a dreadful chilling sound. These guys had only one thing on their minds — our deaths.

They only had about 20 or 30 yards to cover and they would be on our heads in no time. The Japanese were masters of the bayonet charge and were screaming out to scare us. The Gurkhas started firing and I rose to a half-crouching position. I had the trench spade in both hands and stared straight ahead, swallowing hard as two Japanese charged in my direction. It was bedlam. There were shouts, screams and cries of agony. Rifles and revolvers were firing and grenades were exploding. The first Japanese lunged towards me. My heart was pumping as if I was in the last lap of the Ibrox Mile. I neatly sidestepped him and hit him as hard as I could with the sharpened edge of the spade. He went down with a cry of agony and I struck at his arm to get the rifle away from him. After that, I went into a world of my own. I ignored everything around me and concentrated on smashing the shovel into the Japanese soldier over and over. It was as if I was on automatic pilot and heard or saw nothing around me. I just concentrated on him. One of us was going home and it was going to be me.

When everything went quiet and the Japanese stopped moving, I straightened up in a daze. I looked around at the battlefield. We had won. Our wounded men were groaning and the Gurkhas were moving among the Japanese wounded, finishing them off with their curved kukri knives. I was stunned, shocked to the core, and so were a lot of the other guys. Only now did I become aware that I was covered, absolutely drenched, in blood. It was too much to have come from my attacker. I immediately feared that I had been shot and started feeling my body for a bullet wound. Then I realised what had happened. While I had been dealing with my Japanese, one of the Gurkhas had taken his kukri across his throat, sending great arcs of blood over me as I was bent over bashing him.

We were all shaken by the attack and a lot of us were physically sick. We had not trained as infantry and were strangers to hand-to-hand combat. Not for the first or last time, I thought to myself, "Thank God for the Gurkhas." Often we would come across them in the jungle and not see them until the very last minute; they were masters of staying stock-still perched up in trees and lying in thick vegetation.

We celebrated Christmas in our dugouts under a more intensive barrage of artillery than usual. The Japanese were making a point and keeping up the pressure to demoralise us on Christmas Day. We were a sorry lot by this time. We had been fighting — and running — for a fortnight. We were filthy, exhausted, hungry and often thirsty. Most of us were suffering from shock and various skin diseases. Ringworm attacked the groin area, making walking difficult, and painful footrot was common and seemingly untreatable. Some men were completely covered in tormenting prickly heat. A lot of the lads were reluctant to take their boots off in case they couldn't get them back on again. As we huddled in our waterlogged scrapes, swatting the dive-bombing mosquitoes that carried dreaded malaria and dengue fever, it was hard not to feel depressed. I thought of all my friends and family and wondered how they were celebrating Christmas. The cold and damp streets of Glasgow and the Gorbals never felt more inviting.

We had retreated 176 long miles under constant attack and were completely done in. From our concealed positions, we overlooked a destroyed bridge located between two tin mines. At dawn, four Japanese staff cars approached to inspect the demolished bridge. As the officers left their cars, we lobbed in eight rounds and killed them all. Our resolve had been stiffened and, on 31 December, Colonel Murdoch decided to celebrate Hogmanay. We saw in the New Year by firing a salvo of 12 shells timed like the strokes of Big Ben at Japanese positions. I thought wistfully of the folk back home enjoying a good dram to mark the bells. How I longed to be back in Glasgow, which seemed a world away.

On 1 January 1942, the Japanese launched a ferocious infantry attack supported by tanks, but we fought them off, providing cover to a battalion of Gurkhas to our left and right. We were outnumbered by more than five to one, but we ambushed the Japanese with the guns and we held the enemy at bay for four long days. We nicknamed our position "Hellfire Corner" because of the punishment we took from Japanese dive-bombers, which screamed in on top of us and had us clawing into the earth. It was our first real victory and the effective fire of the artillery played a big part in pushing the Japanese back. Five hundred Japanese died over those four days against British losses of a hundred and fifty. The Japanese were licking their wounds, but tragically the British failed to capitalise on it. Once again, we were outflanked after the Japanese landed on the beaches behind us.

We were the last artillery battery to leave and provided cover for the Gurkha rear-guard action.

On 4 January, we were on the move south again — one step ahead of the pursuing Japanese. We hitched our guns to the limbers and prayed the lethal enemy Zeros, which screamed in from nowhere to strafe and bomb us from the air, were otherwise engaged. We streamed south heading for the Slim River where we were again to fight the Japanese and slow their by now relentless progress. The Japanese were snapping at our heels all the way, and in Kuala Lumpur they discovered huge stockpiles of food and supplies to fuel their campaign.

Our defensive line at Slim River was about four miles long and ran through the Cluny rubber estate. The battle was to be a disaster for the British, but the Lanarkshire Yeomanry could at least claim the glory of holding back the advancing Japanese tank column. At around 8a.m. on 7 January, headquarters sent word that a force of Japanese tanks was advancing and that we should go forward from our location six miles south of the Slim River road bridge. However, the news was out of date; headquarters had been overrun and the Japanese were advancing more quickly than was realised. Unknown to us, they had actually crossed the Slim River road bridge and had come two miles down the road towards us. Colonel Murdoch and an advance party went forward to scout out the situation. The colonel was on the back of his trusty BSA motorbike when he had the misfortune to run straight into the first Japanese tanks. The bike screeched to a halt and turned around, but it was too late. As Colonel Murdoch tried to head back to alert the advancing column, the lead Japanese tank opened up with a burst of machine-gun fire that killed him. Sergeant Major Billings was also killed and two officers were captured.

Twenty-year-old Captain Maurice Eustace — a tall Irishman and one of the seven thousand volunteers from the neutral Irish Republic to fight with the British army in the Second World War — got away and sped back to raise the alarm. Under the orders of our adjutant, Captain Charles Gordon Brown, our advancing guns pulled over and set up an ambush. Howitzers designed to lob shells three and four miles were now to be used as anti-tank weapons. When the first Japanese tank appeared around a bend, Sergeant Oliver Keen showed nerves of steel and waited until the range was down to 30 yards before firing. The first round hit the tank but failed to stop it. A second round set it on fire and the Gurkhas shot the fleeing Japanese crew. A second tank arrived, firing as it went, and Sergeant Keen only managed to fire four more rounds before being ordered to retreat. Wee Johnny Guthrie, the quiet postie from Springburn, showed incredible bravery when he came tearing out of the line and threw grenades at the tanks.

During the exchange of fire, Captain Brown had his right arm torn off and was hit in the leg. He was lying wounded in the road when two Japanese soldiers jumped down from the second tank and ran towards him. Despite also being wounded in his other hand, he managed to draw his pistol. Lance Bombardier Mair also opened fire with a pistol and the Japanese were shot dead. Unfortunately, Sergeant Keen was killed by machine-gun fire. The Japanese were stopped in their tracks, though, and forced to retreat. Captain Gordon Brown was awarded the Military Cross for delaying the Japanese advance and Sergeant Keen was mentioned in despatches. The Lanarkshire Yeomanry had paid a heavy price, though. On that day, we lost our commander, and two other officers and seventeen men of the Royal Artillery were killed. A further three officers and two men were wounded.

The Japanese took the infantry positions to our north with bayonet charges and the battle was ultimately lost. Around 500 men were killed and 1,200 were captured. Another 2,000 men took to the jungle and were captured weeks later after much suffering and privation. One Gurkha corporal managed to evade capture and hid in the jungle until 1949 — four years after the war was over. The Japanese also captured large numbers of undamaged heavy guns, armoured cars and Bren carriers — all of which they turned on us.

We dashed south to Yong Peng where, from our observation post, Captain Mackenzie could actually see over the rubber plantation to the coast and watched the Japanese landing at Batu Pahat — out of range of our guns.

On the morning of 19 January, the Japanese attacked the Norfolks and I felt sorry for the young, inexperienced reinforcements who were rushed forward through our positions. The Japanese were closing on us all the time and we fought off Japanese patrols with grenades and bayonet charges. The guns were firing at point-blank range over open sights against the charging Japanese and only just managed to avoid capture.

We pulled back to a place south of Ayer Hitam. We had troops protecting the guns, but, on the night of 21 January, we came under attack again and were encircled. At 9 a.m. the next day, I was standing in the middle of the road directing stragglers towards an abandoned school building when a Bren-gun carrier sped past me, heading north. It was carrying Major Wilson and a driver. It had only gone about 20 yards when it screeched to a halt. I never heard the crack of the sniper's rifle that killed Major Wilson, but he was shot cleanly through the head in the speeding vehicle — so much for the poor eyesight of the Japanese soldiers. I would later mourn the loss of a popular officer who, at the age of 30, was far too young to die, but my immediate reaction was to crouch down. "It could have been me," I thought, and prayed that we would all get the hell out of this benighted place in one piece. We were surrounded and it was looking bad for us until about 50 Argylls arrived riding captured Japanese bicycles. What a welcome sight they were! They soon had the Japanese pulling back.

Captain Mackenzie was now in command, and we were deployed to blast a way through the surrounding

Japanese by taking out machine-gun nests. But it was a lost cause, and at 6p.m. on 26 January the order was given to destroy the guns. It was a case of every man for himself — the four most dreaded words any soldier can hear. Most of us made for the coast, wading through a treacherous swamp. The rivers were swollen with rain and at one point the Sikhs took off their turbans to make a rope to get us across a fast-flowing current. I was worried some of us might be hit by the logs floating down the river and was even more alarmed when I was told that they were not logs but crocodiles. Around 1,500 men were rescued by the Royal Navy, but in the chaos of the retreat I became separated from my comrades.

I headed south, following the road but taking care not to break cover. With the jungle canopy over my head, I kept going. Japanese planes were buzzing up and down the road and every now and again I came across smouldering British vehicles. It was a depressing rout and as I pressed on into the jungle I began to wonder if I would ever get home. Tormented by the bugs, humidity and prickly heat, every step became an effort, but I dug deep and remembered my training. I thanked God that I had kept my fitness and discipline as an athlete. Whenever I tired, I could hear rifle shots of the Gurkhas and Argylls fending off the advancing Japanese in the distance. They spurred me forward and I told myself, "Keep going, Coogan, keep going."

Finally, the jungle was engulfed by blackness and I sat down, totally shattered, with my back against a tree. The jungle came alive with noise at night but not even the racket of the crickets and chattering of the monkeys could stop me from slipping into oblivion. A shaft of sunlight on my face awoke me with a start in the morning. I wondered where I was at first, and then I was hit by the sickening reality of being on my own and fleeing through the dense vegetation like a hunted animal. My stomach sank and as I rose to my feet my dried-up mouth reminded me of my dehydration. I had to find water soon.

I started off heading south again with unchallenged Japanese aircraft driving me forward. As the sun rose, the jungle began to steam. The humidity was incredible and I was sweating heavily. By late afternoon, I was totally exhausted. I was at the end of my tether when I came upon a little pond with two or three dozen white ducks swimming around a wooden pole six to eight feet in height. It was such an idyllic and peaceful sight. I scooped some water from the pool and slaked my thirst. Then I lay down on the bank of this magical oasis totally overcome by exhaustion. I was beginning to drift off when I felt somebody shaking my shoulder. I opened my eyes to find an ancient Chinese man with a long white wispy beard leaning over me. He had a kindly face and gestured to me to follow him.

His wooden hut was built on stilts and roofed with palm thatch. He beckoned me to enter his humble abode. My legs felt like lead and I was ready to drop as I wearily followed him into the hut. He rolled out some matting for me and invited me to lie down. Then he produced a Chinese wooden pillow, which looked very uncomfortable. I reluctantly laid my head on the block

163

and instantly fell into the deepest of deep sleeps. When I awoke, I was totally refreshed. The old duck-herd came into the hut with a kettle. He gave me a refreshing little cup of tea and a couple of boiled duck eggs. They tasted delicious and I washed them down with more of the tea. Then he took me out and, using sign language, explained that his ducks would never stray beyond a certain radius of the pole. For a few minutes, I was able to forget the war that was raging a few miles to the north. The Chinaman was so friendly and smiled all the time. He refilled my water canteen and gave me three hard-boiled duck eggs to take on my journey. I was sorry to leave the old man but I knew that the Japanese were not far away. If they discovered him helping a British soldier, we would both die horrible deaths. The Chinaman signalled the direction I should take for safety. I thanked him for his kindness and waved goodbye before I once again plunged into the jungle.

The distant rattle of machine guns and the occasional crump of mortar fire kept my pace up. It was another long, hot and humid day. I tried to ration my water — wetting my lips and taking occasional sips rather than greedy gulps — but, even so, all too soon my water canteen was empty. I was tortured by thirst and, as I pressed on, I even began to wonder which of the succulent plants might not be poisonous and which could yield some thirst-quenching juice. I was getting quite desperate when I stumbled into the most amazing and unexpected encounter. Standing in front of me were two tiny figures — a man and a woman with a small baby. They were black and looked more like black

Africans than Asian Malays. They were completely naked apart from tree bark tied around their waists to protect their modesty. I had heard of Pygmies in Africa but didn't know they existed in Malaya. These were the shy and primitive Pygmies known to the Malays as Negritos. They were obviously scared of me and were on the point of melting away into the jungle, but I desperately needed their help. They were nomads who knew the jungle like the back of their hands and could take me to water.

"Please! Please! Don't go," I said, smiling, and slowly raised my hands with my palms open, trying to look as friendly as possible. Then, ever so slowly, I moved my right hand across to the left breast pocket in my shirt and slowly produced a hardtack army biscuit. I put it to my mouth, bit on it, chewed and swallowed. Then I slowly extended my hand with the biscuit to the male pygmy, who was clutching a spear. He took it and chewed, looking at me all the time. He swallowed some of the biscuit and handed it back to me. I took another bite and, when I had eaten some more biscuit, I handed it to the woman. She nervously accepted the biscuit and chewed on it. Then I carefully removed a duck egg and gave it to the man. He smiled. The ice was broken. I indicated that I needed to drink water and showed him my empty canteen. He motioned for me to follow him and his wife into the bush. After about 20 minutes, we came across a small stream. I threw myself down and stuck my head in the cool water. I was about to drink but the pygmy stopped me. The water was no good. We went on for another 20 minutes and then

165

came to a deeper, faster-flowing stream. The pygmy took my canteen and pushed it right down to the bottom of the stream and filled it. I drank great draughts of the crystal-clear water as he looked on nodding. I drank as much as I could, then filled the canteen. I thanked the Pygmies as best I could and headed south once again.

As I walked away, I thought how strange it was that these stone-age people could help a stranger, a fellow human being in need, while people in the so-called civilised world were busy using every means at their disposal to destroy each other. Who was really the more primitive?

I didn't travel far that day before at last I met up with some other stragglers. I was overjoyed to recognise one of the lads from the Yeomanry. His name was Carter and he came from Castlemilk. He was with a Gurkha and a big red-haired Argyll we called Ginger. It was such a relief not to be alone. Even better — Ginger had a rifle and so did the Gurkha who also had his faithful kukri. We shook hands and set off for the south.

We were following a road from the safety of the jungle's cover. On the other side of the road were open paddy fields. We never let up the pace, and there was no talking as we went on in single file. The Gurkha was in the lead, hacking his way through the overgrown path choked with tangled vines and lianas. It was hard-going and we were all exhausted, longing to sit down and rest. I was on the point of suggesting a break when the silence was broken by Ginger up ahead.

"Oh, Christ! The bastards!"

Ginger had stopped and was staring ahead. Carter and I caught up with him only to be confronted with the most shocking and sickening sight. There, tied to two trees, were the mutilated bodies of four Australians. Their stomachs had been ripped open and their entrails spilled to the ground where ants were having a feast. They also had stab wounds on their torsos and shoulders. It was clear that they had been used for bayonet practice. They had died in agony and had most probably endured the torment of watching their comrades die before it was their turn. The bodies were beginning to smell in the heat of the jungle, but they had not been dead long. The Japanese were close — we had to keep going and fast. We had to get out of this bloody jungle and down to the safety of Singapore.

There was no time to bury the poor Australian lads, and as we moved forward Ginger vowed, "If I have to go, I'm gonna take ten of those Jap bastards wi' me."

Later, we would learn that this type of sadistic atrocity was typical of the Japanese Imperial Army. A few days earlier, on 22 January, the Japanese had captured over 150 wounded Australian, Indian and British troops at Parit Sulong. The men were shut up in a warehouse and denied water, food or urgently needed medical treatment. The next day, they were told to march to a nearby row of burned-out shops for medical attention. The walking wounded carried those too ill to walk. When they arrived at the shops, three concealed machine guns opened up on them. Survivors were bayoneted and burned alive with petrol poured over them. One brave Australian survivor crawled for six weeks in the jungle with two broken legs and survived the war to give evidence at the trial of General Takuma Nishimura, who was found guilty of ordering the massacre and was hanged by the Australians.

We were all hungry now and after a few miles we saw a planter's house on the other side of the road. It was built up off the ground and painted white. Many of these houses had been abandoned in a hurry and there was a good chance that it would have stocks of tinned food. It was risky but we were starving.

We hesitated before showing ourselves and crossing the road, which was just as well, because as we were about to leave the safety of the jungle we heard a car coming and shrank back into the shadows. A Japanese staff car with two officers in the back screeched to halt outside the house. As the two officers got out of the car, leaving their driver alone smoking in the front, the door of the house suddenly burst open and a Eurasian woman bolted for it. The Japanese officers quickly grabbed the screaming woman and pulled her back into the house.

We looked on in horror. The woman's screams were heartrending. I couldn't bear it. I looked at Carter, whose face was creased with anguish. Then I looked to Ginger. His jaw was grimly clenched.

"Ginger, come on. We can't let this happen. Let's get the buggers," Carter implored.

Ginger looked serious. "Keep the heid, keep the heid! If we start firing guns, the place will be swarming with Japanese." He turned to me and commanded, "Right, Andy, follow me."

168

We dashed across the road and into a ditch when the driver wasn't looking. We crept up the stairs at the back of the house and glanced in a window at the rear. One of the officers was lying on the bed and the other one was trying to tear the clothes off the Eurasian woman, who was still fighting them off. Ginger signalled to me to stay put, then he went into the house through the back door. I watched through the window as Ginger burst into the room swinging his Lee Enfield rifle above his head. He brought the butt crashing down on the head of the Japanese officer who was standing. It was incredible. The officer's head burst like a balloon. The other Japanese seemed paralysed and was dumb-struck. In an instant, Ginger spun around and smashed his head in too.

The Eurasian woman was in hysterics and collapsed in tears onto the floor. She was sobbing when I went into the room, and we helped her to get dressed and compose herself. She spoke fluent English and said that she would lead us through the jungle to the British lines. We went out by the front door and I was horrified to see the Japanese driver still sitting behind the wheel. I had forgotten all about him. But I needn't have worried. The driver's head was still on his shoulders — but only just. The Gurkha had crept up behind him with the silent stealth for which the Nepalese fighters were famed. He had unsheathed his kukri — and the kukri must draw blood before it can be re-sheathed. The driver would never have known what hit him.

The Eurasian woman led us into the jungle and took us to a cave in a Malay village. Inside the cave, they had stored water, bananas and rice, and they gave us a share of their food. The woman told us that the Japanese had been to the village, taken the young men away and raped all the women and young girls, leaving just the old people. The villagers told us that the Japanese had already been there looking for British soldiers and urged us to be careful.

We walked and walked and the next day we arrived at a place where the head man came out and said that the woman should stay with them, as it was not safe for her to continue. The head man gave us another guide and we set off following the man who was to take us to the British lines. We walked silently behind him and had been going for a few hours when a group of young armed Chinese men appeared from nowhere and surrounded us. They were carrying Japanese rifles and pointing them at us. We were worried and our guide looked terrified. We didn't know that, a couple of weeks before the Japanese invasion, the British had done a deal with Chinese communists and freed them from jails in Singapore to set up a guerrilla army.

One of the Chinese asked what was going on. We told him that our Malayan guide was taking us to safety. The guerrilla turned to his comrades and ordered two of them to take the Malayan away. From the jungle we heard a single shot and looked at each other with alarm. Then he spoke to us. "He was not taking you to the British. He was taking you to the Japanese! They are paying the Malays by the head for prisoners. We will take you to the British. Don't worry about that traitor. He will not be helping the Japanese any longer."

But we were worried, and not sure what or who to believe. We did know, though, that a lot of the Malays were not to be trusted and that some had fallen for Japanese propaganda. The Chinese, on the other hand, nearly all hated the invaders because they knew all about the cruelties they had committed in China. Sure enough, the Chinese were as good as their word and brought us to a clearing where we found a group of Argylls, Gurkhas and Aussies.

We had walked seventy miles through the jungle in five days and were relieved to clamber aboard a lorry. It took us to the causeway that linked Singapore with the Malayan peninsula. It was 31 January 1942 and, as we crossed, bagpipers in full regimental regalia were piping us out of Malaya. We had got out just in time. Shortly afterwards that night, the last of the Argylls and the Gurkhas slipped across the causeway and the engineers blew it up behind them.

At last, we had arrived in Singapore but the thought now struck me: "Would we ever leave it alive?"

CHAPTER
SEVEN

Trapped!

We were dropped off on the Singapore side of the causeway and joined a few other lads who had commandeered a van to drive into Singapore city. It was easy to find our way. In the distance to the south, we could see great columns of smoke: Singapore was burning. But at least the Japanese weren't breathing down our necks.

As I relaxed in the back of the van, I looked around at my fellow passengers and took stock. We looked like a real motley crew. We were sweaty, sticky, unshaven, filthy dirty and covered in bites, scrapes and scratches. Our long hair was matted and we were hungry, thirsty and exhausted. Our ragged uniforms were in tatters and covered in mud and bloodstains. We stank to high heaven and each of us looked gaunt. Our eyes were sunk into our heads and some men just stared ahead wide-eyed, as if in shock. We had been to hell and back, and it felt like it. We had been fighting non-stop for 54 days, and 5,500 of us had been killed and 5,000 wounded. Another 40,000 had been taken prisoner.

Suddenly, somebody shouted and the van stopped. We got out and were presented with an astonishing vision of elegance and tranquillity. In front of us was a beautiful English-style bungalow with a well-manicured lawn and lovely gardens. We could have been in the Home Counties on a Sunday afternoon. Swirling round on the lawn in front of the house was a sprinkler spraying water on the neatly clipped grass. The fine mist from the sprinkler caught the dying light of the day and looked so cool and inviting, particularly as we were so parched that our lips were cracked.

We walked onto the lawn and were in the process of uncoupling the hose from the sprinkler to quench our thirst and douse ourselves when the lady of the house appeared. She was not pleased to see us — to say the least. "Get off the lawn! Get off my lawn!" she shouted. "What do you think you are doing? Leave that hose alone. Leave it alone! Put it down!"

My blood was boiling. This was our welcome committee in Singapore. It was outrageous that we were being treated like this after all we had been through. I had heard stories about the arrogant colonials in Singapore with their clubs and bars that were out of bounds to servicemen and their armies of domestic servants. So it was true enough: they did look down their noses at us. I was just about to give vent to my feelings when her husband came out — dressed for dinner in a black tie and evening suit. Talk about fiddling while Rome burned. They clearly didn't have a clue that their endless social whirl of cocktail parties and Singapore slings and long days of siestas after tiffin were about to be brought to a very abrupt end.

173

The man was red-faced and angry. He pointed to our van, shouting, "Get that bloody thing out of here. We don't want you military types around here. You'll just bring trouble to us."

We were seething with rage. Ginger squared up to him and, pointing north, shouted, "Don't worry, mate. There's plenty of trouble coming down that bloody road. And it's heading right here!"

He turned to the wife, who looked slightly sheepish now, and told her, "And you won't have to worry about your bloody lawn, missus. There's 30,000 Japs on their way — they'll keep your bloody grass tidy."

I could see that the woman was regretting her pompous behaviour. We glared sullenly at her as she had second thoughts.

"You don't think the Japanese will get here, do you?" she said. "If you want water, go round the back. Use the tradesman's entrance."

Ginger shot back, "No thanks!" As he climbed back into the van, he turned around and shouted, "Say hello to the Japs for us." We laughed wryly as he added, "And remember to be polite to them!"

The first thing that struck us as we drove into Singapore city was the huge numbers of British and Australian troops. They were everywhere — thousands of them all bulled up and spick and span in neatly pressed uniforms. Where the hell had they all been when we needed them, we wondered. Then we learned that Churchill had vowed never to surrender Singapore — we were to fight to the last man. Incredibly, reinforcements were still pouring into Singapore even as the Japanese noose was tightening. It was a shocking and needless sacrifice. Just two days earlier, the British 18th Division had landed on the island; a third of them would die not in battle but as prisoners of the Japanese. Many of these men would be captured without ever having fired a shot. It was all right for Churchill, we thought, sitting in his bunker in London and promising to fight to the last drop of our blood. But how were we supposed to fight without air cover, with no tanks and now no navy?

The idea that we were safe in Singapore was quickly dispelled by the constant Japanese air raids on the city. They had complete mastery of the skies and our anti-aircraft guns frequently seemed to run out of ammunition. The Japanese targeted Keppel Harbour and the British headquarters at Fort Canning as well as our positions. They also targeted the Chinese civilian areas to spread panic and terror. The civilian population of Singapore had swollen to over a million as people fled the advancing Japanese. There were virtually no air-raid shelters and civilians had to jump into fetid monsoon drains to take cover during the ever more frequent raids. Doctors reported that, instead of lying down and covering their heads, Chinese civilians knelt with their heads down and their backsides up, which resulted in their having to treat hundreds of cases with shrapnel wounds to the buttocks.

Singapore was chaotic. Regiments were broken up and scattered all over the place. Eventually, we were directed to the regimental headquarters of the Lanarkshire Yeomanry on the north coast of the island.

Ginger stuck with us. When we arrived at Chong Pang near the Sembawang airfield, "C" battery — which had escaped over the causeway on 27 January — was already dug in with the howitzers pointing out to sea. "B" battery had been issued with new 25-pounders and was located a couple of miles down the road. Observation posts had been set up in the nearby naval base and our defences were being strengthened in preparation for a long siege.

We were starving, and it was decided that a group of us should drive down to the docks to see if we could find some food. As we got in the lorry, I trod on the stalk of green bananas that I had brought with me from Malaya. I was keeping them until they ripened, but, as one of them squashed under my foot, I discovered that they were a variety that was edible when they were green. We had been famished and all the time these delicious bananas were inches away from us. It was galling but we dived on the stalk like a troop of monkeys and munched on them as we drove through bomb-shattered Singapore.

We could see that the docks had taken a real pounding. Civilians, especially European women and children, were being evacuated on the ships which were constantly disgorging more troops into the giant mantrap that was now Singapore. There was a scramble to get out and thousands of people were mobbing the quays, trying to find a place on any boat that was leaving. Some rich colonials were arguing that their expensive motor cars should be allowed on board, but it was too late for all that. Evacuees were allowed one suitcase each and their posh limousines were pushed off the quays into the water. There were ugly scenes too with deserters trying to storm aboard departing vessels. British military police were trying to keep order with revolvers. As the end became inevitable, thousands of Commonwealth troops deserted and went on a looting spree. They would tell us, "We can't fight without the RAF. Where are the planes? It's your bloody war and you bloody Pommies can fight it."

They were definitely not impressed with Winston Churchill or his order to the effect that: "There must be no thought of sparing the troops or population. Commanders and senior officers should die with their troops. The honour of the British Empire and the British army is at stake."

There was still some semblance of order, though, and when Hughie and I told an NCO that we were from the Lanarkshire Yeomanry we were directed to a truck with stuff for us. On the way, we saw crates of tinned pineapple burst wide open. It was scorching hot and we helped ourselves, opening the tins to quench our thirst with the juice and throwing away the pineapple. When we found the truck, we were amazed. It was packed with boxes addressed to men in the Yeomanry. It was saddening to see some of the names on the parcels sent by loved ones to men who had already lost their lives. I raked through all of the boxes and was delighted to find one addressed to me. It had been following me around the world for a year. I ripped the brown paper off the box and opened the lid with all the excitement of a kid at Christmas time. Then I laughed out loud. Neatly folded on top of the contents were a hand-knitted balaclava, a woollen scarf and a pair of gloves: just the job for frozen trenches in Flanders but not much good for the prickly heat that plagued us all the time in the tropics. It was a nice thought all the same. Then I discovered a tin of melted chocolates and another box full of rock-hard doughnuts. I was mystified for a moment then I remembered that, just before my call-up, I was working on the Capital Picture House in Cowcaddens and used to buy doughnuts every day for the cleaners to have with their cup of tea. We used to have a laugh and they nicknamed me "Doughnut". Sure enough, the warm-hearted cleaners had enclosed a letter wishing me well and urging me to look after myself. The doughnuts were inedible by now, and as I showed them to Hughie he tapped one and joked, "Maybe we could use them as ammunition."

We had a nervous couple of days as the Japanese continued to bomb us from the air and then, on 3 February, they opened up with a barrage prompting Sergeant Major Scullion to remark that it was "just like the Somme in 1916". They were obviously massing for an invasion. On 4 February, our guns opened up for the first time since they had arrived at the island. "C" battery under Sergeant Major Roadnight sank five enemy barges loaded with infantry. Roadnight had earlier led the gunners in bayonet charges against the Japanese in Malaya and was awarded the Distinguished Conduct Medal.

On 8 February, just two months after it had invaded Malaya, the Japanese Imperial Army stormed ashore on Singapore Island with 23,000 troops. The island was too thinly defended by the British command, who had men strung out around the entire 70-mile coastline. After a series of dogfights on that day, the last of the RAF's Hurricane fighters were withdrawn to the safety of Sumatra and we never saw a British plane in the skies over Singapore again. The Japanese could bomb us at will, and across the strait of Johore, out of reach of our guns, they set up a huge artillery-spotter balloon to direct fire. They brought in their navy too and we were shelled from land and sea as well as bombed from the air.

There was ferocious fighting in the mangrove swamps where the Chinese militia organised by the British fought to the last man. A Malay unit distinguished itself too, and the Australians and British fought valiantly. However, we were withdrawing all the time to provide covering fire for the retreating infantry.

On 10 February, the Japanese launched an assault on the village of Bukit Timah, which blocked the main road to Singapore City. A fierce battle raged for the strategic village and only after 24 hours' fighting could the Japanese claim the prize. They also took a group of Argylls prisoner. Under their commander Colonel Ian Stewart, the Argylls had been Britain's best-trained and most experienced jungle fighting force. They formed aggressive "Tiger Patrols" and were nicknamed the "Jungle Beasts". During the Battle of Malaya, they had been a constant thorn in the side of the Japanese, who

179

now took their revenge. On 11 February, 12 Argylls prisoners were murdered by the Japanese army. They were tied up with barbed wire, bayoneted and shot in cold blood. A 13th victim got away by playing dead and was helped to safety by friendly Chinese.

We were in position overlooking a reservoir near the village of Nee Soon. I was sent up the hill to relieve my mate Charlie Farmer, who was in a forward observation post. Charlie had acquired a clock as a souvenir and it was his pride and joy. As he left, he told me, "Andy, make sure you look after my clock."

He was not gone long when a Japanese plane appeared from nowhere and dropped a bomb close by. Then more aircraft swooped down and pasted our emplacements below. When they disappeared, I ran down to see if I could help and found the place peppered with craters. Men were recovering and getting to their feet. The first person I met was Charlie Farmer, who promptly demanded, "Andy, have you got my clock? Is it OK?"

I looked about. Miraculously nobody seemed to have been injured, but then we saw an unconscious form lying on his back. We ran over fearing the worst.

I leaned over him. "Are you all right? Are you OK? Where are you hit?"

Slowly, the gunner regained consciousness and I asked him, "Can you move OK? Can you move your legs?"

"Whit are ye on aboot?" came the reply.

"Were you wounded in the air raid?"

"Air raid? Whit air raid?"

As he tried to get up, we could smell whisky on his breath. He had found a bottle and was completely drunk. It gave us one of the very few laughs we had during a very tough time.

As more and more Japanese flooded onto the island, we were pushed back into the city. On 12 February, we were in action at Newton Road and the next day we had fallen back slightly to Farrer Park where the guns from a lot of different regiments were gathered together and pointed in all directions to fire at the encircling enemy. On the night of 13 February, we came under very heavy shelling. It was horrific and felt like the end of the world. There was chaos with twisted trucks and dead and wounded men lying everywhere. Then an ammunition truck was hit and went up in a massive explosion. Young Captain Eustace was hit by shrapnel and died on his way to hospital. We were taking casualties left, right and centre.

That night, Colonel Gold and nine men of our regiment including Sergeant Major Roadnight were ordered to escape to carry on the fight. With the city in flames all around them, they found a junk and rowed out of the burning harbour of Britain's impregnable fortress in the Far East. They survived a gruelling nine-day voyage, during which they were bombed and machine-gunned, to reach Sumatra. Colonel Stewart and a group of Argylls were also ordered to escape to teach the British army the techniques of jungle fighting. They were the lucky ones.

The next day, when the Japanese reached Alexandra Hospital, a British lieutenant approached them under the protection of a white flag but was immediately bayoneted and killed. The Japanese then burst into the hospital and went on an orgy of killing and looting. Doctors, patients and nurses were all murdered. One patient was bayoneted on the operating table. That night, the Japanese crammed around 200 patients and staff into tiny rooms and denied them water. The next day, they took them out in groups and slaughtered them with bayonets and machetes. They had done the same thing on Christmas Day when they invaded St Stephen's Hospital in Hong Kong and massacred doctors and patients before raping and murdering the nurses. It was a cruel terror tactic and utterly typical of the Japanese Imperial Army.

The news of the Alexandra Hospital massacre shocked our High Command. The Japanese were also threatening to massacre the civilian population as they had done in Nanking. We were still fighting but we were running low on ammunition and the Japanese had cut off our water supplies. Unknown to us, the Japanese were in a bad way too. They were also running low on supplies. They were massively outnumbered and had lengthy supply lines. Nevertheless, at talks held in the Ford factory, Yamashita bluffed the British commander General Percival into surrendering unconditionally. If we had known the unimaginable torments that lay ahead for us as prisoners, I believe that Churchill would have got his wish. We would have fought to the very last man.

We had fallen back to Lavender Street, Singapore's notorious red-light area, where only a few weeks earlier a banner had been hung across the street welcoming "The Men of the Australian Infantry". Then the news came that we had surrendered. Men who had fought the Japanese so hard for two months were crying in frustration. We were overwhelmed with despair and despondency. Had all of our comrades died for nothing? Many of us could not accept the surrender and instead regarded it as a "ceasefire". In the Lanarkshire Yeomanry, our pride was intact. Some of the men like Tarn Hannah wanted to flee to the jungle and join up with the Chinese guerrillas but the officers wouldn't hear of it.

Those first hours of surrender on 15 February were worrying and filled with bitter recrimination. We felt let down and betrayed. And who knew what would happen to us now? We knew how the Japanese had treated prisoners in Malaya but surely they could not massacre all of us? We were too many and some of us were still armed. The first Japanese we saw looked frightened of us; we outnumbered them and had fought hard. Men stood around in bewildered groups cursing Churchill and the army planners. We exchanged wary glances with the advancing Japanese as they looked nervously at us and went on to their objectives. It didn't take long for us to witness our first atrocity. A Japanese officer was approached by an upset Chinese man. The man was trying to tell the officer something, when the officer removed his pistol from its holster and shot the man dead on the spot. We looked on horrified. Then, in a separate incident, a young Chinese boy of about nine years old on a bicycle was stabbed in the arm with a bayonet and shot dead on the ground by a Japanese soldier. They seemed quite casual and nonchalant when committing these murders.

We were sitting leaning against a wall when two Japanese soldiers came past with two Chinese prisoners. Their hands were tied behind their backs and the Japanese had placed ropes around their necks to lead them on. The Chinese were terrified and looked at us in a silent scream for help. We knew what their fate would be and it was too much for Ginger. He jumped up and followed the group around the corner and then we heard a hullaballoo. There was a bang, a scream, a clatter and another bang. Then the two Chinese lads came running back past us, free of their ropes. We heard Ginger shouting for help and ran around the corner. The Japanese were wounded but still alive. We threw them in a monsoon ditch and Ginger made sure they would not be murdering any more innocent civilians. We hid the bodies and moved away from the area, mixing with other troops anxiously awaiting instructions, and re-formed into our units, which had been broken up and scattered during the fighting. It was a very nervous time.

We were unaware of the massacre at Alexandra Hospital, but the officers knew because a Scottish officer called Captain Anderson suddenly appeared and asked us to go with him to block a road that led to a field hospital to prevent the Japanese reaching it. He asked for a dozen of us to go with him and we picked up rifles where we could find them. Captain Anderson said that if the Japanese continued to advance towards the hospital, he would shoot the leader and we should shoot the rest. There must have been an agreement that the wounded would not be harmed and Captain Anderson was trying to enforce it. We strung out across the road with our rifles at the ready. Nobody said anything; we just waited in the sun, swallowing hard and trying not to look frightened. It was like a stand-off in one of the old westerns I saw as a boy. Then my heart sank as they appeared — around two dozen of them.

Captain Anderson had tied a white handkerchief on the barrel of his rifle and moved forward to stand in front of us holding the gun aloft. The Japanese were about 40 or 50 yards away. They advanced a little, and their officer came forward and spoke with Captain Anderson. Then he went back and shouted something in Japanese before turning and taking his men away. It was a big relief to us when they disappeared.

There were about 60 or 70 of us standing by some trucks when I saw a Japanese officer coming down the street speaking to groups of our men as he went along. When he reached us, he asked us where we were from in fluent English with a noticeable American accent. We told him we were from Scotland and he asked which part. When one of the lads told him he was from Kilmarnock, the Japanese replied, "Ah, the home of Johnnie Walker whisky."

He was very friendly and put us at ease a little. He told us that he was an American Japanese and had been visiting Japan on holiday when he was called up and prevented from returning home. Then he said, "This is

185

our day today. But when America gets organised it will be their day and bad for Japan."

As he moved on, more Japanese soldiers turned up. They gestured that we should dump our weapons on a nearby tennis court and then line up. After we had lined up, they marched up and down stealing our watches and valuables; I said goodbye to the watch I had won in Paisley. Then we were ordered to form up and march the 16 miles to Changi, the eastern peninsula of the island, which across 19 square miles housed a sprawling complex that included a notorious prison, various British army barracks and the mighty guns that were supposed to have made Singapore impregnable.

We marched four abreast in our tens of thousands in the searing heat. The Rising Sun Japanese flag, which we nicknamed the "fried egg", seemed to be everywhere. A lot of the local Malays and Tamils had been issued with little "fried egg" flags and were waving them as they jeered at us. Sickeningly, the Japanese had also decorated our route to captivity with hundreds of Chinese heads speared on bamboo poles. It was a horrifying sight meant to intimidate us further into submission. When I first saw a clump of heads on poles, I didn't realise what they were, as they were completely black. Then, as we marched past them, the great swarms of flies that had settled on them lifted to reveal the shocking sight of severed heads with tongues protruding and eyes rolled back. It was especially sad to see the bodies of some of our own lads who had died in battle. The air was thick with the fearful smell of decomposing flesh and the stench from the bloated headless bodies, burst sewers and burning buildings hung in our nostrils. Our spirits sank even lower and we were suffering badly in the scorching sun. We were dehydrated and all suffering from a maddening thirst. Every now and again, very brave Chinese women would risk a beating to come out of their homes and offer us water. Then word spread along the column that two of our men had been beheaded for going into a house to seek water. So we plodded wearily on, wondering what lay ahead of us. We were a sorry-looking lot, and sick men who fell behind felt the butt of a Japanese rifle in their kidneys.

Finally, we arrived ready to drop at Changi jail. It had been built by the British as a civilian prison in 1936 and was intended for 600 inmates. Now thousands of us were squeezed into the building, stuffed in four men to a one-man cell. We lay down on the cold concrete floor, crushed up against each other, just glad to lie down. To begin with, the toilet facilities were poor to nonexistent. We had a "rose bucket" in the cell but tried to avoid using it. There were no Japanese around and, as the cells were never locked, we could come and go out of the prison and used nearby bushes for toilet purposes until the army engineers drilled bore-holes and dug out latrines. The sheer number of prisoners had taken the Japanese by surprise and they seemed unsure what to do with us. There were civilians there too — men, women and children of many different nationalities. It was a hellish place but at least British officers remained in command, and to begin with we were more or less free to roam around Changi peninsula.

Those first days of captivity were boring and depressing. Not knowing what would happen to us and how long we might be prisoners was the worst thing. It was all too easy for the uncertainty and sense of helplessness to turn into a feeling of hopelessness. Men endlessly speculated and argued about who was to blame for the biggest military disaster in British history with the capture of 120,000 men. Then the rumour machine started. We called this the "bore-hole news", as gossip was exchanged at the latrines. We felt so isolated and forgotten, and longed to hear news from the outside world. It was also important to counter the demoralising Japanese propaganda, which told us that they were invading Australia and that the Germans were winning everywhere. Later, men would risk — and lose — their lives to build radios to listen to the BBC, but they felt it was worth the risk. Some of the rumours were just fantastic. Hitler was in Sweden for peace talks. The Russians had reached the Mediterranean. The British and Americans had ordered huge fleets with aircraft carriers to sail to rescue us. These wild stories at least gave us something to talk over and think about. None of us ever believed that we would be prisoners for three and a half years. We just assumed that we would be free in a few months after the Germans had been defeated.

Very soon, we had a new subject of conversation and one which dominated all of our thoughts. It even replaced the barrack room's favourite topics of women and sport. It was food. We only had the meagre supplies that we had carried in with us to the camp and, although the cooks worked wonders, we soon felt the unforgettable pangs of hunger. Men began going underneath the wire to trade with the Chinese but it was dangerous. We were guarded now by Sikhs who had orders to shoot to kill and treated us with snarling contempt. Many of the Sikhs had gone over to the Japanese, who promised them independence for India, and some of those who saw through the empty Japanese promises and bravely refused to go over to the Japanese-backed Indian National Army were executed.

A few days after we arrived in Changi, all of us were ordered back out of the jail to form an honour guard for the Japanese commander General Yamashita. Thousands and thousands of us were lined up on each side of the main road to Singapore. Officers, NCOs and privates all stood to attention in the baking afternoon sun. The film cameras followed Yamashita's open-top car, recording for posterity the humiliation of the cream of the British Empire as the conquering general swept past English, Scottish, Australian and Indian soldiers as well as captured personnel from the RAF and Royal Navy. The propaganda film shot that day is regularly shown in television documentaries and I can barely stand to watch it.

The next day, some of us were ordered to form into work parties. We were marched off in the direction of the golden beaches that fringed the Changi coastline. Unknown to us, the Japanese Imperial Army had turned this palm-fringed tropical paradise into a killing ground. The smell alerted us to our new task long before we saw the piles of machine-gunned bodies that had turned the azure sea a dark crimson red. We were shocked but not surprised. Hundreds of Chinese men had been driven into the sea and murdered as part of the Sook Ching massacre, in which the Japanese killed 50,000 Chinese they suspected might be opposed to them — or just because they were Chinese. We completed our gruesome task in silence, sweating in the heat of the day and cursing our captors. We were in no doubt now about the true nature of our enemy. The only compensation for being selected for grave-digging duty was that we were able to collect coconuts on the beach and take them back to the cooks, who used them to supplement the rations for the sick men in the Lord Roberts Barracks, which had been turned into a hospital for 3,000 ill and wounded men.

We knew that we were at the mercy of an army that was capable of anything and confirmation of that soon came with the arrival in Changi of a member of our regiment who had survived the Alexandra Hospital massacre by playing dead underneath the body of a slain orderly. He described the massacre in detail to us. It was a depressing time.

One day, Captain Mackenzie came up to me outside the jail and asked if I would look after a Catholic priest who had volunteered to join up with the 155th. I was quite pleased to be asked to do something for the Church. It was familiar to me and a comfort in a threatening and alien environment. I had seen the priest before and knew that he was a padre from the armband that he wore. We shook hands firmly and I took an instant liking to him. He was an Irish Jesuit called Father Richard Kennedy, an athletic and tough 35-year-old rugby player from Dublin. He was a very committed individual, as befits a member of the Jesuit order — the praetorian guard of the Catholic Church — and had quite a fiery temperament. Father Kennedy had been a teacher in Hong Kong and could speak Chinese. He was from a well-to-do family and his father was a prominent surgeon. He had a brother who was also captured at Singapore and who had fought with the Malaya Volunteers.

We had moved out of the jail to an area of huts and tents in another part of the Changi complex a couple of miles away called Birdwood, and I helped Father Kennedy pitch the little pup tent he had used in the jungle. Then he showed me his portable kit — a tin box about 2 ft 6 in. long, which contained his garments and vestments. It was a bit like a travelling altar and he asked me if I would look after it. He suggested that we should have a Mass for the lads in the morning. I spread the word and quite a few turned up. I used to celebrate the Mass in Latin with Father Kennedy, and enjoyed listening to his stories of working with lepers and the poor Chinese people. I was struck by his dedication when he told us how he used to hide the lepers when Chinese armed units raided the colonies to shoot the victims of the terrible disease, which they wrongly feared was contagious. We would also swap sporting stories, with me relaying tales of the Maryhill Harriers and Father Kennedy recalling his rugby days.

He was good company and took my mind off our predicament.

Birdwood was like a mini-Aldershot with parades, drills and inspections designed to maintain fitness, morale and discipline. So I was pleased to escort Father Kennedy on his duties and avoid square-bashing in the heat. He made regular visits to the Lord Roberts Barracks to comfort the sick men and administer the last rites to the dying. It was a fearful place and the stench had me gagging. As well as the injured with their festering, gangrenous wounds, there were hundreds and hundreds of dysentery cases. There was also a ward reserved for the beriberi patients suffering from "Changi balls" — hideously swollen suppurating genitals that were red raw and maddeningly itchy. The doctors worked miracles with precious little in the way of drugs and medicines. At this point, we had very little contact with the Japanese, who were relying on the Sikhs to guard us, and on our trips to the hospital we would frequently have to run the gauntlet of surly Sikh guards who would punch and slap us.

One day, I was escorting Father Kennedy down to the hospital when we were surprised to see a Japanese staff car pass us with the "fried egg" fluttering on the bonnet. It suddenly slammed to a halt, and, to our surprise, a Japanese officer leaped out and began screaming at us.

"What's he on about, Father?" I asked apprehensively.

"Just stand still, Andy. Stand very still. Look at the back of the car," he whispered.

I looked over and saw a Japanese soldier with a rifle pointing at us. The Japanese officer had worked himself into a fury now and smashed his fist into Father Kennedy's face. I was appalled. Then he turned round and punched me in the face too. More screaming ensued. I was bewildered and the officer struck me again. I didn't know what I was supposed to do.

Then Father Kennedy said quietly, "He wants you to punch me in the face, Andy. Do it."

I was horrified and hesitated. The screaming intensified.

"Do it, Andy. Just do it!"

I hesitated again, mortified at the notion of striking a priest. Then I struck Father Kennedy in the face but pulled my punch. The officer went berserk.

Father Kennedy urged me, "Andy, punch harder. Just punch as hard as you can. You have to, for both of our sakes."

"Forgive me, Father," I whispered, as I punched the priest.

The Japanese seemed satisfied and ordered Father Kennedy to punch me. So it went on, back and forth. For five long minutes, the Japanese enjoyed the spectacle of the two of us beating each other up. Our crime had been not to bow to the Japanese flag. We had endured our first bashing from the Japanese. It was not to be our last.

A couple of months into our captivity, the food situation was getting worse and worse in the camp. We were absolutely obsessed with food, and we talked and fantasised about it all the time. I would regale my pals with tales of Mrs Knott's restaurant and her famous clootie dumpling. We didn't think that we were torturing ourselves because we all expected to be released the following month.

One of the guys in my hut at Birdwood was a very talented painter. We would cut our thumbs and drip some blood into a tin, then he would mix it with oil to create paint so he could decorate the walls of the hut with paintings of fish suppers, steak pies and ham and eggs. He painted a slogan to go with his masterpiece too — "Gone but not forgotten!"

People tried to cope with the starvation in different ways. Some men would spin out their rice by eating a couple of grains at a time and keeping some for the next day. We would eat anything, and everything tasted good. Some Malayan prisoners showed us how to break open coconuts, and the cooks used the fermented coconut milk as a sort of yeast for the rice bread that they cooked on the steel door that we took down from the battery of guns at Changi to use as a hotplate. The Malays also taught us how to catch and skin snakes. To begin with, we cursed the rats, which were the bane of our lives and thrived in the rafters of the hut. They even pinched my mate's false teeth one evening. But soon they became a delicacy, which we all agreed "tasted just like chicken".

Men were taking their lives in their hands to go under the wire and barter with the Chinese. All kinds of rackets were being developed out of dire necessity. Trumpeter Smith was going under the wire to pinch oil for homemade reading lamps, which he sold for three cigarettes — a prized currency. Some of the men like Tarn Hannah had been sent to build a memorial to the Japanese war dead at Bukit Timah and were selling siphoned-off petrol to the Chinese to buy fruit and duck eggs. We were getting weaker and weaker, and men were dying of malnutrition and all of the horrible diseases that went with it.

I was among the men who were drafted into work parties and sent to work in Singapore docks. It was hard work in the hot sun, and there was always a danger of getting a beating from the Japanese, but at least the work parties got us out of the camp and we had the chance to barter with the Chinese and pilfer from the cargoes. We would pinch anything we could. Sewing needles and gramophone needles were especially prized, and how we traded with the Chinese was quite amazing. If we had been caught, the consequences would have been dire — death for the Chinese, and for us at least a severe beating or torture by the dreaded Japanese secret military police, the Kempeitai. As we marched out of the docks in columns three or four abreast, hordes of little Chinese children would playfully dart through our ranks. The Japanese would curse and shoo the children away but they never suspected anything. As the children ran through us, we would pass our contraband to them and the next day they would run through us again pressing a few dollars into our palms. They were very honest and we always got paid. Sometimes, they would pass notes to us asking us to pinch specific things and arrangements would be made to meet at the wire when they would bring bananas and eggs. The Chinese were very brave — if they had been caught, they would have been shot or beheaded.

One day, I was in the docks loading heavy ingots of looted silver onto a Japanese ship. Quite a few of us were in the work party taking the bars of silver — stolen from a Singapore bank — from a lorry and dropping them onto a straw sack on the ship when half a dozen Europeans came along in naval uniforms. They were well fed and carefree, and they were obviously shocked to see us in our ragged and starved condition. They threw us some cigarettes and, when the guards started shouting, they pushed them back and told them to leave us alone. They were German allies of Japan but expressed their disgust at the way we were being treated.

Later that day, one of our guards sat down and fell fast asleep. One of the other Japanese gave him a shake and put his dinner of rice and fish down next to him. When the guard dozed on, the temptation was too much for us to resist and we gulped down his lunch as we walked past. Luckily for us, he had a little dog, which was licking the plate when he woke up. He was cursing and swearing at it as we tried not to laugh.

Boredom was a big problem in the camp. To combat it, we had quizzes and there were lectures by all kinds of experts. Science and politics were popular subjects. A lot of men took the opportunity to improve their education — knowledge was one thing that the Japanese could not take away from us.

At night, to pass the time, we would have a quiz and swap stories about our days in Glasgow. We'd talk about the movies we had seen and reconstruct the plots of the films. We'd also recall skits by famous Scottish music-hall artistes like Jack Radcliffe and Harry Lauder, whom I once saw when I was painting his agent's office. It was great to hear talk about the names of streets and people we knew. It seemed like a dream and a bad one at that. We were a bunch of lads from Glasgow stuck on the other side of the world in a culture that was strange and alien to us. I told the lads about Beeney Dunlop pawning her shawl to give my mother a few bob and about Monkey Reilly taking the dog back off me. "Doc" Sweeney was one of the older lads who had joined us at Lanark. He was 33 and from Plantation, and he had worked for a bookie. He knew Monkey well and he had some great stories from the dog tracks about the betting — of dodgy dealings, great big losses and big wins.

One night, we were lying back having a quiz, and Doc asked, "Who won the Scottish Derby in 1931 at Carntyne?"

I knew the answer right away: "Sister Olive."

"Right enough, Andy. And what was the name of her pup that won it twice?"

My memory was good for this sort of thing. "Olive's Best," I shouted before the others could get in.

"Aye, yer right," said Doc. Olive's Best had won it in 1934 and 1935. Then he asked a question I couldn't get the answer to: "And who won it the year after Sister Olive?"

It bothered me and I went to bed thinking about it. I knew the answer and just couldn't remember. Then it came to me in the middle of the night. I sat up and gave Doc a shake. He half opened an eye.

"It was Laverock!"

"Och! Bugger off, Andy! You're right enough, but the quiz is over!"

I tried to keep my fitness up by jogging around the camp and on the *padang*, or playing field. My body weight was dropping like a stone — the same as the rest of the lads — but I felt jogging was important to keep the circulation going through my arms and legs. We played football and cricket too, but a highlight was always our theatrical productions. Very soon after we were sent to Changi — within days — a theatre group and concert party was established. The camp had an orchestra too, which was about 30-strong. There were a lot of talented people, including professional actors and musicians, among the 60,000 of us at Changi and new productions were aired every fortnight with everybody getting a chance to see the latest show. There were musicals and comic reviews as well, often taking the mickey out of our captors. I enjoyed singing, so volunteered to help out. I sang a popular Deanna Durbin number.

The countryside is green again,
The world is seventeen again,
My heart awakes when April sings.
The skies above are blue again,

The daffodils are new again,
These are the joys that April brings.

It was a positive song of hope, but we sang a lot of songs from home as well. A few of the lads were misty-eyed as they sang the old Scottish favourite "Rowan Tree" along with me.

Oh! rowan tree, oh! rowan tree,
Thou'lt aye be dear to me,
Entwin'd thou art wi' mony ties
O' hame and infancy.
Thy leaves were aye the first o' spring,
Thy flow'rs the simmer's pride;
There was na sic a bonnie tree
In a' the countrie side.
Oh! rowan tree.
We sat aneath thy spreading shade,
The bairnies round thee ran,
They pu'd thy bonnie berries red,
And necklaces they strang;
My mither, oh! I see her still,
She smiled our sports to see,
Wi' little Jeanie on her lap,
And Jamie on her knee.
Oh! rowan tree.

However, I was not prepared for what happened next. I was cast as a reluctant maiden betrothed to a bandit chief in a comic sketch, and Tubby Daly was my horrible hag of a mother. Looking more like a pantomime dame than a desirable maiden, my appearance on stage was greeted with laughter and hoots of derision. We were both wearing brassieres made out of coconut shells and had to walk down the aisle lined by bandits. They played "Here Comes the Bride" then I turned, singing to Don Roberto the bandit chief.

> Dear Sir, this is my mother,
> She's turned 93.
> I am her daughter and you must look after her
> If you are going to marry me.

He looked at me and sang,

> I'm not paying for matrimony
> I haven't got much money,
> Do you see a glint of green in my eye?
> I think you've a cheek to ask it
> So I'll stab her in the bread basket,
> She's got to die! She's got to die!

These concerts fleetingly took our minds off the fact that the food situation was deteriorating even more rapidly. Men were dying like the flies that buzzed round us, carrying the awful dysentery that we virtually all contracted at some stage in our captivity. Father Kennedy was down at the hospital more often than ever to give the last rites.

I decided I had to do something to try to help. I used to go down to the sea regularly to get water, which we boiled off for the salt. We used to swim in the sea there, but because the Japanese had dumped so many dead bodies into the water they had attracted sharks. One of the lads had a leg bitten off one day, and swimming was losing its attractions for me.

One day, when all the lads went in for a swim, I skipped away and came up from the beach on the other side of the wire and through the bushes to some abandoned houses. I waited until there was not a soul in sight and walked up the little stairway onto the verandah and looked in. When I went in, it was obvious that whoever had been in the house had left in a hurry; there was stuff all over the floor. I was looking for medical things, drugs, dressings, disinfectant and things like that, for the sick men in the hospital. I opened up a cupboard and my eyes nearly popped out of my head. I thought I had discovered Aladdin's cave! Neatly stacked up in front of me were tins of bully beef, McConnachie's stew, Spam, canned ham, condensed milk, peas and beans — stuff that we had been dreaming about for months. I was only wearing a pair of shorts and wondered what to do. I went down the stairs and around the back way. I came to a little shed with a lot of rice bags, and I brought one back up and filled it with goodies. Nobody knew about this except me. I knew I didn't have much time because the lads would be coming away from the beach and back up the road. I hid the sack under some bushes near the prison camp hedge and memorised the location, right opposite the giant British guns that had proved so useless in our defence. Then I got a piece of cloth and I stuck it in the wire mesh to mark the spot. I couldn't carry the stuff

201

because the lads would have all have seen it and it would have caused trouble. The men were starving but the sick and wounded needed the food most of all. I joined up with the group coming back and went directly to Father Kennedy's quarters. It was getting dark but I insisted.

"I have something to show you, Father. I've kept this to myself. You'll have to come with me."

I got right to the place. The fence was eight to ten feet high around the whole camp, but, at one point, it was three or four inches off the ground and I started digging with a piece of wood so I could wriggle underneath it. I told Father Kennedy to stay where he was and managed to squeeze below the wire. I got through the hedges towards the bushes where I had left the sack with the stuff in it and I pulled it across. Then I began passing the tins underneath the wire to Father Kennedy. Finally, I wriggled back underneath with the empty sack, which we filled up and took to the medics. I later learned that the Australians were doing the same thing — raiding houses that had been abandoned by fleeing planters.

The doctor was thrilled with all the food; it meant the difference between life and death for some patients. He asked where I got it, and then warned me, "Christ, Coogan, if you get caught, you'll get shot."

It was risky and one man had already been shot for going under the wire, but I made two or three trips back to the house and cut down stalks of bananas that grew in the garden and chucked them over the fence to my mate Hughie Carroll, before wriggling back under the wire. We had to do it in secret to avoid causing a riot. Men were starving and they would have fought over the bananas.

We had to keep quiet too, because in June our officers had reintroduced field punishments. Going underneath the wire was banned and they had established a jail within a jail called Templehill. The place was regarded with dread. Rations were cut for inmates and there was a rigorous exercise and work regime overseen by tough military police. Trumpeter Smith knew men who were in there and was very angry about it. He said that conditions were so bad that some men would catch disease-carrying flies and eat them in the hope of getting sick and being sent to the hospital.

By this time, the Japanese had started to send rice into the camps. Half a cup three times a day with watery liquid of stewed vegetable was to become the staple diet. Once a fortnight, we might get a "stew" with a piece of old pork floating in it. Some men would count out the grains, trying to spin it out. Everyone had their eyes glued on the rice cauldrons we called "kwalies", to make sure they got their fair share. The cooks did their best and ground the rice down to flour to make rice cakes and chapattis. We were always on the lookout too for the burned scrapings from the "kwalies", which at least had some taste. Often, the rice was the sweepings off the warehouse floor, and it was full of weevils, vermin droppings and maggots, but it was all we had. Frequently, it had been sprayed with a foul-tasting liquid that we thought might be lime or sulphur. Even worse, the rice was polished; it was shiny white and the husks had been removed. The simple failure of the Japanese to leave the husks on the rice deprived us of vital vitamins and would sentence thousands of men to death. Lack of thiamine or vitamin B_1 led to beriberi, which caused swollen legs like the Indian people I had seen in Bombay and swollen testicles too, painfully inflating scrotums to the size of footballs. Men were crippled and couldn't walk. They suffered agony from a burning sensation in the soles of the feet which we called "happy feet". It attacked the nervous system and the heart, but, above all, it caused a terrible lethargy and breathlessness. If you suffered from beriberi, it took every ounce of energy to shuffle along like a zombie. All too often, it was fatal. The cause of beriberi had been discovered in the late nineteenth century by the Dutch, and the Japanese knew all about it, but they didn't care what happened to prisoners.

Another affliction had appeared in the camp. Our immune systems were wrecked by starvation and the slightest scratch on a limb almost invariably led to the development of tropical ulcers. In no time at all, these suppurating ulcers ate down to the bone and rotting flesh seemed to peel away. Doctors tried to treat them with maggots but all too often men were having limbs — usually legs — amputated. The operations were performed without anaesthetic and many of the patients died of shock.

At night-time, Father Kennedy and I prayed to God that we would survive and keep our legs so we could play sport. We both dreaded losing a leg.

Father Kennedy's regular services for Catholics in the camp were proving popular as men sought hope and comfort. To begin with, we gathered in a dusty corner behind a hut. But, over time, we gathered scraps of wood and bamboo and made a makeshift chapel. I worked with Tammy Donnelly and "Doc" Sweeney to build the chapel that was dedicated to St Ignatius of Loyola, the patron saint of the Jesuits. We somehow acquired paint and brushes and I enjoyed painting the chapel — it brought back memories of all the laughs we had as painters in Glasgow and I regaled the lads with some funny stories. I painted the Lamb of God on the altar and when I finished it looked quite good.

I made new friends among the English lads who came along. One of them, the son of a top lawyer in London, became quite a pal, but he was suffering terribly from starvation and was wasting away in front of us. I tried to keep his spirits up but he went downhill rapidly, and when I went to visit him in hospital with Father Kennedy he asked me to visit his parents when I got home — he knew he would never get back. I promised I would, and as I walked away I was both sad and angry that a young life was being sacrificed so needlessly. (After the war, I kept my promise and went to see his parents. His mother hugged me as if I was the son who had never returned. It was so sad.)

One night, after prayers, we were sitting talking and Father Kennedy suggested we add a tabernacle — something to represent a sacred place to say our prayers and have Holy Communion. There was nothing lying about the camp to use; every single piece of wood or metal had been scavenged or cannibalised and hammered out for another purpose — the place was bare.

I was thinking about Father Kennedy's tabernacle. I remembered a planter's house we passed when we were out with a working party, and thought maybe there would be something in there that we could use for our tabernacle. I felt sure I could remember how to get there. One morning after roll call, Father Kennedy and I decided to have a go. We slipped under the wire and crept away from the camp, making our way through the thick rustling bamboo that towered high above our heads. We stuck close together and soon found a thin path through the bushes. After a while, we came to a clearing with a small wooden hut. It had been someone's home, but there was no sign of life; it had long been abandoned.

We stood for a while listening to make sure there was no sound, then nodded to each other and made for the hut. I crept in the door, Father Kennedy at my back. The room was sparsely furnished with a table and broken chair. We looked around for water and tinned food but there was nothing except the rotted remains of a half-eaten meal.

There were stairs to a cool basement where a small chest, about 12 by 18 inches, was fastened to the wall. It looked like a painted tin cupboard, and we thought it might have been an icebox. I opened it to find it was completely empty.

"There's your tabernacle, Father."

"Yes," said Father Kennedy, "that'll be grand."

I looked around for something to prise the cupboard from the wall and found a piece of bamboo. I slipped the bamboo stick behind the icebox and tried wrenching it from the wall but it was well stuck. I was determined we would have the box and tried over and over again to get it free. Then I was aware of a sudden movement. Father Kennedy was nipping up the stairs. At the same instant, I felt a tap tap on my shoulder. I turned to see a Japanese soldier in uniform smiling at me — the sort of broad smile that used to chill our bones. I nearly fainted. It was petrifying.

He took the stick from me and, without much effort, pulled the box from the wall. He pointed from the box to me as if to say, "There you are — take it."

I stood still, not sure what to make of it. I could feel myself surrounded by Japanese, in the bushes outside and maybe in the hut. They would be waiting with their swords and were very cunning. The officer beckoned me outside, and then took my arm and led me round the back of the hut where a motorbike was lying against a tree. Smiling, he pushed his gun into my arms, lifted the bike and pushed his foot hard down on the pedal, again and again trying to start the bike. It was peculiar. I had his rifle and could easily have shot him, but all the time I was wondering, "Where's Father Kennedy? Where are the other Japs?" The soldier had another go and the bike spluttered but then fell silent. He took his gun back from me and pushed me towards the bike, indicating that I was to try starting it. He leaned his rifle against a tree and held the bike steady. I put my foot on the pedal and pushed down sharp and hard.

Not a splutter. I tried again, this time twisting the rubber grip on the handle bar. A miracle happened, and the bike coughed into life but then just as quickly fell dead again. Next, the soldier stamped down as I twisted the grip. At last, we got it going. The soldier mounted the bike and I passed him his rifle.

He slipped it over his shoulder and with a smile and a wave he was off through a clearing in bushes. I stood for a long time, listening to the bike getting further and further away. I felt sure I was being watched. I stood still, looking round for Father Kennedy, but there was no sign of him. It was completely silent.

Then there was a noise, faint at first, but then the far-off puttering of the bike was getting closer again. He was coming back. Oh, God! I prayed for my mother and my father, God rest him. I prayed for Frank, Eddie, Pat and Betty. The Japanese soldier reappeared, smiling at me. He drew up and beckoned me over. I took a few steps towards him, terrified not to. He asked me for my hand, reached out and placed a small package in my palm. I nodded thanks. He smiled, revved up the bike and was off the way he came.

I stood still, confused, still waiting. Where were the Japs? What had happened to Father Kennedy?

After a while, I went back to the hut and sat on the doorstep. I was soon joined by Father Kennedy, and we sat silent for a while. Then the priest started to sob. "May God forgive me, Andy. If he had gone for you, I was ready for him." He let a heavy piece of wood fall from his hand.

We sat still, hardly believing we were still alive. I showed him the rice paper parcel in my fist. We opened it up and inside was a little piece of ginger.

The Japanese were working on a plan. The era of quick victories was behind them and they realised that their army needed all the men it could get. Like the Nazis, who used concentration-camp prisoners for labour in their war machine, the Japanese had decided that their Allied prisoners would become slave labour. However, first, they had to break our spirit and take control of Changi where British officers still ruled and were served by their batmen. Changi would then become a transit camp for working parties shipped out across their conquered territories and ultimately to Japan itself.

In August, a new Japanese commander, General Shimpei Fukuye, arrived at Changi. He moved quickly to establish his authority on the camp. Escape from Singapore was futile, as we were so easily spotted as Europeans. Survival in the jungle was virtually impossible and then you had the problem of getting off the island. Nonetheless, four men — two British and two Australians — had tried to get away and had been caught. On 30 August, Fukuye ordered that we should all sign an undertaking not to escape. Our officers told us not to sign. It was not just a symbolic battle over authority for us; the right to escape is enshrined in the Geneva Convention and we were trying to get the Japanese — who were not signatories to the Convention — to observe its terms.

Fukuye was enraged at our mass refusal to sign, and the next day we were all ordered to report to the Selarang Barracks and warned that any man found outside Selarang after 6p.m. would be shot. The only exceptions were the civilians in Changi jail and the 3,500 sick men in the Lord Roberts Barracks. The Selarang Barracks had been built in 1938 and was home to the Gordon Highlanders. It consisted of three flat-roofed barrack buildings constructed around a small parade ground. It was designed to house 800 men and now the Japanese were to squeeze in 17,000 of us, just to show who was boss. Early on that morning, there was a mass exodus of men taking everything they could with them to Selarang.

When I arrived with Father Kennedy, the square was already filling up and people were jostling for space. Some men had already staked out a space on the flat roofs of the buildings, which were crowded but open to the sun. Others had crowded into the barracks in a bid to escape the blowtorch rays of sunshine. The rest of us had to make do with the barracks square and the strip of land behind and to the side.

The first and most pressing problem was the total lack of latrines. The half a dozen or so toilets in each of the three blocks would have been totally inadequate even if the Japanese had not cut the water off. The engineers immediately directed us and we set about digging. We made good progress and dug a lot of bore-holes, but there were so many people that we could hardly dig fast enough — and there was too little space. When a bore-hole was full up we would put a big slab over it and leave it. We were constantly digging bore-holes but quickly they became too close together and the vile contents of the filled-up holes would start to seep into the new ones as we were digging them. It was hellish, but we did what we could and what we had to do. The flies had a field day and the cases of diarrhoea and dysentery multiplied.

Men started to die but we still refused to sign. It was an electrifying game of cat and mouse. We would sing "Land of Hope and Glory" or "There Will Always Be An England" to keep our spirits up, and the Aussies would kick in with "Waltzing Matilda". Then the Japanese would retaliate by setting up machine guns and training them on us. There was only one standpipe to supply water and men queued all day to get a full bottle. The Japanese blustered and bullied but we stood firm.

On 2 September, they decided to execute the four escapees and ordered our commanding officers to attend the execution. The firing squad was composed of Sikhs, who were to fire up a slope at the condemned men. Before the execution, the Australian corporal took responsibility for his escape attempt in a bid to save the life of his younger colleague. However, the Japanese ordered the executions to proceed. It was bungled and it took several volleys to kill the men.

Still we stood fast and refused to sign. Our medical officers were becoming seriously concerned and feared massive loss of life. We were baking in the tropical sun with more men going down with malaria and dysentery. It was unbearable but our resolve held until the

Japanese threatened to transfer all the sick men from the Lord Roberts Barracks. It would have been a death sentence for hundreds and our leadership finally agreed to us signing "under duress" on 4 September.

The next day, we wearily made our way back to our camp. The Selarang Squeeze, as it became known, was a sign of things to come.

The following couple of weeks were spent in the usual drudgery of the camp routine. Then, one day, there was a call for volunteers. The Japanese needed men to go up north to "a holiday camp" in the hills. We would work three days and have four days off — and the food would be much better. It sounded like a great improvement on Changi and I was tempted. I had been in the camp for seven months and was fed up. Father Kennedy counselled me against it. "Don't go, Andy," he said. "You can't trust the Japs. Goodness knows where you might end up. Better to stick with the crowd here. There's safety in numbers."

I decided not to go and so missed out on the first train north to the Death Railway and the Bridge on the River Kwai where 100,000 Asian labourers and 16,000 Allied prisoners died in atrocious conditions, building a railway through virgin jungle to allow the Japanese to supply their armies fighting in Burma. But the Japanese had something else in store for us — an ordeal that would become a hell on earth and would make all of our previous sufferings look like a Sunday-school picnic.

CHAPTER
EIGHT

The Depths of Hell

Soon, quite a lot of men from our regiment were being sent up to the Death Railway on work parties that were no longer voluntary. They were stuffed into stiflingly hot overcrowded metal railway trucks for a five-day journey that was followed by a lengthy death march into the jungle. The journey alone was an ordeal for ill, weak and starved men, and cost many lives. The wrecked survivors of the railway had yet to return to Changi so we knew nothing of their sufferings.

On 24 October, we were ordered to get our stuff ready as we were moving out the next day. We were told we would be sailing from Singapore Harbour but had no idea where we were headed — which was just as well.

The next day, we were driven in Australian lorries to the harbour where just over a thousand of us lined up for a bizarre medical inspection. There was a small table with a couple of Japanese officers sitting behind it and a couple of medical orderlies standing around. One by one, we all had to go forward and in full view of all the other men drop our trousers and bend over to allow a glass rod to be inserted into our backsides. God knows what this was supposed to diagnose because there were no records of any kind kept. The dogs in the street could see that we were all starving and sick men ravaged by diarrhoea, dysentery and malaria. It was embarrassing but if it was intended to humiliate us it didn't work. There were too many wisecracking wits among us to allow it to get us down and we managed to laugh at the whole procedure. Some men said that they saw a Red Cross inspector down at the docks. However, personally, I never ever saw one at any time in my captivity, nor did we ever receive any of the Red Cross parcels that were sent to us but stolen by the Japanese army.

Next, we were marched over to the quayside where a rusting old tub called the *England Maru* was waiting for us. It was a 5,000-tonne vessel with four cargo holds. Some of the lads recognised it and said that they had unloaded cattle from it. Sure enough, as the Japanese rushed us up the gangplank and onto the deck, we had to step over cowpats that littered the deck. Then we were forced down into the holds where the animals had been. The men below were shouting that the hold was full but our guards forced us down at bayonet point. We were packed in tighter than sardines. It was hellish. The floor was covered in manure and the hold swarmed with biting bluebottles, which competed for our attention with the rats and cockroaches. The smell made us feel sick, but it would get a lot worse as men went down with dysentery and seasickness took hold of us. There were wooden buckets to serve as latrines for the men who were too sick to clamber up the stairs to a wooden contraption nicknamed the "stage", which hung over the side. I felt very sorry for the lads with dysentery who had to fight their way to the buckets 20 or 30 times a day. If they didn't make it, there were cries of disgust and curses from the men squashed next to them. Soon we would all be spattered with faeces. The cattle had been transported in better conditions than this. At least they had been fed and watered — unlike us, who had to survive on an occasional rice ball and water that was lowered down in a bucket when the Japanese felt like it.

When they battened down the hatches, a terrible cry went up. We were plunged into darkness. It felt like we were entombed in a floating black hole of Calcutta. How long would they keep us down here? How long before we started dying? If we had guessed that we would be trapped like rats in the hold of this foul-smelling rust bucket for three long weeks, I think many of us might have lost the will to live or lost our sanity. It didn't seem likely that we could survive three days, never mind three weeks. The heat was unbearable, the atmosphere was airless and men were crying out for water. We were kept there in the dock for a full day and could hear other ships leaving the harbour. By the time we sailed out of Singapore Bay, some men had lost their senses altogether. I was lucky to have Hughie Carroll, Tammy Donnelly, Tammy Dodds and Father Kennedy near me. Father Kennedy's calm words of faith and reassurance helped me to get through a terrible time.

We were aboard a Japanese hell ship — one of a fleet of old freighters that plied the waters around the Japanese empire in the east, shuttling slaves from one outpost to another. The Japanese never marked these vessels with a red cross or POW markings, and many ships were sunk by American submarines unaware that the holds were packed with Allied prisoners. Conditions in many of the ships were so horrific that sometimes men welcomed being torpedoed. In some cases, the Japanese just sealed the hatches and forgot about the prisoners, leaving them to rot and go mad with thirst and starvation. Twenty-two thousand of us died on these ships and within seven months the *England Maru* itself was sunk by the American submarine USS *Grayback*. The treatment of Allied prisoners on the hell ships was undoubtedly a major war crime yet nobody was ever prosecuted.

Father Kennedy and I took our turns to empty the evil-smelling wooden pails over the side. We had a job getting through the crush of men with the vile buckets. It was pretty horrible and invariably the contents spilled over the side onto our legs. We went up to the deck in our bare feet using the rough ladder but it least it got us out of the stinking hold for a few minutes and sometimes we could use a hosepipe for cleaning the deck to hose ourselves down with seawater. The toilet we called the "stage" was so named because the Japanese guards used to gather in front of it to laugh at us trying to use the wooden structure that hung out over the ship. It was dangerous and you had to hang on for dear life. If men were weak, we would hold on to them. The Japanese found all this hilarious. Sometimes, to amuse themselves further, they would open the hatches to urinate on us down below, but we were usually just so glad to get those hatches opened. We could hardly breathe when they were closed. When they lowered water down in buckets, men would go crazy fighting each other to get a drink. Decent men were reduced to animals. We had reached our lowest point. It was truly awful.

After about a week, the boat stopped and at last we heard the anchor chain rattling down the hull. Men were beginning to die and our officers argued that we should be allowed on deck for air. We were let up in batches and hosed down. Eventually, I got up on deck with Father Kennedy and I could see we were anchored in the bay of a port. A cutter glided past carrying well-fed and immaculately dressed European naval officers — not Germans as we first thought, but French. We were at Saigon, the capital of what was then French Indochina and under the control of Vichy France. The Vichy French regime under Marshal Pétain was collaborating with Nazi Germany and they had a working relationship with the Japanese. It was strange to see these normal-looking white men laughing and joking, and it made us realise what a state we were in as we looked at each other.

Some of the men tried to shout to the French, to let them see how much we needed help, but the Japanese started to brutally force us back down into the hold. They were now being led by a new officer. It was my first encounter with him, but we would all come to know him well and dread the mere mention of his name: Lieutenant Nobuo Suzuki. He was small, lean and very mean. Always clad in his oversized ill-fitting uniform, he particularly enjoyed beating men who were older or bigger than himself. He was a Formosan who seemed to want to impress his Japanese masters by outdoing them in the cruel treatment of his victims. Suzuki would terrorise our every waking moment and haunt my dreams for years to come.

A convoy was being assembled in Saigon as protection against patrolling American submarines. Our next destination — although we never knew it — was Taiwan, or Formosa as it was called then. The Japanese had seized the island from China at the turn of the century to make it part of their empire. The long journey to Formosa was a nightmare. It became cooler, which was a blessing, but we were thrown about on top of each other as the Weather in the South China Sea turned nasty, banging the anchor endlessly and deafeningly off the hull. Conditions were worsening and so was our health. The hatch was opened to let in air but the men underneath it were soaked and lay in mud and filth. We now had cases of diphtheria and a case of typhoid. The Japanese allowed some of the worst dysentery cases to go on deck closer to the "stage", but this meant that they were exposed to the wild weather. It was no surprise that more men died and were thrown over the side to feed the sharks.

For hours on end, I watched the rats running around and tried to think of pleasant things. The fitful sleep that came with exhaustion and dehydration brought dreams of running freely along the lovely sands and shores of the Firth of Forth. How I yearned to escape this claustrophobic hell, to stretch my legs and run free again. Cramped in that inferno, I thought of home and better times to come. I always tried to use positive thoughts in my mind to escape the horror around me.

Finally, the ship stopped and we heard the longed-for rattle of the anchor chain. We had arrived in Keelung, a port in the northeast of Formosa. It was 6a.m. and, appropriately for a town nicknamed the "rain port", the rain was coming down in stair rods. We had to stand to attention in the downpour for two hours at the dockside. We were exhausted and drenched. The sick men had to be supported and anyone who fainted was beaten by the guards. We were freezing too, and were only clad in our shorts and shirts for the tropics. It was just the beginning of a dreadful day that would claim the lives of ten of my comrades. We had put our boots back on and taken all of our kit from the boat, but none of us had proper waterproofs.

We were split into two groups of around 500 men, and, as my group marched through the town, thousands of townsfolk and children had been assembled to jeer us and witness the humbling of the British. We arrived at a small station and boarded the third-class compartments of a small train. Just to sit down felt like heaven. After about an hour and a half, we arrived at another small station where yet more townsfolk had been marshalled to ridicule us. We still wanted to look on the bright side, and when a group of women dressed in white came among us with baskets of bread and dished out little loaves to us, we really thought that things were getting better. We were off the hell ship and nothing could ever be worse — or so we naively told ourselves.

Then we were told that we were to march into the forbidding cloud-shrouded mountains to the north of the town at which we had arrived. The road soon became little more than a rocky mountain track and we seemed to be forever going uphill. The sick men had to be helped and were constantly beaten by the vicious Japanese guards. We were driven along like animals through poverty-stricken villages where the villagers didn't yell at us but instead looked sorry for us. Suzuki and his men slammed their rifle butts into our backs and dished out slaps and punches — I received my first broken nose on that march. Some of the men had blood running down their backs. On and on we went. As the going got harder, struggling men ditched their non-essential kit. Father Kennedy was completely done in so I took turns with Hughie Carroll and Tammy Dodds to carry the tin containing his vestments and portable altar. It dug into our ribs all the way but we couldn't let the priest down. Anyone who fell behind was brutally beaten up. We had no idea where we were going or why. We started to see miserable-looking men and women wearing what looked like little mining helmets. Surely, we were not going to a mine, not away up here in these mountains?

Finally, we arrived at the top of a hill and could look out to the sea in the distance and, far below us, a camp perched on a rocky slope — our destination. The Japanese cried, *"Yasume,"* the command for "rest", and we collapsed onto the ground, our chests heaving and hearts pounding. We were all desperately thirsty as we hadn't been allowed water since our arrival. The guards knew as much and enjoyed taunting us by drinking water from their canteens in front of us and splashing it around their faces. Some of the sick men looked like they were ready to die. One man could hardly breathe; he was as white as a sheet and had a swollen throat — the tell-tale sign of diphtheria, the childhood killer that thrived on poverty and squalor.

With difficulty, we got to our feet again and finally arrived at the camp on the side of a rocky hillside, where we were again made to stand stiffly to attention in the pouring rain — this time for two and a half hours. It was too much to bear for many men, but anyone who collapsed was pounced on by maniacal screaming guards who kicked and punched ill prisoners to their feet to be held up by the men on each side.

Finally, an overweight Japanese officer appeared on a small makeshift podium. He proceeded to harangue us for an hour. He told us we were at the Kinkaseki copper mine, which we later learned was the main source of the vital conducting element for Japan's war machine. He ranted on about how despicable we were for having surrendered and how we had let our country down. We were a disgrace and would work now in exchange for a bed and food. The Japanese were winning everywhere and when they conquered Australia we would have bread and meat. If we laughed at the Japanese, we would be punished. Punishment would be meted out for breaching a host of rules and regulations. It went on and on as we swayed on our feet. When he left, we were still standing in the rain, and we were made to do so for a further three and a half hours. The hell ship began to seem better than this. Our misery was complete and the pain in our legs was indescribable. Men were collapsing and sleeping on their feet or were out of their minds, their teeth chattering and their bodies shaking.

Next, we were taken inside in groups of four and strip-searched. Every fourth man was beaten, punched and slapped. We were issued with a shirt, short green pants and a pair of wooden clogs with a piece of inner tube for a strap to hold them onto our feet. They were murder to walk in and we hobbled back outside where we stood until all the men had been processed.

We were divided into groups and sent into long low huts with leaking roofs. There were platforms about 30 yards long and a foot off the ground down each side for the men to sleep on with a space of around 2 ft 6 in. per man. With the exception of two men in every hut who had to remain up to guard their fellow prisoners, we flopped down absolutely shattered. It was 2 a.m. on 15 November. We had been on our feet for nearly 20 hours. For some men, it was a death sentence.

Major Freddie Crossley was our commander and he meticulously noted our sufferings in a secret diary that would later be used in war-crimes trials. He directly charged that the death march of 14 November had resulted in the deaths of ten men. They were: Gunners

Griffiths, Waring, Shaw, Gunn, Brain, McKew, Adamson, Ellerby, Warnoch and Jordan.

It was nearly the death of me too. We were so thirsty that we were tormented. Next to the hut we were allotted, I spotted a rain barrel brimming with water and couldn't resist it. I stuck my head in the barrel and drank like it was the horn of plenty. The water was foul but it tasted so sweet and cold to me. I hadn't noticed the decaying carcasses of dead rats in the bottom.

We didn't go down the mine to begin with but were made to do exercises in the camp. In fact, as we were the first prisoners to arrive at Kinkaseki, we were still unsure why we were there, as the mine entrance and workings were concealed behind a steep hill and not visible to us.

Within days, I was struck down with dysentery. It was miraculous that I had avoided it so far, but now I would learn all of the pain and suffering that went with a disease that wasted us away to matchstick men. The constant running to the latrines — a long ditch with a log over it upon which we had to balance — sapped away at the strength of skeletal and depleted bodies. And there was another hazard. We constantly had to bow to the Japanese, and failure to do so resulted in a beating. Guards would rush into huts just after we laid down for the night and repeat the process time and again to force us back onto our feet. We were all nervous wrecks, never knowing when we were to be beaten next or why.

There were armed guards with bayonets fastened to the end of their rifles at each corner of the compound.

To intimidate us, the Japanese would often stage bayonet practice in front of us. Escape was impossible. Even if we got out of the mountains, we would still have to get off the island and face a lengthy sea journey. It was pointless to torture ourselves with dreams of escape. However, a couple of lads from one of the other camps on Formosa did try. They were quickly caught and badly tortured before they were executed as a lesson to us all.

The reign of terror in the camp was constant. Men counted how often they were beaten in a day — the unlucky winner was beaten nine times in a single day. Some of the guards would hide in the shadows on the way to the latrine. Sick men scurrying to the toilet might not notice them and it gave them a chance to torment another poor soul. One night, I was making my umpteenth dash of the day when a guard emerged from the gloom. To my dismay, it was a guard we had already learned to fear, and had nicknamed the Beast. He shouted at me and pointed to my bare feet. He was roaring and getting worked up. Maybe I ought to have been wearing the cumbersome clogs, which we had not got used to yet. Suddenly, he punched me in the face, knocking my specs off. As they landed on the ground, he brought his rifle butt down and smashed them to pieces. My heart sank. I knew I would never get another pair. Then he started to smash my toes with his rifle. Again and again he brought the rifle butt down, as I was crying out in pain and hopping from foot to foot. Then I lost control of my weakened bowels. When he noticed my accident, the Beast began laughing like a hyena. It drove him into an even greater frenzy and he continued to strike my legs and thighs. I went down and he kicked my face, breaking my nose and knocking my front teeth out with his rifle butt. As I lay there at the mercy of this maniac, I just wanted to die. I hoped he would kill me.

Eventually, after what seemed like an age, he cooled down and let me go. I limped to the latrines, a sobbing, bloodied mess. I feared my left foot was broken. Some of the other sick lads came to my help. They washed the blood from me and helped me clean myself up as tenderly as any caring nurse and tried to repair my specs.

After that beating, my dysentery got worse and I ended up in the hospital hut. It was the same as all of the other huts except that there was a little section screened off at the end of the platform. It was nicknamed the "Death Hut" — it was where you went to die. I was in a bad way but there were others even worse. I was getting sicker, though, and ominously I was starting to move along the platform closer to the partition, which meant only one thing. I drifted in and out of consciousness and in my dreams I would be back in Glasgow with the lads in the Maryhill Harriers, only to be suddenly confronted with a horrible vision of Suzuki's snarling features. I was drifting off in an inviting tunnel of blue when a gentle tapping on my cheek brought me round. It was Father Kennedy; he sat by my bedside for hours, saying prayers for me and willing me to stay alive. I could hear his voice in the distance: "Come on, Andy. Come on! A lap to go! A lap to go!" It was Father Kennedy's words that brought me back from the brink and slowly I began to move back up the platform — away from the dreaded Death Hut where shrunken husks of men died miserable deaths.

There were three big killers in Kinkaseki — dysentery, diphtheria and despair. You had a chance with the first two, but if you were struck by despair as well, your chances of survival were next to nil. I was a very fortunate man to have Father Kennedy at hand. He kept my spirits up. It would have been so easy to have just slipped away to that peaceful place.

When they began to send the lads down the mine, I was too sick to go and was kept in the hospital hut. However, as the Japanese had cut the rations for sick men, we had no reserves of strength to fight the disease. We also had no medicine. All Captain Seed — the doctor who had been with us since the Battle of Jitra — could prescribe was rice water, then ground-up charcoal and then a few grains of soft-boiled rice. The dysentery tore at my guts, stripping out my stomach lining and causing agonising stomach cramps.

As the worst of it began to pass, I was desperate to get down the mine — for an extra ball of maggoty rice. It was a tiny ball of food that meant the difference between living and dying. I also wanted to escape the brutality of the camp where the sick men were constantly beaten.

After a week or two, I tried to get fit enough to go down the mine. I was moving my legs, trying to get them working again. The lads sent word that they would get me on an easier job and I would get more rice. My legs were stick-thin but the wounds from the Beast's rifle butt had healed. Four of us patients volunteered to go down the mine, which meant that Captain Seed could admit another four sick men to the hospital, as we were only allowed to have so many sick men at any one time. I was glad to get out of the hospital too. We were not allowed to lie down during the day in the hospital hut and were denied even a blanket. The Japanese were also prone to bashing the sick men. In particular, a mad medical orderly we nicknamed "Sanitary Syd" used to rush in wielding a kendo sword stick and beat all of the patients who were totally helpless. We were always on edge when he was on duty. Father Kennedy and Captain Seed would regularly intervene and place themselves between the ill men and the Japanese, only to be thrashed for doing so. They were both very brave and selfless men. It was awful to see them being beaten. One day, Sanitary Syd charged in and viciously kicked a patient in the back. Many patients died within hours of these attacks. Father Kennedy pulled him off and was beaten black and blue. As we lay there unable to do anything, I closed my eyes and tried to close my ears to the cries and screams that went with those beatings. It was heart-rending.

The next day, we joined the rest of the men for *tenko* or roll call. Shortly after our arrival, the Japanese had issued little booklets and announced that we were to learn Japanese. It was a tall order. Out of our five hundred men, only one lieutenant spoke a smattering of the language, which seemed fiendishly difficult to us.

We were also fingerprinted and photographed with a number which became our identity and which we had to learn in Japanese. My number was 128 — *ichi ni hachi*. Now men were reeling off their numbers in broken Japanese and woe betide them if they got it wrong. Any mispronunciation was met with slapping and punching by guards who seemed to compete with each other in their viciousness. *Tenko* took place twice a day, before and after working in the mine. It could take forever as these beatings were dished out, and we had to stand in the rain until it was completed to the satisfaction of our masters. Eventually, I became quite good at Japanese — it was either that or daily beatings.

We joined the tail end of the column that was to ascend the brow of a hill and then walk down to the mouth of the mine. To men in our state, even the climb up the hill out of the camp seemed impossible, never mind a 12-hour shift down the mine. We were all issued with little carbide lamps, which were to be our only source of light in the mine, but ours were broken. Nervously, I reported this to the guards, at which point I was horrified to see Suzuki walking towards us. When he saw what was going on, he went berserk and screamed at the guards, who hauled us out as the column set off to march up the 1,186 killer steps out of the camp. I was terrified that we were in for a beating. Suzuki accused us of breaking the lamps to avoid going down the mine, even though we had volunteered to work; we needed that extra rice ball that was shoved in the wooden lunchboxes the men took to the mine. We were ordered to stand to attention in the rain and stood anxiously awaiting our fate. We dreaded these beatings. We were so weak that they were potentially lethal, and if the skin was broken there was always the danger of infection and flesh-eating ulcers that could end up in amputation. We had no flesh to absorb the blows and every single one seemed to send pain shooting through our skeletal frame. The beatings were demoralising to witness and humiliating to endure; after each one, deep depression came with the throbbing pain that wracked our bodies. That was when our comradeship was so important. We never knew how to take the beatings. If you dropped to the ground and curled up, the guards might beat you even harder. But, if you stood your ground and took it, they might look at you as being defiant and go into a fury. We could never work out the best strategy to adopt.

We stood to attention in the chilling rain as the rest of the men marched off up the hill. The rain was cold and seemed to be getting colder. Captain Seed made a point of measuring the rain, and in one month alone he recorded an astonishing 90 inches falling. The downpour was so incessant that some of the lads who were former miners joked that they couldn't wait to go down the pit to get out of it — that was before they discovered the horrors of the mine. The two guards who were appointed to watch over us settled down in a small hut, rested their rifles across their knees and casually lit up a cigarette. I remained alert waiting for Suzuki to reappear. One of his specialities, I had learned, was to creep up on his victims and smash a rifle butt into the back of a knee, sending them tumbling to the ground and then kicking and pummelling them senseless. But, as we stood freezing, shaking and shivering, the time dragged on and on. As our chilled bones ached and shooting pains shot up our legs, our punishment became clear. We were forced to stand in that freezing rain all day until the men came back from their 12-hour shift in the mine. Some of the officers tried to object to our treatment but they were slapped and ordered away. We were not allowed to go to the latrines and had to suffer the indignity of relieving ourselves where we stood. When the first man collapsed, the guards rushed out to kick him to his feet, but they soon tired of that, and, as we all collapsed in turn, the standing men had to hoist the fallen man up. It was unbearable and eventually we welcomed the chance to help a fallen comrade just to get our circulation moving and momentarily ease the pain. As the cold, cold rain and wind whipped in from the sea, the man next to me kept saying over and over, "God, take me. Please God, take me now."

I said my prayers and by some miracle we did survive that day — all of us. We were in a state of collapse when the lads returned from the mine and helped us into the hut. Tammy Donnelly had been given such a terrible beating that he couldn't work down the mine again and was put on to latrine duty.

The next day, we somehow managed to get up at 5.30a.m. as usual and parade for *tenko*. Breakfast was the usual rice but my comrades in the hut all gave me some of their precious rice to help me recover. We set off for the mine barely able to walk the mile or so up and down the hill to the mouth of the mine, which waited to devour our bodies and our minds. I was supported on each side by one of my mates. The Glasgow boys stuck together; we really looked after each other and tried hard to keep each other going.

Later, when the Japanese reduced the sick-man quota even further, sick men would be carried into the mine. Officers remained in the camp and some of the older men were given lighter camp duties. Among them was Sergeant Major Scullion, who was now stick-thin and a poor soul who was barely human. We lost a lot of men in their fifties; Captain Seed said that their hearts simply wore out. But he was surprised at how it was the youngest men who died first. He felt that they were still growing and had not matured — nor did they have wives and families to live for. The truth was that we never knew who would be next to go, and sometimes we envied the dead — at least they were out of it.

I wondered what lay ahead of us as we stopped at the entrance to the mine and bowed to a little shrine that was meant to protect us. We entered the mine and walked for about a quarter of a mile through a low tunnel and then descended 800 of the most hazardous steps imaginable. They were almost vertical and you had to proceed with the utmost caution, clutching your carbide lamp in one hand and a rope in the other.

We were sent to the very depths of the mine where temperatures in the galleries that we climbed up into reached 130 degrees, and men could only work for seven or eight minutes at a time without collapsing. So we would dash out and jump in a big drain of cool foul water and try to regain our breath. It was so hot that the Formosan labourers who worked in the mine refused to go down to the bottom levels. However, we were expendable and so were the Formosan political prisoners. Contact with them and the Formosans generally was strictly forbidden but they often tried to help us.

The stench in the mine was unbelievable. There was no drainage and, of course, no toilets, so at times we were ankle-deep in human waste. It was a real health hazard. The mine shoes that we were issued with had canvas uppers with a compartment for your big toe and rubber soles, but they quickly rotted and we went barefoot in the mine. Scrapes, cuts and gashes were inevitable and I was always worried about getting an infection that might end up in the loss of a leg. Another hazard was the sulphurous acid that constantly dripped on us, burning into our eyes and wounds. It would eventually turn our skins a golden yellow and some men were congratulated on their wonderful tans when they got home. By far the biggest danger was from roof collapses and rockfalls. After we climbed into room-sized chambers, we would drill up into the roof and bring down slabs of ore-bearing rock. Then we would gather the rocks up with our chunkels — a cross between a shovel and a hoe — to fill up the punkies, as we called the baskets, and drag them over to the chutes where bogeys waited below to catch the ore. The whole procedure was primitive and potentially deadly.

Because I was so weak when I went down, I was given the job of pushing the bogeys out of the mine, but it was hard work all the same. One day, I was shoving my bogey along when it came off the rails, which were about 18 to 20 inches wide. I was struggling to get it back on the rails when a female Formosan miner came to my assistance. She got her back down against the bogey and pushed it back onto the track for me. I couldn't believe it. She was as strong as a horse. I thanked her profusely, and as she turned to go she slipped me a half a cigarette. It was a simple act of solidarity but it meant a lot to us. I didn't smoke, so I gave it to my pals, who were pleased to get a few puffs.

It was not the only act of friendship the Formosans extended to me. One day, I was struck by a rockfall and ended up with some really bad cuts on my back. In the furnace heat of the mine, we worked virtually naked. I was winded and leaning with my hands against the wall of the mine with blood running down my back. Two black panthers — the political prisoners who wore black pyjamas — came up to me chewing their tobacco and they spat the mixture of nicotine and saliva into the open wounds. It hurt like hell and had me yowling, but it stopped the bleeding. On another occasion, I was going crazy with acid in my eyes. Three of the Formosan drillers rushed over. One of them held me down, the second held open my eyes and the third spat into my eyes to wash the acid out. After a while, it worked. I marvelled about this, but then, when I was telling the lads back at the camp, I remembered my father doing exactly the same thing to Jerry, our greyhound who had a bluish-white film over his eyes.

Not long after that incident, I lost my sight completely for about a fortnight. My blindness was a by-product of extreme malnutrition and vitamin deficiency. It was dubbed "camp-eyes" and affected quite a few men. My eyesight was already poor and Suzuki had smashed my specs, so I was worried when my sight started to shorten and fail. It was very frightening when it went completely. To survive in Kinkaseki, we needed all of our senses and we needed to keep all of them finely honed. I felt even more vulnerable as a blind man in the camp. Incredibly, going blind was not a good enough reason to be excused from going down the mine with its mantrap floor of broken planks and potholes. For two weeks, I tramped up the hill and down the mine with my hands on the shoulders of the man in front of me. Once in the mine, I was led to a bogey and shoved it full and empty up and down the mine all day long. This was true slavery and I thought how similar my plight was to that of the pit ponies in the mines of Lanarkshire that went blind from never seeing daylight.

By this time, a lot of the men were showing signs of madness. They talked to themselves or turned their faces to the wall and just gave up.

The brutality of the *hanchos*, the cruel overseers, was criminal. They would snuff out their lamps and creep up on us to hit us with their hammers or throw rocks at us. The worst ones were listed in a subsequent war-crimes trials as "guilty of particular bestiality and indirectly responsible for many deaths". We had nicknames for them — the Eagle, the Ghost,

Frying-pan, the Black Panther and "Blackie" made our lives unbearable.

The targets always became more difficult to meet as we dug into the rock advancing away from the chute and the entrance to the drive, but no allowance was ever made for that and there were beatings at the end of every shift. These beatings were administered at the bottom of the pit, after which battered and exhausted men had to climb back out and up those 800 steps. It took every ounce of our remaining strength, and nobody ever spoke on the climb out of the mine. Men dreaded the mine, and every day weeping prisoners joined the lengthy queue at sick parade begging Captain Seed to declare them too ill to work.

Even in these extreme conditions, we still tried to sabotage the mine. Rocks were put in the bogeys instead of ore, and we broke rails and tore out electrical wiring.

With the help of what little extra food my comrades could find for me, my sight gradually returned, and, not long after, I was working alone in a chamber when I felt a sudden puff of air. It blew out the tiny flame in my carbide lamp and I was plunged into the thick black darkness that can only be experienced underground. The lamps were always flickering out of existence — sometimes due to a lack of oxygen — and a delay to production would mean a beating for not meeting the target. At the end of every shift, men were forced to lean over a bogey to be beaten black and blue from the neck to the thighs with the three-foot-long hammer handle that the brutal *hanchos* called the "*hammero*". I cursed my luck and, as I did so, the earth collapsed on top of me. It was the rockfall we all dreaded. I was engulfed by panic and fear as the roof came down. I covered my head and coughed as the dust choked my airways and dried out my mouth. It was terrifying. My worst fears had come to pass — I was buried alive. I groped in the dark and reached out to find that I was next to a kind of pipe used by the drillers, which was holding up some of the ceiling above me. I picked up a piece of rock and began banging on the pipe. Eventually, after what seemed like an eternity, I heard tapping back. My mates and the black panthers had heard the noise of the collapse and seen all the dust billowing out of the chamber entrance. I was trapped for two long hours and it felt like a lifetime.

Accidents were a daily occurrence and I had my share of lucky escapes. During the lunch break, the Japanese would blast the rockface with dynamite and we would go back to the drive and clear the debris. One day, I went back as usual but I couldn't see any debris. Then one of the *hanchos* shouted for me to come out. I came back and just got back into the main shaft when there was a terrific explosion which brought the roof down. It was a faulty charge. I was almost blown to bits. Once, while I was working with Maurice Rooney, another Gorbals lad, in a drive 50 yards from the main shaft, we suddenly hit water and were washed back into the shaft, bouncing off rocks all the way. We were cut to ribbons and were lucky not to have suffered broken bones.

Not all of us were so lucky down the mine. Men died, backs were broken and skulls fractured. Later, in August 1943, my pal Dominic "Doc" Sweeney fell some 30 feet down a chute and was crushed by falling rocks. We were not allowed to dig Doc's body out until the shift had finished — neither the injured nor the dead were allowed out of the pit until the work was over for the day. We took Doc's body out in a bag, but when we got him back he was put in a wooden coffin and placed in the hut that contained the big communal bath where we were allowed to bathe once a week. (If you were among the first hundred men, it was vaguely clean but, if you left it too late, it was like washing in mud.)

Then something strange happened. The Japanese who had starved Doc almost to death during his short life adorned his coffin with colourful paper flowers, bowls of fruit and rice cakes to send him off to the other world. He was respected in death because he had died a noble death in the mine.

Doc's death depressed us all. He had been such a cheery and supportive comrade.

Just after we arrived in Kinkaseki, a terraced paddy about half a mile from the camp had been set aside for a cemetery — the Japanese knew that they were going to work us to death. We called the place "Boot Hill" after the cowboy movies. I was on the funeral parties several times and it was always a grim experience. The flimsy coffins allowed the dead man's blood to seep over us, and by this time we were all so close that we felt like we were losing a family member. All we had in the world was each other and we had bonded together

237

to survive this hell. When a man wished he had died in Malaya or prayed not to wake up the next morning and pulled the blanket over his head to cry, one of us was always there to say, "Don't worry, mate. You'll get through it. You'll get home — we'll look after you."

To begin with, there were four men to each funeral party, but we were never able to dig the graves deep enough and the nonstop rains would wash the earth away, horribly exposing the dead. The funeral parties were increased to six men and, with Japanese guards harassing our every step, two men would scurry around the terrace re-burying our dead. It was always a depressing duty but we gladly volunteered in the hope of being able to snaffle an orange or banana.

Kinkaseki was a grim, grey prison in a bleak, barren and colourless landscape. Every day I looked in vain to see a bird in the empty sky. There were no concert parties or light relief of any kind. Playing cards was banned and we were terrorised by the guards around the clock. We were all covered in lice and the bedbugs were so bad that some men tried to make sleeping bags out of their blankets with drawstrings around their necks to try to keep out the biting tormentors. Religious services were banned, although Father Kennedy would come around to the sick men and say prayers with them.

Our first Christmas in the camp was a miserable affair. We had worked as usual and sung carols down the mine during *yasume*. The Japanese relaxed the ban on singing for half an hour and as a treat we were allowed some pickled turnip. It was our first Christmas in captivity and a time for thoughts of home. We were dying at a rate of three a week and it was hard not to wonder if we would ever see home again. I knew from my athletics training that it was vital to keep a positive attitude and not give in to despair. I kept praying to God to get me out of the camp and to let me keep my legs.

We tried to keep our spirits up as best we could. We held wee quizzes in the hut about sport, boxing and greyhound racing. We talked about Glasgow all the time — the dancing and the picture houses — and about our families and pals. A lot of us dreamed of a new start when we got home. Tammy Donnelly was a great character. He was older than me but we talked about starting a piggery with the money that we thought we'd get from the army when we got home. It was important to do what you could to get your mind out of the camp.

The Japanese were out to break us all the time. They despised us and told us so regularly. The militarist leaders who ran Japan were extreme nationalists who harked back to a mythical samurai era of Japanese history. Under the code of bushido, it was ignoble to surrender. Warriors were supposed to take their own lives rather than surrender, although, funnily enough, none of our tormentors did so when they were finally captured. We were less than human to the Japanese and they wanted to crush us utterly. Maintaining any sort of spirit was a way of fighting back at them and, on the occasions that we had the strength, we used to rile our guards by singing on the way in and out of the mine. There was one song they hated in particular. It was written by Trumpeter Smith, our talented bugler who became the Rabbie Burns of Kinkaseki. It became our anthem and a cry of defiance, and we all knew it by heart.

There's a song in old Formosa that the Nips they loudly sing
In the billets every evening you should hear the music ring,
Now they sing to British soldiers who have travelled from afar,
To fight for king and country, now they're prisoners of war,
But they know they'll see their homeland in the future once again,
Listen, while I sing to you the Nipponese refrain:

Down the mine, bonnie laddies, down the mine you'll go,
Though your feet are lacerated you dare not answer no,
Though the rice is insufficient and we treat you all like swine,
Down the mine, bonnie laddies, down the mine.

You should see us work with "chunkels" and we work with baskets too
Though the method is old-fashioned, to the boys it's something new,
And we'll work away with patience till the dawn of freedom's day,

But until then the Nippon men will all be heard to
 say:

Down the mine, bonnie laddies, down the mine
 you'll go,
Though your feet are lacerated you dare not answer
 no,
Though the rice is insufficient and we treat you all
 like swine,
Down the mine, bonnie laddies, down the mine.

The drillers had their own lament too.

Come with me to old Formosa
Down the mine beneath the skies
Where the acid water trickles in your eyes
I call my mate who's with me — bring that oil can
 over here
To oil this bloody drill, the bugger makes me swear
The Jap guard keeps a-screaming he wants 12 holes a
 day
But he'll be bloody lucky 'cos the Yanks are on their
 way.

Yet, no matter how hard we tried, we could never
escape the cruelty of our captors. Prisoners who got a
black mark in the mine were made to run up and down
the rough steps to the hospital over and over — or they
might be made to hold heavy stones over their heads
and were beaten when they dropped them. When camp
commandant Wakiyama visited the hospital and found

two patients sitting up and playing cards, he ordered a terrible punishment. He instructed that seven sick men all suffering from dysentery be handcuffed together for three days and nights. It was a cruel torture as it meant that the men, handcuffed in three groups, could never get a rest as one of them always had to go to the latrine. Four of the men later died. Most feared of all was the "icebox", a tiny hutch open to the elements in which a prisoner had to crouch or assume certain positions. Rations were reduced to a bowl of rice a day; it was heavily salted to induce a raging thirst and then a bowl of water was placed within sight but out of reach of the poor soul in the "icebox" — it was tantamount to a death sentence.

By May 1943, we were all in a very bad way. The official camp records showed that in that month the average number of sick men was 206 as compared with 257 "fit" men, but most of the sick still had to go down the mine. Starved and suffering from various stages of beriberi, most of us also had worms from the contaminated rice. Many of us were also suffering from bronchitis caused by the dust in the mine and the constant changes in temperature. Captain Seed was a miracle worker but he was not immune from the extreme conditions in the camp. He worked seven days a week, twelve hours a day, and he endured the stress of constantly standing up for us against Sanitary Syd and the Japanese camp commandant. His health was broken and we feared that we might lose him. He was a very ill man.

My health was going downhill rapidly too. I looked with pity at the worn-out men who shuffled around like zombies and feared becoming one of them.

By August, so many men had died that the Japanese were forced to send reinforcements. Men arrived from other camps on the island and it was great to see fresh faces with news of friends and comrades in other camps — and with fresh rumours. Among the group was a Canadian doctor who had come with us from Singapore on the *England Maru*. The arrival of Major Ben Wheeler was a godsend and he would be revered by the men. He was horrified by what he found at Kinkaseki and persuaded the Japanese to issue 100 sick cards. Seventy red cards allowed prisoners to rest in the camp for a day but not to lie down. Thirty white cards were issued to allow seriously ill men to lie down. It was totally inadequate but it was something. We were allowed to have 100 "officially" sick men.

Major Wheeler collected moss and lichen to apply to sores and wounds. He seared tropical ulcers closed with a red-hot poker; it was agonising for the patient but it worked. He improvised all the time to make medical instruments, and operated on men with a razor blade and no anaesthetic. To get desperately ill men out of the mine, Major Wheeler resorted to deliberately wounding them to draw blood as the Japanese made allowances if a man was bleeding. Every day, he had to play God and decide who he would save by issuing a white or red card, knowing full well that being sent down the mine was a death sentence for pitifully weak men.

At around the same time, Father Kennedy, who had been living with the officers, was moved out of the camp. He was sent to Manchuria with some of the officers to a camp where high-ranking officers were held as possible hostages. I was sorry to see him go and thanked him for all of his help. He told me to look after myself. I wondered if we would ever meet again as he left the camp.

When the cold winds and freezing rain of November arrived to lash the camp once again, I was a very sick man. Dysentery and beriberi were playing havoc with me and I had shrunk to skin and bone. Major Wheeler and Captain Seed had organised with the Japanese to arrange what became known as "thin man parades". During these selections, men held in what little stomach they had and sucked in their cheeks making every effort to look even more pathetic and get a ticket out of Kinkaseki in the sure and certain knowledge that no place could be worse. I didn't have to make any effort to exaggerate my condition — I could barely stand. Captain Seed told me, "We have to get you out of this camp, Andy, or you won't last another six weeks."

On 13 November, almost a year to the day after I had arrived in Kinkaseki, I was selected — along with Sergeant Major Scullion, Tommy Donnelly, Hughie Carroll, Jim Brennan and around 50 others — to leave the mine. We were helped into trucks but there was no banter or air of celebration; we were so shattered and ill that we could barely speak. We didn't know where they were taking us and wondered if we were being taken away to be slaughtered.

As we lay in the back of the trucks, we all became sick from the sweet smell of the fuel, which was some kind of petrol made from sugar. After a while, we arrived at a railway station and were shoved into wagons for animals. We wondered what would happen next — being helpless and not knowing what your jailer has in store for you is a fearful thing.

At the end of the train journey, we were put into lorries and driven to a camp in the countryside. The camp at Heito in the south of the island was one of fourteen dotted around Formosa.

There were no men from my regiment in the camp at all. There were Americans who had been captured in the Philippines, Dutch taken in the Dutch East Indies and Australians. There were plenty of British too, including a contingent of Argyll and Sutherland Highlanders. They looked so much better than us and they couldn't conceal their horror at our appearance. They just couldn't believe their eyes. One of the Argylls asked, "What the bloody hell has happened to you lot?" And what a sight we were. Even by the standards of Heito, we were painfully thin. The long matted hair down our backs and straggly beards made us look like the poor wretches who had slaved on a Spanish galley for years on end. One of the prisoners was the camp barber and he shaved our heads before we went into our new huts, which were much brighter and bigger than we were used to.

The Argylls were great lads and so were the Manchesters, and they brought us sweet potatoes, edible leaves, pieces of sugar cane and molasses. As we started to get better, we learned about our new home. The Americans had arrived first, and then, in August 1942, General Percival and the top commanders captured at Singapore had arrived after a hellish journey on the *England Maru*. American and Dutch commanders were also held at Heito before they were all shipped off to Manchuria. The place had been a camp for local construction workers and the prisoners were either engaged in backbreaking agricultural work or worked in a sugar-cane factory. The commandant, we were told, was "a nasty piece of work". Lieutenant Koji Tamaki was a vicious sadist who, when the camp first opened, vowed that he would fill its cemetery. He was as good as his word and 131 men died in the camp — worked, starved and beaten to death. As well as suffering from the usual dysentery, beriberi and diarrhoea, prisoners at Heito also faced sunburn and sunstroke from labouring half-naked and unprotected under the blazing sun. Malaria was a big problem too, and the camp was alive with mosquitoes that zipped and zapped around our heads all night.

I was too ill to be put to work lifting stones to clear land for planting or to do a 12-hour shift in the cane factory, so instead I was assigned to clear out the latrines and empty the disgusting contents onto rows and rows of tomato plants. It was great to be in the open and I enjoyed the fresh air after a year down the mine. The fertiliser seemed to work really well, and we would pinch one of the huge crimson tomatoes whenever we got the chance.

One day, we were lined up and some men were selected to plant peanuts. I was disappointed not to be selected. Those nuts were packed with protein and I was salivating at the thought of them, and I was not the only one. When the work party returned to the camp, they were all lined up. They had been warned not to eat the peanuts or else, and now they were asked if they had eaten any. Terrified, two men stepped forward to admit that they had. The Japanese told the others to open their mouths. Two more men were discovered to have pieces of peanut wedged in their teeth. They were forced to beat each other up while the men who admitted it were not touched and allowed to go.

In many ways, Heito was worse than Kinkaseki, where 87 of us died, but at least we had more opportunity to scavenge, scrounge and steal food. Stuff was growing all around us; there were banana plantations, fields of sweet potatoes and sugar cane. There were snakes and snails. Men who worked in the refinery risked life and limb to smuggle a handful of brown sugar back into the camp.

Shortly after I arrived, I fell ill again. My leg was badly infected at the top of my thigh. It was full of poison and had swollen up, making it difficult to move it. There was no doctor in Heito but there was an American orderly who helped out. I was worried about blood poisoning and then I remembered something my father had done to treat horses with a condition we used to call "greasy heel". It was an old folk remedy from Ireland, but it worked on the horses, so maybe it would work on me. I had watched fascinated as Dad had boiled up cattle manure and urine in a bucket and then put the horse's foot in it — within two or three days, the horse was cured. I decided it was worth a go. I got some water buffalo manure and an old piece of cloth. I boiled up the manure in an old tin can outside the hut and then put the cloth over my wound. Then I applied the manure on top of the cloth like a poultice. It was agony. Some of the blokes thought I was bonkers, but I did it over two nights and it worked, slowly drawing a lot of dirty green yellow stuff out of my thigh. Soon, I could straighten my leg and I could walk again. I still have the scar but I was so relieved as I really feared that I was going to lose my leg.

To survive in the camps, we had to keep our wits about us all the time. I was taking my bearings in the new camp and noticed that a bullock cart would come in loaded with bananas. The bananas were sent for the prisoners by the company that owned the sugar-cane factory, but the Japanese always stuck them in a hut and let them go rotten. I looked at the hut and could see it was made of bamboo. I reckoned I could pull it back and get in. I mentioned my thoughts to my friend Claude, a Glaswegian from Springburn.

"Claude, I'm going to have a go at those bananas one night."

"For Christ's sake, Andy, watch what you're doing. It's awful risky."

Eventually, I plucked up the courage to give it a go. Claude gave me an old shirt and I tied it tightly around my shrunken waist. I sneaked out of my hut as it was getting dark and went to the banana shed. I pulled at the bottom of the bamboo, prising it back far enough to allow me to wriggle through. It was quite dark inside but, sure enough, there were the mounds of precious bananas. I put my hand on a pile to start pinching them and thought I saw movement. In the next instant, I was overrun by swarming rats that ran over my shoulders and head. I almost cried out in disgust and shook a bit after I brushed them off. The bloody rats had beaten me to the bananas. I filled my shirt anyway and headed back to the hut. The lads fell on the bananas when I got back. Claude was so hungry that he ate the skins too and ended up getting badly constipated and was in pain. The American orderly had to perform a procedure on poor old Claude to give him some relief. I raided the banana shed quite a few times in the coming weeks but I was always wary of the rats.

Then I hit on a new idea. I always wondered why the Dutch were so obviously fitter and better fed than us and the Americans. We were all walking skeletons, while they looked almost normal and one of them looked like Tarzan. The Dutch were in charge of the bullocks and pigs, and suspicions began to form in my mind. I was sure that they were pinching the animal feed. One day, I saw Tarzan disappear into a stable where a Japanese officer we called the Snake kept his horse. He was carrying a couple of buckets and when he left I decided to investigate. The stable was about 50 yards from the Japanese guardhouse at the entrance to the camp. I looked over the three bars at the entrance to the stable and could see a partition beyond the horse — a sort of shed attached to the stable. I got into the stable and pulled myself over the partition. It took a bit of acrobatics but when I got into the shed my eyes popped out of my head — there were three or four barrels of boiled sweet potatoes. I wolfed down as many as I could and stuffed some more down the front of my shirt to take to my pals. It was great. It was risky and I would have been beaten to a pulp if I was caught, but I kept it going for weeks.

Of course, all good things come to an end. One day, I went to the stable as usual, but, instead of the horse, I was taken aback to discover a fierce young bull. It didn't look very friendly, and while its horns were short, they looked pretty sharp. The black bull was snorting at me, and I nearly turned back, but the boys were relying on me — we were literally starving. I was watching the bull and waited until it turned its back on me. I climbed up and pulled myself over the partition. I could feel the heat from the bull's nostrils on my feet, but I got to the other side, filled myself with what was left of the sweet potatoes and stuffed a few down my shirt. I got back up and the bull was standing glaring at me. Then, to my horror, the bell went for *tenko*. If I was missed, it would be a disaster. I had to do something fast. I put my hand into my shirt, took out a couple of sweet potatoes and threw them to the far end of the stable. Sure enough, the bull turned round. I got my foot onto its back and from its back sprang right onto the top bar of the gate. The bull was not very impressed at my using its backside as a stepping stone.

I had a bad landing on the pathway and the sweet potatoes got mashed. I was all skinned and bruised but got up and ran to the hut. The boys quickly wolfed down the squashed potatoes as we rushed out to *tenko*. It was a close shave — too close for comfort — and I decided to call a halt to the sweet-potato racket. It was too dangerous.

My next target in my new career as a thief almost ended in disaster too. Not far from the toilets — the benjos, as we called them — was a henhouse made out of the same bamboo construction as the banana shed. I waited until it was dark and crept into the henhouse. I pulled back the bamboo and squeezed inside. I heard the cluck-clucking of the hens and moved slowly so as not to disturb them. Soon, I had a clutch of four gleaming white eggs. But, just as I started to push out the bamboo wall to make my escape, I heard footsteps and could make out the shape of a Japanese sentry through the bamboo. He lit up a cigarette and then another guard arrived and they started chatting. I was sweating — it was so nerve-wracking. Then, to make matters worse, the clappers went for *tenko*. Oh, no! I waited for what seemed like an age until the guards finished smoking. As soon as they moved off, I got out of the henhouse and back to the hut. The eggs were all smashed. I took off the shirt with the sticky gooey mess inside it and formed up with the rest of the lads for *tenko*. When we got back, we scooped up the raw broken eggs and savoured every drop as if it was the finest of delicacies.

Ironically, the only time I got into trouble over stealing in Heito I was completely innocent. As we went out to work on the rocky old riverbed we were clearing for the planting of sugar cane, we were issued with shoes like those given to us at the mine. There was a great pile of them, but, when a count was done, there was a pair missing and the balloon went up. I was accused of pinching them but knew nothing about it; in fact, unknown to us, one of the Americans had gone off with a pair. A Japanese sergeant started punching me in the face, and every time he hit me his dog would bite the back of my legs. After my bashing, I was made to kneel in a stress position on small stones that dug into my knees and caused agony. If I moved, I was beaten. It went on for hours until the mystery of the missing shoes was solved.

I had the last laugh, though. One day, the Japanese sergeant came into the camp looking for his dog. It was nowhere to be found and that night we were served up with an unusually tasty soup with grease floating on top. I asked a Chinese-American cook what was in the soup and he smiled. "Well, that bastard won't find His dog, that's for sure!"

We had eaten the dog, and very tasty it was too. We still tried to have a laugh — it was so important to keep up our spirits.

As soon as I had recovered my strength after the Kinkaseki ordeal, I started doing some exercises to build myself up. Just simple stuff like bending and stretching and a little bit of running. Some of the lads warned me against it, saying I should preserve my energy, but being active seemed to make me feel better.

After a few weeks, I joined my mates in the work party. The work was to clear fields of stones, where the Japanese were preparing to plant sugar cane. We would lift the stones, chuck them in bogeys, then push the bogeys up planks and empty them into the trucks. Trucks were lined up for about half a mile, and the track twisted away from the field. The trucks at the top of the track were nearest the field and so it wasn't so far to carry your stones. When the lads lined up in the morning, there was always competition to get to the front of the queue of trucks. A Japanese guard would shout, "Go!" and all the prisoners would run to get to the first bogey. Once the trucks were full, there was nothing else for us to do, so you would get a longer rest if you bagged the first few trucks.

I noticed the Dutch lads were the strongest in the camp and were able to sprint to the first truck. It was usually a race between them and some of the Argylls. We worked in parties of four, and I was with a Javanese, an American and an Argyll. After a few days of being in the last trucks and getting worn out, I was determined to get to the front. When the guard shouted, "Go!" I ran flat out as fast as I could and got to the first truck. It was very close, with the rest of the lads at my heels. I won the race and threw my hat in the first truck to claim it. I paid for it, though, and collapsed breathless onto the ground. My Argyll mate came up and clapped my back and helped me to my feet.

The Japanese guard was watching. "Ah, *ichi ni hachi, ichi ni hachi*," he said over and over.

I don't think he could believe that I'd beaten the Dutch. I couldn't believe it either.

After about ten months in the camp, I got a letter from home. It was my one and only communication from home and I treasured it, reading it over and over again. I had to share it with the rest of the men and it was carefully passed around the camp from one man to another because it was something from home; we were so starved of information that we shared our letters. Mine was in a fragile state because chunks had been cut out by the censor. It was from Freddie Graham, secretary of the Maryhill Harriers, and it read, "Dear Andy, Your mother and family are well and your two young brothers have joined the Maryhill Harriers — they will make good sprinters. Jackie Paterson beat Peter Kane in the world flyweight championship and knocked him out in the first minute."

The letter had taken a year to reach me but it was so wonderful to hear from home. We had not been forgotten and I would later learn that, in the first few weeks after the fall of Singapore when we were posted missing, Jack Scott, the Gorbals policeman, and some of the Maryhill lads had formed a committee to bombard the International Red Cross with demands for our whereabouts and assurances of our safety.

As well as lifting stones off the land, I also helped with the burial parties, and one day Sergeant Major Scullion came to ask me to go with him. We took a barra to the hospital hut and collected the body of a

Nottinghamshire lad called Harold Speed. He was a popular guy in the camp and we knew him as "Speedy". Starvation and illness had finally done for a man who had been tall and fit and was now dead at the age of 25. We placed Speedy's shrivelled frame on the barra and left the camp for the burial ground in the jungle. Suzuki, who had transferred from Kinkaseki, and a small rotund Formosan guard we nicknamed Yo-yo came with us. When we got to the burial ground, Suzuki ordered me to dig a shallow grave for Speedy of about only 18 inches. I protested in Japanese that it wouldn't be deep enough to deter scavenging animals but Suzuki told me to get on with it. When I got to 18 inches deep, I kept digging.

Suzuki went nuts, cursing me in Japanese, *"Dammi, dammi, buggero, buggero."*

Sergeant Major Scullion warned, "Andy. You had better do what he says. He is going off his head. He's dangerous."

"OK, OK," I replied, as I climbed out of the grave.

We took Speedy off the barra — he was wrapped in an old sheet — and laid him on the ground. Suzuki booted his body into the grave. I glowered at him and felt like strangling the bastard. After Suzuki had beaten up Father Kennedy on one occasion, a group of us at Kinkaseki had taken a solemn oath that we would get Suzuki one day, no matter what. I longed to keep my word. I filled in the grave and put stones on top to try to deter the animals. When I had finished, I put my chunkel back on the barra and made to return to camp.

Suzuki stopped me. "Now you dig another grave."

I wondered what he was on about; we only dug graves as we needed to. "Why?" I asked.

"For you. Tomorrow you die!"

My heart fell into my stomach. Sergeant Major Scullion looked grim and even Yo-yo looked sorry for me. I dug the grave and then wearily made my way back to the camp and a sleepless night.

The next morning, we were summoned again and took the body of another English lad up to the makeshift cemetery. In a way, I was relieved that we had somebody to bury. I laid the poor lad in the empty grave I had dug the previous day.

As I filled in the grave, Suzuki stood smoking, watching me intently. When I finished, he ordered me to dig another grave. He was enjoying himself and told me again, "For tomorrow — for you, *ichi ni hachi*. Tomorrow you die."

Suzuki had absolute power over us and was capable of anything. I dug the grave in silence, longing to put Suzuki in it, but we were so powerless. I had another uncertain night in the camp but the normal routine was interrupted by the first ever air-raid alert that we had experienced, and Suzuki forgot all about me and my waiting grave.

Suzuki was the cruellest of the cruel and was hated even by the other Formosan guards, whom he bullied at every turn, but one day we saw him get his comeuppance. We were filling the railway trucks with stones and there were hundreds and hundreds of Chinese labourers — men, women and children — close by. Suddenly, Suzuki turned on a little Chinese boy of seven or eight and began to beat him up. It was awful to see and we all began to boo him and shout that the boy should be left alone. He was kicking the boy, who was screaming on the ground. When he finished, the boy was unable to move.

About ten minutes later, a Chinese man came along the railway and picked up the little boy and took him back up to the Chinese labourers. Then he came back, walked right past us, past the first guard and up to Suzuki. Suzuki must have guessed what was coming because he made a lunge at the man. He missed, though, and the man set about Suzuki, knocking him to the ground. We were all shouting and cheering, "Yes, yes. Give him more, get stuck in."

Suzuki was lying on the ground trying to cover himself as the man gave him a real hiding. He was in a hell of a state and, even worse, he had lost face in front of the other guards. None of the guards moved to help him — they just let the Chinese man get on with it. Then the man stood up and, as Suzuki lay bleeding and battered, he walked off, but he turned to us and said in perfect English, "It will not be long now until the Americans come here."

How right he was. A couple of weeks later, we were clearing the land and filling the trucks in a big long line. We worked in silence, keeping our heads down, while Suzuki and his men strode among us, lashing us with bamboo canes. It was another long, hot, thirsty day, and I was in a team led by an American with two Javanese prisoners. Our sole distraction was counting out the Japanese fighters from an airbase around eight or nine miles away and then counting them back in again. Usually about ten went out on patrol and, to begin with, they all returned, but then maybe one or two failed to return and we speculated feverishly that something had happened and that the Americans were getting closer.

That morning, we counted out ten as usual, but then about two hours later only two returned. The line was abuzz with murmured excitement. We thought that the Yanks must be close with aircraft carriers. Then our hearts sank as we saw the missing planes fly back in from the sea. I looked up at the sky to count them, but, as they got closer, I saw stars painted on the wings. I had never seen American planes before and I asked the Yank what they were. He stared for a few seconds then started jumping up and down, waving his arms. He was going bananas.

"Oh, Jesus Christ, they're ours. They're ours, they're ours! Over here! Over here!"

All the prisoners right up the line were cheering and waving our arms in the air. It was incredible. As the planes swooped in low over us, Suzuki and the guards ran in to mingle with us; they were frightened of getting machine-gunned. We roared and cheered as the Yanks flew down towards the airbase and gave it hell. We couldn't see the base but we could hear the explosions and see columns of smoke, and after a while we smelled the cordite. We cheered ourselves hoarse. We had not seen an Allied plane since the fall of Singapore more than two years earlier. We felt forgotten and utterly isolated. Now men were laughing and crying as they waved and shouted. One of the planes must have seen us and it came back over and dipped its wings. Then the pilot pulled back the canopy and dropped shoeboxes down to us. He must have radioed his mates and they came over and did the same. We rushed to open the boxes. Inside, we found cigarettes and notes pre-printed and addressed to prisoners: "Hang on, boys. We know you are there. We will be coming to get you soon. The Allies are winning the war. Hang on and stay safe."

We were ecstatic and the morale in the camp that night was sky-high. We rushed to tell the sick men, "The Yanks are coming. Hang on, lads, hang on. They dropped leaflets. They bombed the airport."

We knew that the news alone was enough to save men who had given up — without hope, it was so easy to give up the ghost. All the talk in the huts that night was about the American planes, and the smokers savoured the American cigarettes. That night, the Japanese locked us in the huts, but, when we heard an aircraft overhead, we were able to lift the banana leaves on the atap roof and see purple flares being dropped; we knew that must be the Americans too.

The next day, the Japanese retaliated. They stopped all food in the camp and said that what we had seen were manoeuvres and that there would be no fires or smoke because of these exercises. It was a completely ridiculous claim but amazingly some men in the camp believed it, as they had been so ground down by the Japanese. We argued with them, "It was the Yanks — we saw them. They dropped cigarettes. Can you not smell the cordite from the airbase?"

With no food in the camp, the mood became sombre once again. We still had to work, even though we were in a state of near collapse with no food. A couple of days later, I was up at the trucks when Suzuki came along and kicked my basket of rocks over. I saw red, picked up the empty basket and threw it at him. Then I braced myself for a beating but it never came. Instead, Suzuki went off and reported me to Tamaki for a more severe punishment. We were all scared of Tamaki. He spoke English and had been in London as a commercial sales representative before the war, and he harboured a bitter hatred towards us. He was a cruel war criminal who enjoyed making speeches saying how the Japanese would rape all the women in London when they won the war and he enjoyed his life-and-death authority over the prisoners.

Tamaki strode towards me. "On your knees!" His broad features creased into a twisted sneer of hatred and contempt, as his black moustache drew back in a vicious snarl.

"Oh, Christ! This is it," I thought. I had survived a *banzai* charge, bombs and flying bullets during the bloody Battle of Malaya and the fall of Singapore. I had come through a hell-ship voyage and the forced march to the Kinkaseki death mine where we slaved and starved and withered and died. Now my luck had run out, and as I sank to the parched Formosan soil I felt warm water run down the inside of my legs.

I looked up at Tamaki in mute appeal. He was short and squat but towered above me now as he drew his samurai sword and held the glinting steel aloft in the tropical sun.

"Say . . . goodbye . . . to . . . your . . . friends."

As the ragged skeletons behind me found their voices, I was suddenly transported out of that terrible camp. They say a man's life flashes before him as he faces death. And as my comrades shouted out for mercy in accents honed in Australia, America, England, Scotland and Holland, my mind raced back in time. I saw again the kindly faces of my mother and father, and the smiles of my brothers and sister. At last I had escaped the Japanese Imperial Army. I was back in the streets of my beloved Glasgow.

Then I felt a stunning blow on my head as Tamaki hit me with the flat of his sword. I blacked out and was dragged away by two mates. My head was bursting. I was stunned for a while and came round later that night when rice was sent to the huts and we ate again. I had survived another close encounter with death.

A couple of days later, all the "fit" men were taken away in trucks and I bade farewell to the hell camp of Heito where I had spent 14 miserable months. We were driven to a small town where we were put up in a school that was run by the first civilised Japanese we had met since our capture. He wore a uniform but spoke very good English. He told us that he did not like the war and that he had visited America as a wrestler. He introduced us to his wife, who was immaculately dressed. She asked if we could make a rice box for her.

Myself and another lad volunteered and were taken to a workshop full of tools. On the way, we passed a framed picture of Tojo, Japan's militarist leader, on the wall. The Japanese man stopped briefly. He never said anything but smiled as he quickly showed us that on the other side of the photo was a picture of Christ on the Cross. They were Christians. We did our best to knock up a rice box but it was not up to much. Nonetheless, his wife thanked us. Their behaviour towards us was a surprise and Suzuki did not like it. When he got the chance, he started showing off and pushing us around in front of them.

The next day, 27 February 1945, we were herded onto trucks once more. We were to return to the port of Keelung, where a hell ship named the *Taiko Maru* waited to take us to a slave camp at a coal mine near a Japanese city called Nagasaki.

CHAPTER
NINE

The Lights of Home

The *Taiko Maru* was a good bit smaller than the *England Maru*, but, as we trudged up the gangplank, we all knew what was in store for us. There were 700 of us squeezed into the holds of the 3,000-tonne freighter for our journey to the Japanese coal port of Moji. To the Japanese, the 3,000 tonnes of sugar that she carried were infinitely more valuable than her human cargo. The journey was more hazardous than our first voyage. America had flexed its mighty industrial muscles and the seas around Japan's shrinking empire were full of hunter killers more lethal than the hungry sharks that followed the hell ships — submarines. They had already sunk dozens of hell ships, and thousands of prisoners had been drowned, so our convoy zigzagged all the way from Formosa to Japan during a voyage that took 11 long days.

Down below, it was the same old story of cramped misery, starvation, illness and filth. I had a spoon with me. It was a precious item, but I had little chance to use it on the *Taiko Maru* where men stampeded for what little food or water we were given. One day, as I lay watching the rats run along the planks laid across the hold, I wondered what kept them alive — they looked pretty healthy. Then I dropped my spoon between the planks I was lying on. I cursed myself for my carelessness and managed to squeeze my hand through the rough timbers to fish around for the spoon. I could feel bulging sacks and then to my relief I found the spoon. I had sharpened the handle and stabbed one of the sacks. I had struck gold — the sacks contained sugar. I quietly started removing a handful at a time and passed the sweet granules to my mates. They were all sworn to secrecy as we were fearful of starting a panic. Men were starving and there would have been a riot. The lads let the sugar dissolve in their mouths, enjoying the taste and making it last. We thought it might be a lifesaver, but there was a horrible sting in the tail to the sugar racket — it drove us all mad with thirst and we had to give it up.

My luckiest break on the *Taiko Maru* came one day when it was my turn to empty the rose buckets over the side. As I went to get a hose to clean down the deck and hull, I passed an old Japanese seaman who was cooking fish on a kind of grill. There were six or seven of them sizzling away on his barbecue; they looked great and smelled even better. It was risky but they were irresistible and I thought I would pinch one of the silvery delights to share with my mates. When he looked the other way, I took a chance and whipped one of the fish off the grill. I was only wearing a loincloth and had nowhere else to hide it, so I stuffed it down beside the most delicate part of my anatomy. I was dancing around like a scalded cat — that fish was hot! The old

Japanese cook saw what I had done and he signalled to me to come over to him. My heart sank; I was sure I was in for it, but he must have felt sorry for us in our starved condition and just indicated that I should eat the fish there and then. It tasted great to me and brought back memories of fish suppers in Glasgow.

Our guards travelled with us, and they included Suzuki, who had haunted us right the way through our imprisonment on Formosa, from Kinkaseki to Heito, and now on to Japan. Also on the ship was the Snake, the cruel second-in-command at Heito who was supposed to be the translator but spoke only a little broken English. I always stayed out of his road, but on the *Taiko Maru* I had a near-fatal encounter with him. I had been emptying the toilet buckets along with big Charlie Farmer. We had hosed down the ship, the buckets and ourselves with the freezing cold icy salt water because we were so filthy, covered in everybody's muck. We went to hang up the hose by throwing it over a mast, but it slipped and fell on the deck, breaking the nozzle. The Snake saw it happen and flew into a rage. It was a moment of absolute dread. He started shouting, "You no good, no good. Got to be punished."

He ordered the guards to take us up to the ship's mast. We were tied to it with our arms around it, facing each other. I thought we were going to be flogged. We were clad only in our "jap-happy" loincloths. It was freezing, bitterly, bitterly cold with flecks of snow coming through the rain and spray from the ship's bows in the heavy weather. This was to be our punishment. We were tied there for hours. Charlie was crying out in pain and I got excruciating colic. I was in agony and fully expected to die. How we didn't freeze to death or die of exposure, I will never know. Our officers tried to intervene but the Snake wouldn't hear of it. They must have got word to the ship's captain, though, because he came down and told the Snake that we had suffered enough and should be taken below.

The next few days were pure hell. We lay close to each other and wept. I had never known pain like it. Charlie was a big man of 6 ft 2 in. but he was suffering from beriberi, malnutrition and a host of other diseases. Now he was a shaking skeleton.

When we arrived at Moji, it was early evening. We staggered onto the quay and were ordered into a huge empty warehouse and told that we would spend the night there. We lay down on the cold concrete floors dressed only in our jap-happies and all cuddled into each other for warmth. Our teeth were chattering and we were violently shivering, as if we had malaria. Charlie had a kilt that he had clung on to after Speedy, its previous owner, died in Heito. It was swarming with lice, which had infested the pleats, but we put it over us anyway to try to gain some warmth. We lay all night huddled together in that freezing warehouse, trying to stay warm.

In the morning, the guards came in, clapping and shouting, kicking at us to get up.

I sat up and gave Charlie a shake. "Come on, Charlie, come on. Up you get, Charlie, up you get. Time to get up."

Charlie never moved. I knew right away he was gone. I had been sleeping with a dead man. Charlie was only 26 years of age when he passed away on that quayside. He was the first of my comrades to die in Japan, but 16 more would die through starvation, brutality and neglect during our time there.

I took Charlie's kilt, and we brought his body on the trucks with us to our new camp, where we cremated him in a funeral pyre. We arrived at Senryu, also known as Fukuoka 24B, on 10 March. It was attached to a coal mine owned by the Sumitomo Company and was part of a network of slave camps serving mines, steel mills and shipyards in Japan. There were about 130 of these camps in Japan, and of the 35,000 men held in them 3,600 would die of starvation, dysentery, beriberi and pneumonia. When we arrived at Senryu, there were already around 150 Australians in the camp who were survivors of the Death Railway and had arrived in January 1944. There were also some Americans who had been slaves on the Death Railway; a lot of them had been sailors on the USS *Houston*, which was sunk in the Java Sea in February 1942.

Conditions in the camp were a lot better than in Formosa. The huts were warmer, but they were still crowded and heaving with lice. Suzuki and the Snake were assigned elsewhere. Apart from petty harassment from the guards, there was not much brutality and fewer beatings. The camp commandant was an old man and most of the guards were home-guard types who did not bother us much. Starvation and disease were our biggest problems. I weighed around seven stones, and we were all ill. Sergeant Major Scullion and Tammy Donnelly were very ill and were put in the hospital hut. They were both veterans and should never have been out in the Far East. We were worried about them and tried to get extra food to them. They would surely die on the diet of rice and watery soup that was our staple at Senryu.

Soon after we arrived, I hit on a way of helping Tammy and Sergeant Major Scullion. Near the American huts, the Japanese kept a few chickens. I started pinching the eggs. By now, I had become as skilled as the Artful Dodger at swiping food. We would hard-boil them and I would take one each along to the two old soldiers, who were both so grateful for those eggs. I was always worried that the Japanese would see the eggshells, so we buried them in the earth floors underneath the beds. The racket went on for quite a while, but then the Japanese noticed that their hens had stopped laying and blamed the Americans. The Americans were worried and came to ask us to stop pinching the eggs.

I had two jobs at the camp. Like the rest of the men, I worked down the pit, but I also looked after three fat black pigs. The work in the coal mine was hard and dangerous. We didn't burrow into the roof as we did in Kinkaseki, but the seams that we were working at Senryu were narrow — only about three feet thick — and even the small Japanese miners found it hard-going as we hewed at the coalface with pick and shovel. Men worked the seams lying on their sides for ten to twelve hours a day, and we worked for thirteen days straight with one day off a fortnight. The Japanese miners showed us the ropes; if they heard a distant rumble, they knew it was time to run. Roof collapses and injuries were common. The rations of the Japanese miners were not much better than ours and they were not nasty towards us. There were no brutal *hanchos* or beatings down the mine. Most people would be horrified at the conditions, the long hours and the lack of health and safety. It was slavery all right but it was nothing like the horror that we had endured at Kinkaseki.

I was always glad to get back out of the pit into the fresh air and look after the pigs. They had asked for a volunteer who knew about pigs, and, although I didn't really know about pigs, I said I did because I thought it might give me a chance to snaffle some extra grub. I had an idea that there might be some edible stuff among the pigswill and remembered the healthy Dutch prisoners at Heito. Sure enough, the pigswill included leftover rice from the guards' cookhouse and other leftovers. Sometimes, we were not very sure what we were eating, but we just ate it anyway; it didn't do the pigs any harm and we were so hungry all the time.

Part of my job was to go into the nearby village and gather up old vegetable tops and things like that from the market. I was usually accompanied by a tired old home guard we called Dogface. Loudspeakers in the village, which had a railway station to service the mine, constantly played military music and propaganda announcing the latest Japanese military successes and how many American ships they had sunk. I was not supposed to speak to the local people, who were mainly women, as the men were either at the front or working, but I was able to converse quite a lot with them because of the Japanese I had learned in Kinkaseki. I got the impression that the Japanese women felt quite sorry for me — I was a walking skeleton, clad only in a loincloth and walking in bare feet. One of the women would occasionally slip me a leaf with soya paste in it — they knew we were starving. I only got caught speaking to the women once and was beaten up by one of the guards on the spot. I could see that the women sympathised with me.

My pigswill racket was going fine and the lads in the hut waited eagerly every night to see what swag I had managed to liberate. I liked going down to the village with old Dogface too. It got me out of the camp and broke up the monotony.

One day, when I was in the village, I looked up the slight hill into the place and saw a runaway horse with a cart careering towards us. It was making for its stable behind the market and was really going like hell with its ears back and its teeth bared. I shouted to old Dogface and pointed up the hill. He immediately shouted a warning to the civilians, telling them to get back. Just then, a little boy of about three appeared out of a house on the other side of the road and started to walk into the path of the horse. I dived across the road and grabbed him. I fell heavily but managed to push the boy to safety. He was a lovely wee boy and was crying his head off. His mother came out, scooped him up and took him inside. I had bashed my head and was bleeding. As I lay stunned and skinned, the lady came out again with a bowl of water and she started to clean me up. She spoke a little English and said, "My son. Thank you. Thank you."

The guard who had beat me up for speaking to the locals looked on approvingly. Then the lady went inside again and came back out with a small bag of sugary little cakes and handed them to me. "Thank you. Thank you. *Presento*."

The next day, I was still pretty raw, but, when I was due to start my shift down the mine, the guards told me, "*Yasume!* You rest, no work today."

It seemed somebody had told the commandant what I did.

Shortly afterwards, I narrowly avoided getting into serious trouble. The singing of patriotic songs had been banned in all of the Japanese camps ever since we had sung "There Will Always Be An England" in Selarang in Singapore to defy our captors. One evening, after a dayshift down the mine, some of the lads had gathered in the hut for a sing-song, which was one of our few entertainments. I was on the mouth organ when one of the lads said, "Come on, Andy, give us 'There Will Always Be An England'."

I picked up the tune and we had a rousing chorus of the anthem. We finished with a cheer and in high spirits. Unknown to us, though, the Japanese camp interpreter had been lurking about outside and had heard everything. He came in and looked at us, but didn't say anything and turned around and walked out.

The next day, he sent for me and I went to his office. He put a mouth organ on the table and said, "You. You play mouth organ. You play for me. You play 'Englando — Always Be Englando'."

I realised it was a trap straight away and told him, "I am from Scotlando. I am Scottish not English. I not know 'Always Be Englando'. Cannot play 'Englando'."

He was furious and knew I was lying. If I had played the song, it would have confirmed to him that I had played it the night before and I would have been given a severe beating.

I went to the hospital hut to see Tammy Donnelly to tell him my tale and to cheer him up. He was in a terrible condition — shrivelled and shrunken by dysentery. I tried my best to keep his spirits up, talking about our plans to set up a pig farm together after the war with all of the money we would get from the army. I told him the latest rumours that the Yanks were getting close and urged him, "Hang on, Tammy, hang on, Tammy. We'll soon be hame."

It was too late for Tammy, though, and he died on 10 April. Taking Tammy's body to a place where a funeral pyre had been built was the saddest day. He had been a big-brother figure to me and we had come through so much together. Now he was dead at the age of 43 in a strange land that could not be further away from his home in Burnbank in Lanarkshire. It put my head down a bit. We had been prisoners for three long years and I wondered how much longer it would be, how many more of us would die and never see Scotland again.

I tried not to let the Japanese propaganda get to me, and I began to detect a softening of attitude by the Japanese towards us. Maybe they knew that they were losing the war.

One day, just after I had come up from the coal mine, we were all told to bring out the bags in which we kept what little possessions we had for an inspection. The guards wanted to see whether or not we had been trading with the Korean prisoners who were also slaves in the mine. We all lined up with our bags at our feet. One of the Japanese started to go through my things. He looked at a photograph of me with my mother and brothers and said in Japanese, "Ah, mother, your mother." I nodded, then he picked up the picture of me running at Ibrox when I was ahead of Wooderson. It was the photograph that had got me into trouble at the Redford Barracks, which now felt like a lifetime earlier. He studied the photo intently then said, "*Ichi ban?* Number One? Mile. Woodosan."

He couldn't say Wooderson but he knew fine who he was — the holder of the world record for the mile. Then he looked at the picture again and stood back to look at me and compare the matchstick man before him with the young athlete of five years earlier. "*Ichi ni hachi?* You, number 128? You?"

I nodded. "Yes, that's me."

Then he summoned the other two guards over, showed them Wooderson and pointed to the photo, then to me again — *ichi ni hachi*. They looked in wonderment. Then he barked an order: "*Sunda, yasume*" ("Finished, go back and rest.")

273

The lads started putting their belongings back in their bags, but the guard started gathering my things and putting them back nice and gentle. Then he handed the bag to me, looked sad and said, *"Sensa dammi dammi, sensa dammi."*

"Yes," I agreed. "War no good."

My comrades in the hut were beginning to look a little better for the pigswill, but the trouble was that, as my pals grew fatter, the pigs grew thinner. One day, the commandant sent for me. I had to go down and see him at the pigpen. He was standing looking angrily at the pigs. The once-portly porkers had shrunk and looked more like greyhounds. The commandant pointed at the pigs, saying, *"Puta dammi dammi."* ("Pigs no good, no good.")

I was well and truly rumbled but I tried to explain to him that they needed more food, more vitamins. I was supposed to be the pig expert, so I told him the pigs were suffering from the porcine equivalent of beriberi. They needed more potatoes. Thankfully, the commandant seemed to fall for my story and I was sent back to the hut. There I told the lads, "The ball is burst. The Japs are on to the pigswill racket — we'll have to cool it for a bit."

However, it didn't take me long to find another illicit source of food. One day, the Japanese asked if there were any skilled men among the prisoners to repair and replace the thin panels in some of their accommodation. I put my hand up right away — well, it sounded easier than going down the mine. I went to the huts and was issued with some tools. I could see that in some places the panelling needed to be glued back on and told the Japanese that I needed rice flour to make paste. They returned with buckets of rice flour and we made up the paste — and gorged on it. I doubt if there could ever be a more tasteless meal, but to starving men the paste tasted like the ambrosia of the gods and we wolfed it down.

I tried to cut back on pinching the pigswill, but some of the lads were in a bad way. Johnny Matthewson, a pal from Springburn in Glasgow, had pellagra and was in a hell of a state. His whole body was covered in sores and he badly needed whatever nourishment he could get. The commandant had ordered more potatoes for the pigs, as I had suggested, so I got a canvas bag, put the potatoes inside and boiled them up in among all the gunge for the pigswill. Then I would smuggle the bag back to my hungry mates at the hut. This was working fine, but, unknown to me, the commandant was watching me. One evening, he saw me lift out the bag after I had boiled it. The guards pounced, and when the commandant saw the contents he got really angry. I was ordered to his hut where there was much screaming and shouting, then three or four of the guards started to beat me up with bamboo sticks. I was bent over the commandant's table and they beat my back, legs and backside until they drew blood. It was bloody agony but the strange thing was that one of the guards — the one who had recognised Wooderson — was just going through the motions. He was drawing back all of the time.

After a sound thrashing, I was dismissed but, as I made my way back to the hut, I met the Japanese camp translator. I told him, "The commandant no understand. I cook potatoes for pig's breakfast in the morning. So I not have to build fire before I go down mine."

The translator took it all on board and went off to see the commandant. Later that night, one of the guards came to the hut with a bowl of rice and some whitebait. It was a way of saying sorry — the commandant had fallen for my pigs' breakfast story! Shortly after, the Japanese guard who had tried not to beat me also came to the hut. He gave me a leaf with an ointment in it — a salve to put on my painful and shredded backside. He made me promise not to tell anyone he had brought me ointment. Then he said again, "*Sensa dammi dammi.* War no good."

A week later, the same Japanese guard came to the hut and told me to go with him. I grabbed the old shirt that we kept in the hut and always wore when we got a beating, so that the skin wouldn't get broken. I wondered what was up and expected to get another hiding. We walked through the camp to the hut where we were issued with the tools for the coal mine every morning. We went into the hut and he turned to me, swearing me to secrecy once again.

Then, to my amazement, he whispered, "*Ichi ni hachi, Deutschland sunda. Deutschland sunda.*" ("128, Germany is finished. Germany is finished.")

Incredulously, I repeated the words: "*Deutschland sunda? Deutschland sunda?*"

"Yes, yes." He indicated with his pinkie turned down. "Very shortly, Nippon cannot carry on alone. You will go home to Englando to your father and mother." Then he produced from his pocket a photograph of himself and two mates — they were runners. He smiled as he showed me the photo and then his brow furrowed. "*Sensa dammi dammi*. War no good."

When I got back to the hut, my mates were waiting anxiously. "What's the matter, Andy? Did they hit you? What did he want? Are you OK?"

"Yeah, yeah," I said breathlessly. "He just told me the war with Germany is finished!"

"Are you sure?"

"Yes, he just told me. He says very soon Japan cannot carry on itself."

"Why would he tell you?"

"Because he's a runner too. Remember how he brought me the ointment? He showed me a photo of him and his mates running."

Even though we had heard so many false rumours, and so often our hopes had been dashed, morale in the hut was sent sky-high. We had never been told anything like this by a Japanese soldier. All of the guys started speculating about what might happen. I went over to give the good news to old Sergeant Major Scullion, who was still very ill and living in the officers' hut.

"Hang on now, Sergeant Major. The Germans are finished. It won't be long now and we'll be getting home. It'll be fish suppers and plenty of drams for you."

"How do you know, Andy? Are you sure?"

The officers asked me what all the excitement was about.

"I can't tell you how I know," I told them, "but I have been told from a good source that the war with Germany is over. Take it from me, the Germans are finished."

The Korean prisoners in the mine had a good news network and, soon after I was told about the defeat of Germany, they confirmed it. The morale in the camp was better but there was always the nagging doubt about what would happen to us. On the one hand, we hoped that we might soon get home, but, on the other, we feared that we might be killed. We had good reason to be fearful, as the Japanese army was capable of anything.

I had my own suspicions too. For several weeks, we had been employed driving a new tunnel into the hill near the camp. One of the Korean guards was approachable and I asked him what the tunnel was for.

"Air-raid shelter?" I suggested.

He shook his head solemnly. "No," he said. "Tomb."

We discovered later that they planned to drive us into the tunnel and set off explosives to bring the roof down on us.

The headquarters of the Japanese Imperial Army had already issued an order for our elimination. In an echo of the Nazis' treatment of the Jews in Europe, we were to be subject to a "final solution". The order went on to state: "Whether they are destroyed individually or in groups, or however it is done, with mass bombing,

278

poisonous smoke, poisons, drowning, decapitations, or what, dispose of them as the situation dictates."

There could be no doubting the determination of the Japanese to carry out these massacres. In December 1944, as the Americans advanced in the Philippines, troops under Yamashita, who had defeated us in Malaya, had massacred 150 American prisoners at Palawan camp by herding them into air-raid shelters and burning them alive with barrels of flaming gasoline poured into the shelters.

It was unthinkable that we could have survived so much only to be slaughtered on the eve of liberation. I prayed that we would all survive. We needed to be liberated, and right away. Men were still dying in the camp. A pal of mine from England we nicknamed "Stan" had always been a great support to me. He was popular with the rest of the lads too and used to entertain us with a moving rendition of his party piece "The Lights of Home" — a song recorded by my favourite, Deanna Durbin. Stan had contracted bad dysentery and had been admitted to the hospital hut where the medics treated patients with their only available medicine — kind words. I went to see Stan and was instantly saddened to see his condition. I had seen it so many times before and we had all become experts in the progress of the diseases that wracked our bodies. I knew that only a miracle — or food and the simple medicines that we were denied — could save Stan now. I kneeled down beside his bed and tried to offer words of encouragement and hope. "It won't be long now, Stan. The Yanks will soon be here and we'll be going home."

He smiled weakly. His breathing was laboured but he managed to whisper, "Sing for me, Andy. Sing it."

I knew what he meant and fought back the tears as I sang:

I can see the lights of home
Shining brightly o'er the foam,
Beckon to me while I roam
Away from lights of home.
I can see somebody there,
Loving eyes and silver hair,
I can see her kneel in prayer
Beneath the lights of home.
In that little old sleepy town,
Nothing happens when the sun goes down,
Not a thing but moonbeams run around,
In a starry dome.
Turn the hands of time for me,
Let me live my memory,
Once again I long to be
Beneath the lights of home.

I knew as I left Stan that night that I would never see him again and that he would never see the lights of home.

One day, I came out of the mine after another hard shift. I was always pleased to see the sky when I emerged from the mine but this time it looked strange. I could see great dust-laden clouds in the atmosphere to the south of the mine. They were a strange colour and I asked one of the lads what had happened.

"We think it was a volcano," he said.

They had heard a rumble from the direction of Nagasaki 30 miles away. The camp optimists thought it might have been a naval bombardment or a direct hit on a huge ammunition dump. We never gave it too much thought and had no way of knowing that history had been made that day. Just after 11 a.m. on 9 August, an American B-29 bomber had dropped "Fat Man", which detonated above Nagasaki, instantly vaporising and incinerating 39,000 people.

In the camp, we carried on as usual with the boring routine of mine-camp-mine, but we began to sense that something strange was going on. Guards kept disappearing in twos and threes and then returning to the camp looking grim. They were huddling and conferring among themselves, looking mighty worried. It was likely that they had been to Nagasaki, perhaps in search of family or comrades, and had seen the carnage. We knew that something serious had happened.

Six days after the bomb dropped, I had finished my shift down the mine and was in the village, down at the marketplace to collect the scraps for the pigs. The loudspeakers were playing martial music as usual, but then a voice broke in and called for attention. I stopped to listen and couldn't believe my ears. Over and over it repeated, *"Sensa sunda! Sensa sunda!"* (The war is finished! The war is finished!)

At last, the moment I had dreamed about for years had arrived. Old Dogface looked as stunned as I felt. Then the women all came running out of their little houses, cheering and shouting, *"Sensa sunda! Sensa sunda!"* They were all glad, so pleased that the bitter years of loss and sacrifice were over. The women were hugging and embracing us.

Old Dogface clapped me on the back. *"Sensa sunda.* Soon you go home to Englando to Mama and Papa."

I couldn't wait to get back to the camp. I loaded up my barra and started pushing it back up the hill. Old Dogface was burdened with his heavy rifle and placed it on top of the barra. I was eager to tell my mates the news and hardly noticed the camp guards as I entered the camp. Suddenly, a Japanese sergeant appeared and started slapping and punching the old man for laying his rifle on the barra. I felt sorry for Dogface and heard myself shouting in a voice of authority, "Stop! Stop! Leave him alone. *Sensa sunda! Sensa sunda!* War is finished."

The sergeant stopped and stared at me, amazed that one of his slaves could speak in that way to a Japanese guard — I was a little amazed myself. The sergeant was dumbstruck and the other Japanese guards looked at each other incredulously. The sergeant stopped beating Dogface and looked at me. It was a tense moment. I thought I was in for a hiding, but then they turned around and, to my relief, moved off.

I ran on into the camp and came across a group of about 50 Australians and Yanks who were ready to go down the mine with pickaxes and shovels. Some had crutches and sticks, which meant that they didn't get the hardest job down the pit, although they still had to go down for a 12-hour shift.

Big Bob Smith, a 6 ft 4 in. Australian whose once-powerful frame now looked pathetic, asked me, "What's the matter, Jock? What's the matter?"

"The war has finished! The war has finished — it was on the loudspeakers in the village. It's over! It's over! We've won. We've won!"

He looked stunned. "Are you sure, Jock? Are you sure? How do you know?"

I began to wonder myself if I had imagined it. Then over the hill came half a dozen Korean prisoners, waving flags and shouting, "The war is finished! Japan finished. *Sensa sunda! Nippon sunda!*"

I turned to Bob. "See, there you are. It's finished. It's over. The war is finished."

All of a sudden, the Aussies threw their sticks and crutches in the air and began dancing about like crazy men. They had been hamming it up to dodge working at the coalface — I had cured the lame! Men were laughing and crying, hugging each other and punching the air. We had survived.

Our officers appeared and sent for the Japanese commandant. He came out shaking. All of the regular guards had run away, and he and his interpreter were the only Japanese in the camp. He informed us, "We have been told war is finished but we have received no orders from the Japanese Imperial Army headquarters and you remain under the orders of the Japanese army."

As our officers pondered the situation, Bob Smith shouted at the commandant, "Bloody hell! You can bugger off! We're under nobody's bloody orders. Where's the bloody food? Where are the Red Cross parcels you buggers have been stealing all these years?"

A mob of hungry men ran round to the hut where the Red Cross parcels were kept. Sure enough, we found parcels that had been there for months and months. There were boxes and boxes of stuff that could have saved the lives of men who died in the camp. A lot of it had gone off and a lot had been pilfered. The Japanese had smoked or traded all of the cigarettes, but there was enough food for us to have a feast of canned ham and condensed milk.

A few days later, American aircraft flew overhead and dropped leaflets telling us to stay where we were and that we would be rescued soon. They said that food and supplies would be dropped soon but warned that we should not eat too much, as it would be dangerous for us to overeat. We killed the hens and a pig and made a half-hearted attempt to cook them. Then American planes parachuted canisters to us, which landed in the countryside around the camp. We knew where they were because Japanese civilians came to the camp and took us to them. They helped us bring the canisters into the camp and we rewarded them by giving the silk parachutes to the women and the ropes to the men. We rushed to open the containers. It was marvellous! As well as tins of Spam and potatoes, there were shirts and trousers, boots and toiletries — everything we could want and never could afford in Scotland. Some lads ignored the advice not to eat too much and suffered terrible pains after gorging themselves.

We were responsible for ourselves and enjoyed our new freedom. We had no ill will towards the ordinary Japanese people, and some of the men went on hikes out to the countryside to trade with farmers. One day, I got a loan of a horse in the village to ride up into the countryside to barter with the farmers for fresh eggs. I rode up to a lake where some of the lads were enjoying a swim. One of the Aussies there asked if he could have a go on the horse. He explained that he had been a jockey in civvie street. I said OK and handed him the reins. He was riding around the lake quite the thing, enjoying himself in the saddle again, but then the horse threw him and bolted. It ran round and round the field and then made for the gate. I made to stand in front of the gate and stop it, but it was out of control and I had to jump aside. The horse ran off towards the village and I followed it back down to the stables. As I went through the village, people came up to me and said that the horse had knocked down and injured a little boy. I feared the worst as I went with the villagers to the little boy's house. He was skinned and bruised, but, apart from feeling pretty sorry for himself, he was fine. My pockets were stuffed with cigarettes and sweets to trade with the farmers, so I gave the boy sweets and his father cigarettes. The man thanked me very much and I promised to return the next day to see how the boy was.

When I went to the stables, a Japanese man was stitching up the horse — the little boy had been lucky.

I apologised for the incident and loaded the Japanese man up with food — the Americans had given us more than we could ever consume. The next day, when I went back to see how the wee boy was, I was besieged by young boys all claiming to have been knocked over by the horse and demanding sweeties.

When word came through that we were to get our stuff ready and that we would be leaving on a train from the village, we sent word for the villagers to come up to the camp. We gave them the pigs and then spread blankets on the ground and gave them all of the excess stuff that we had. They couldn't believe that we were so forgiving but we had nothing against these people. They were not fascists or militarists. They were just poor folk who were suffering. I gave old Dogface shoes, socks, boots and trousers, as well as cigarettes and foodstuffs. All the lads were doing the same, and the Japanese were overwhelmed.

As we marched down to the station, the villagers waved us off. There were around 250 of us — British, Australian and Yanks. There were no officers with us, but the Japanese commandant came down and watched as we piled aboard the train that took us to Nagasaki. We still had no clue about the atom bomb, but as we got closer to the city, maybe about 12 miles or so from it, we started to see flattened farmhouses and wondered why the place had been bombed. We were mystified too by the lack of bomb craters. Everything was demolished, and there were no leaves on the trees. The closer we got, the more devastation we saw. We were travelling through an atomic wasteland.

When we arrived at the platform in Nagasaki, the Americans had a band playing for us. They were belting out "California Here I Come" and a group of American nurses — the first white women we had seen for three years — were handing out doughnuts and coffee. The women cried when they saw how feeble we were. The American servicemen were also shocked at how starved and ill we were and gave full vent to their opinions of the Japanese. They could not have been more helpful or kind. They helped us off the train and carried our bags for us. The very sick men were taken away on stretchers to a hospital ship, and Johnny Matthewson was among them.

As we walked to the trucks that were to take us to the harbour where an American aircraft carrier awaited, we were met by civilian survivors of the atom bomb. Their faces were horribly burned and their hands bandaged. The poor souls were on their knees begging for food. We had brought food with us, as we didn't know where we were going, and so stopped to give what we had. Some of our American escorts were surprised that we wanted to help these people after what we had been through, but we knew what it was to be hungry, and it was the Japanese army who had been cruel to us, not the ordinary folk. I gave them what I had and prayed for these terribly injured people. It was clear that some of them would not make it.

Down at the dockside, the American navy had another band playing "Anchors Aweigh", and they had set up a production line to process us. Hundreds of prisoners were arriving from all the surrounding camps.

We heard now that a special bomb had been dropped on Nagasaki and that a few prisoners had been killed too. The US marines took our clothes and the stuff we had brought with us and, apart from our personal effects, burned the lot. We were filthy, smelly and lice-ridden. They issued us with a bag of toiletries — I had a toothbrush and paste for the first time in three and a half years. We had our hair closely cropped by a bloke with electric clippers and then it was into the showers. I had forgotten what a hot shower was like. It was just like the Maryhill steamie after a run — pure luxury. After we were disinfected, we were issued with new uniforms and then it was all aboard the USS *Chenango*.

As I walked up the gangway, I looked back at what was left of Nagasaki — a pile of flattened rubble as far as the eye could see. At last I was leaving Japan. At last I was free. Hundreds of beds had been set up on the carrier's flight decks and in the hangars. An American sailor was appointed to look after each group of eight of us. I was given a plate of scrambled eggs and buttered toast. It was the most wonderful thing I had ever tasted. When I asked our American minder if I could have some more, he returned with a huge mountain of it piled high. We got bread, butter and lovely jams. It was hard to believe sometimes that we were free.

That night, the Americans played movies for us and we caught up with the new songs and fashions. I looked around at Sergeant Major Scullion, Hughie Carroll, Tammy Dodds and Willie Moffat and wondered how the hell we had all survived.

Our next stop was Okinawa, a Japanese island 400 miles south of the mainland. There had been hellish fighting to take the island, which the Americans planned to use as a springboard for the invasion of Japan. American doctors were waiting for us there and we were assigned in groups of eight or so to big bell tents. We were given pills that made us swell up, and once again the food was great. We enjoyed stews and plenty of chicken and rice. The American in charge of us took our names and addresses to send messages home to our families saying that we were all right. He also dished out cigarettes and chewing gum and gave us a crate of a fizzy black drink called Coca-Cola — it was the first time we had seen it.

One day, the Yank came along and said, "Hey, guys, a dame is doing a bit of a sing-song tonight at the main camp." It was Gracie Fields!

Normally, we would have loved to go, but we were exhausted and simply glad to be alive. We were quite happy to just sit and talk about how lucky we were to be there.

Prisoners from all over Japan were being collected at Okinawa. There were Canadians, Australians, Dutch and Americans, as well as British scattered about in all these camps. As we got stronger, we walked all over the camps looking for mates and trying to get news. I walked along and couldn't believe it — there was Father Kennedy. It was wonderful to see him again. I'd been at death's door the last time I saw him and many's the time I thought about him, praying he was alive. He told me he'd been shipped to Manchuria with other officers and had been liberated by the Russians. Apparently, the Russians had wanted to shoot the Japanese guards but Father Kennedy persuaded them not to do it. He also told us that the Americans had bombed Heito and that quite a few of the lads had been killed.

Father Kennedy looked pretty gaunt but he was in good spirits and was glad to see me. He had met an American padre who was going to take him sightseeing and he invited me to join them. The American had a jeep and took us to a castle where he told us about its history and how Marco Polo met the emperor of Japan there because it used to be the ancient capital. Then he took us to some cliffs, but, when we looked down, we saw the most awful sight. At the bottom of the cliffs, there were hundreds and hundreds of dead bodies bobbing up and down in the tide. A lot of them were women and children who had jumped off the cliffs rather than surrender. The fighting had been fierce, with 100,000 Japanese soldiers and 12,500 Americans killed. The Japanese government had tried to stiffen the resolve of their people by telling them that the Americans were cannibals who would slaughter them and eat them, so they had committed suicide. We shook our heads at the pitiful sight below us, and, when the American priest said that some Japanese had still not surrendered and didn't know the war was over, I suddenly felt very exposed on that cliff-top.

We travelled in silence back to the camp, trying to take in the horror of what we had just seen and pondering on the stupidity of war. On the way back, we saw Japanese soldiers who had been taken prisoner too. They were mending the roads, but they were smoking and drinking Coca-Cola — what a contrast to how they had treated us, we thought.

We had spent a fortnight in Okinawa when word came that we were to leave. We were lined up the next day with what we had and told those magical words: "OK, guys. You're going home."

They took us to this huge airstrip and at the very end there were aircraft waiting. They were coming along like taxis, picking up 20 guys at a time. We had no idea where we were going, only that it was the beginning of the long journey home. I was in the queue with Tammy Dodds, Hughie Carroll, Willie Moffat and one or two other lads from the regiment who were all trying to keep together. One of them shouted, "Look, there's Father Kennedy over there!"

He was about 50 yards away from us, and I ran up and asked him, "Are you going home with us today? Where are we going just now?"

He told us he thought we might be going to Manila in the Philippines.

Because we had run across to him, we missed our plane, but we got on the next one and away we went. We flew for about an hour or so but it kept circling round and round the aerodrome in Manila. We couldn't land because the plane before us had crashed and a lot of lads were wounded. It was the plane we should have been on.

We spent a couple of days being looked after by the Filipinos, who never missed a chance to tell us how much they hated the Japanese. Then we embarked on a British aircraft carrier HMS *Implacable*. While on board the *Implacable*, we had to sign undertakings to the British government that we would not talk about what we saw in Nagasaki or how we suffered as their prisoners. They took us to Pearl Harbor, where we gaped at the damage and wrecked ships from Japan's sneak attack in December 1941.

The ship spent a couple of days in Pearl Harbor, and we were allowed off to exercise. I had made a new friend in Ginger, a Scots lad who had also been a prisoner, and I decided to take the ferry across to Honolulu with him. The ferry was full of American sailors, and, when they heard us speaking, one of them shouted, "Hey, guys, we've got a couple of Limeys here."

Then a couple of voices shouted out, "They're not bloody Limeys, they're Scots. Come over here."

We went over to be greeted by two Scottish lads in US naval uniforms. They had been working as engineers in America when war broke out and had to join up. They took charge of us and declared that we were their guests on the island. They took us into a big saloon with a long bar like we had seen in the movies; they told the barman that we had been prisoners and that we could have what we wanted and they would pay for it. We didn't drink very much, and I stuck to soft drinks, but the barman would not accept any payment. On the way back to the ship, they took us to all these great clubs with bands playing and beautifully dressed women in brightly coloured dresses. People were enjoying themselves but it was hard for us to take in.

A couple of days later, we sailed on to Vancouver in Canada where there was a big reception for the ship, which was carrying hundreds of Canadian soldiers who had been captured in the fall of Hong Kong. We travelled by train right across Canada, stopping in Edmonton, Calgary and Toronto. Crowds thronged the platforms of all the stations to greet the returning Canadians and we were fantastically well looked after. Canadians came on board the trains at every stop to give us chocolates, fruit and cups of tea. The Americans had given us some dollars, and in Toronto I bought clothing and stockings to take home for my family and filled the kit bag the Yanks had issued me with.

Finally, we arrived at a huge camp in Nova Scotia near a town called Truro. My mate Ginger and I went out for a walk one day and we saw a lorry coming along the road with "New Glasgow" written on the side. We stuck out our thumbs and the driver stopped to offer us a lift. We told him we weren't going anywhere but that we were interested in New Glasgow because we were from Glasgow in Scotland. The driver said, "Why don't you come along and see it for yourself?" so we jumped on board.

We travelled for nearly half an hour before we came to a nice little town with no high buildings. We walked into the town and went into a restaurant. We were pretty hungry and the menu was too much of a temptation, so we ordered all we could eat. Then we asked the waitress if she could bring us the manager.

"Is anything wrong?" she asked.

"Naw, it was great, but we haven't got a bean — we're broke!"

The manageress came out and we offered to wash up or do any jobs she needed done. We told her we were billeted at Truro and were just in New Glasgow for a short visit. She was nice about it, and soon Ginger's hands were in the sink while I got started with a vacuum cleaner. When everything was cleaned up, the manageress asked us back to her house. She wanted us to meet her mother. It turned out her elderly mother was Scottish — from Bathgate. We had a grand evening. The mother just wanted us to talk and talk, and she was tearful. She was missing home and just wanted to hear the Scottish voices.

We stayed at the Canadian Legion that night and asked where the nearest chapel was. Someone made enquiries and soon a Canadian arrived to take us to Mass. Bernard Martin was a local councillor and took us along with his family to Mass. He invited us to stay at his house, where we had a great time of it with the Martin family. There were three young ones, all friendly and great musicians. The first few evenings we had sing-songs. It had been four years since we felt happy and among a family. They were so kind to us.

It was a lovely home, a real Canadian home. Mr Martin was very interested in our coming from Glasgow and wanted to hear what it was like. He told us how New Glasgow and most of the other villages and townships in Nova Scotia had been founded by Scottish settlers — a lot of them victims of the

Highland Clearances. His wife came in, then two daughters and a son arrived. Mrs Martin was a lovely, kind person and she made us a beautiful meal. It felt so strange to be in a normal family situation again. I had a brief sinking moment when I thought of the wasted years as a prisoner and five years in the military. When we told them we had to get back, they insisted that we stay and got word to the Legion that we would stay with them. They were fascinated about our experiences, but we couldn't answer all of their questions.

After our meal, Mr Martin revealed that he was of Scottish descent too and asked his daughter to play a tune on the piano that his grandparents had often sung to him as a wee boy. His other daughter produced a fiddle and then they began to play with Mr Martin singing.

> Ye banks and braes o' bonnie Doon,
> How can ye bloom sae fresh and fair?
> How can ye chant, ye little birds,
> And I sae weary, fu' o' care!
> Thou'll break my heart, thou warbling bird,
> That wantons thro' the flowering thorn!
> Thou minds me o' departed joys,
> Departed, never to return.

A lump came to my throat. It was the Burns song my mother used to sing. I had not heard it since I fell out with Flaherty during the drill at Lanark. I joined in with Mr Martin, and Ginger joined in too. We were harmonising and it sounded great. We gave ourselves a little round of applause when we finished and then I thought of home. How was Mum? Had her health stood up to years of cleaning floors? How were my brothers and sisters? Had Eddie been conscripted? Had he survived the war? Had the Germans bombed Glasgow? Were they all OK?

Mrs Martin showed us to our room and said, "I'm sorry you have to sleep in the one room. Bernard has been decorating the other one and he has been on it nearly a fortnight now. He doesn't have much time to finish it."

The next day, when we got up and everybody was away, I asked Mrs Martin to show me the spare room.

"He's going to get round to it sometime," she said. "We've been arguing and fighting about it."

"Don't worry, Mrs Martin, I'll do this for you," I offered.

"Oh, no, you couldn't do that. You're going home, no, no."

Nevertheless, I insisted that we would do it. I looked to see what they had and discovered enough rolls of paper to do a whole mansion! Ginger and I got to work and started damping down the paper on the walls, ready to strip it.

Mrs Martin was horrified. "What are you doing?" she asked. "It took Bernard ages to put that up. He thinks it's lovely."

"Yes, but it's upside down. Don't worry, you have plenty of paper."

It was six years since I had papered a room but I was pleased to discover that I had not forgotten the skills I had learned at Pollock and Traill. Mrs Martin watched as I measured the paper and matched it all up. I went to the walls that hadn't been done and started papering them. It was the best feeling, smelling the paste and having a brush in my hand. She stood amazed. We finished the room at about half past five and she was getting dinner ready for about half past six. We got all the furniture back in place and the curtains up, then went downstairs to join the family. We had another nice musical evening, and accompanied by the daughter on the piano we all sang a beautiful song we had first heard in Vancouver, "Goodnight, Sweet Dreams".

It had felt good going back to my old trade, and one day, when walking in New Glasgow, I had another opportunity. A Chinese gentleman was painting his shop and making an awful hash of it. At lunchtime, he put the paint tin and brushes down to go for something to eat. I couldn't resist it. I picked up the brush and in no time had the job finished. He got the surprise of his life when he came out. He called for his wife and daughters to come out and we all had a great laugh. They were bowing and gave us sweets as a present. I knew now that I would be able to do my old job.

The Martins' room had been decorated for about three days, but we decided that we would let Mr Martin discover it as a surprise. The night before we were due to leave, we were sitting at the table when we heard Mr Martin discovering our handiwork: "My God, who did this? Oh, God. Did you get a decorator in?"

297

Everyone was in stitches laughing. They were so pleased. Mr Martin wanted us to stay in Nova Scotia and said he could get us all the work we needed in New Glasgow. He told us that our work was as good as any professional decorator!

We were sorry to leave the Martins, who had been so kind and welcoming to us. It was our first experience of civilian life for years. One of the girls had taken a shine to Ginger too! We exchanged Christmas cards for many years and I was delighted to receive a Christmas present of beautiful silk ties from them. We would have loved to stay in Canada, but we were desperate to get home and see our families.

We got back to the camp at Truro and clambered into trucks that took us to the Nova Scotian port of Halifax, where we boarded the *Ile de France* liner to sail for Southampton. We were told that we couldn't take bags aboard and that they would be sent on to Scotland. I had to leave all the stuff I had bought in Toronto for my family and all the boots and clothing I had been given by the Americans. I'm still waiting for that bag! I arrived in Southampton with only the Canadian uniform that I had been issued with and a pair of brown boots.

The *Ile de France* was a luxury liner but there were no luxuries for us. In sharp contrast to how we had been treated by the Americans and Canadians, it was a miserable affair. We were reminded that we were British soldiers and were forbidden to mix with the passengers or even to go on deck. The food was poor and there was so little of it that we nicknamed the ship the "Ile de Hunger". We just wanted to get the voyage over with.

It was a cold, slate-grey rainy day when we arrived at Southampton. There was no razzamatazz or welcoming bands. We came down the gangplank to be processed by sour-faced British officials and given our rail warrants to get us back to Scotland.

Only 24 hours to go and we would be back home — at last.

CHAPTER
TEN

Back on Track

It was a long, arduous train journey from Southampton through London and back up to Glasgow. It felt so weird to be back at last. It was a shocker too. The country had been through the mill all right. Ruined buildings and bombsites bore witness to Hitler's blitz and a lot of the buildings looked dowdy and in need of painting.

We rattled and shoogled our way north on the night train, sitting on top of bags in a smoke-filled corridor. As the day broke, we were back in Scotland at last, and, about an hour from Glasgow, we all started to become quite nervous because we didn't know what it was going to be like when we got there. There were hundreds of ex-prisoners on board. A lot of the men were married and were anxious about what kind of welcome they would get. We had been away for more than four and a half years. All of a sudden, the return we had dreamed about became quite scary. I was surprised at how worried I became. It did not seem real. I was not a pretty sight either. I had been through the wars quite literally. My nose was broken, my teeth were smashed, my head had been shaved, my childhood squint had worsened in the camps and the pills that the American doctors had issued had caused me to balloon up in weight. All kinds of thoughts were running through my head. Would there be anybody there to greet me?

The train steamed slowly into Central Station and we were amazed to see the platform thronged with hundreds and hundreds of people. As I descended from the carriage, there were men and women, especially women, running up and down anxiously looking for their loved ones and shouting out names. A lot of them carried photographs and came up to me frantically enquiring, "Do you know my son? Do you know my father? Have you seen my brother?" Sometimes it was sad and some of the women were a bit hysterical. By now, it was well known in Britain that prisoners had suffered terribly at the hands of the Japanese and that many of them would not be coming back. A lot of people were asking about lads that we had left behind, wanting to know what had happened to them.

One woman came up to me with a little picture. "Do you know him? He's my son. Johnny Matthewson."

I studied the smiling young soldier in the picture who looked so different from the shattered skeleton I knew of that name.

"Is he from Springburn?"

"Yes, yes! That's my Johnny."

"I know him, Mrs Matthewson. He's OK, he's OK. I've seen him not long ago. He's coming back on the hospital ship. I was in the camp in Japan with him."

"Oh, thank God. Thank you, son." She scribbled a quick note. "Here's our address. Please come and see us when you can."

Her husband gave me a tight cuddle. Through tears, he said, "Thanks, son. Ah'll be able to get a sleep the night."

There was bedlam on the platform with people screaming, hugging and crying. I stood on the platform in my Canadian uniform with my little bag at my feet, as people desperately searched for their relatives. I saw two chaps walking up and down looking for somebody. They walked past me and then came back again.

When I heard one of them say to the other, "Naw, he's not here. He's not here," I recognised the voice.

"Is that you, Freddie? Is that you?" I asked. My heart soared. It was Freddie Graham and Dunky Wright from the Maryhill Harriers. They had come specially to meet me.

They hugged me. "Oh, Christ, Andy — it's good to see you."

Then a woman walked by and I whispered, "Dunky, that's my mum. It's Maw."

Dunky shouted her over. "Mrs Coogan, Mrs Coogan!"

Mum's hair was streaked with a little more silver now and she walked up to Dunky. "I cannae see him, Dunky. I can't see him anywhere. Maybe he's on another train."

"Here he is, Maw. It's me," I said softly.

She rushed to me and we cried in each other's arms. "Oh, Andrew, Andrew, what have they done to you?"

"Nothing, Maw, nothing. I'm fine. Let's go home. Let's get the tram and go home."

Everyone around me seemed to be in tears. Dunky and Freddie said there was no need for a tram. We got outside the station and there was a big black car waiting for me with a Maryhill Harriers banner on it. We set off for the Gorbals and home to Hospital Street.

When we arrived, it was just amazing. All the neighbours were out, and banners had been stretched between the tenements right up the street with the message: "WELCOME HOME ANDY!" Never did it feel better to be back among "my ain folk". It was the moment I had dreamed of for three and a half years.

My brothers and sister were waiting for me. It was very strange; we were all looking at each other and we all seemed so different. Eddie had a story to tell too. He had been in the navy and, just like our father, had survived being torpedoed. It was a miracle we had both survived the war.

We had a lovely celebration with friends and family, and the next day they held a street party for me. Tables were set up in the street and the children were given whatever goodies that were available under the rationing. I felt shy and embarrassed, and I wasn't sure of myself, but the folk had gone to such trouble to welcome me back that I made a real effort to join in. They were all so happy to have me back but I felt awkward.

For weeks afterwards, I still had my doubts that I was actually home, and as I walked the streets I constantly found myself looking over my shoulder to see if the

Japanese guards were there. I wandered around the Gorbals in a bit of a dream at times. A couple of weeks after my return, I was walking down the street and stopped at the corner of Clelland Street and Hospital Street. I was standing looking up at the street signs when a policeman came along and asked, "Are you all right? Can I help you, lad?"

"Aye. Can you tell me what the name of that street is?"

"That's Hospital Street."

"Thanks. Thank you. I just wanted to be sure. I thought I was imagining things."

The policeman laughed and shook his head as he walked away. I'd thought I was dreaming, because in the camp I'd had dreams when I thought I was home. They were so vivid that it was always a disappointment to wake up and find myself still a prisoner.

I was dreaming at night too. In fact, the nightmares have never left me. Even in my nineties, my sleep is disturbed by the two brutal faces of Tamaki and Suzuki. When I first came home, though, my nightmares were more frequent and very frightening.

One day, my mother said, "You were very warm last night, Andrew. You were sweating. Are you all right? I had to take your sheets away to wash them."

I didn't want her to think that I was having nightmares and never told her. However, one night, I was sitting at the table with my brothers, Eddie, Pat and Frank, when Eddie asked, "Andy, who's Tamaki?"

"Tamaki? How do you know that name?"

304

"Last night, you sat bolt upright in your bed. You were still sleeping but you were shouting, 'You bastard, Tamaki. I'll get you, Tamaki. I'm coming back for you, Tamaki, and you, Suzuki.' Who were they?"

"They were prison guards. I don't want to speak about it."

I knew I wasn't right. Today, they would call it post-traumatic stress but we had no awareness of such a condition in the days and months after the Second World War.

I used to walk round the streets and the places I had known as a younger man, telling myself over and over, "You're all right. You're home. You're all right. You're OK."

I visited the cobbler's shop to see the two Irish brothers who ran it, and they made me feel at home. They had a greyhound, a good dog, and I would sit beside him, stroking him and talking to him — it made me feel welcome. I started taking the dog for walks round the Gorbals, up and down to Gorbals Cross and by Dixon's Blazes, streets that were so familiar, and it brought me back to myself a bit.

The winter of 1945 was very cold and I kept myself busy going to the gas works to collect coke for my mother and the neighbours. I hired the barra from Hyslop's. They gave me bags to put the coke in, and we paid the gas works a shilling a bag for the coke. It was the poor man's fuel and was very difficult to light.

I was sitting around the house a lot, moping and getting under Mum's feet. I was still lacking in confidence and feeling lost.

The nightmares were terrible, and I couldn't stop them. I would wake to find myself sitting bolt upright and soaked in sweat. The effect of the pills had worn off and my weight had plummeted again; I wasn't feeling too well. I saw an Irish doctor, Dr Colville, who arranged for me to attend the Red Cross headquarters in Woodlands Road. They gave me Marmite, powdered eggs and cheese to build me up. Then I was sent to Maryhill Barracks, where the army dentist removed my broken teeth and gave me a set of falsers. I was technically still in the army but was certainly not fit to serve.

One day, Dr Colville came to the house to see how I was. I mentioned the nightmares, and the fact they were becoming a problem. Dr Colville frowned and then said, "Andy, I think the best thing would be for you to get back to running with the Maryhill Harriers again. You can ease yourself in gently and I will keep an eye on you. It would be good for you physically and mentally."

I was very unfit but felt ready to try a little light jogging, so I got in touch with the lads at the Maryhill Harriers. It was the best thing I ever did. All the members of the club took a great interest in me, and most of them hadn't been in the war. Some, like John Emmet Farrel and Gordon Porteous, were top athletes at the time and I was treated as a valued member of the team. They took me out for gentle runs, building me up to a mile and a half, and then declared that was enough. After our run, we would go back to the hall, and Bob Bell had me doing some exercises with the skipping ropes, punch bag and speed bag.

It was painful at first, especially the press-ups, but Bob would say, "Come on, one more, Andy, one more. Come on, you can do it." He'd say, "I'm an old man and I can do it, so you can do it." He was very good with me.

I began to get pretty fit, and eventually Dunky Wright encouraged me to take part and start racing. "Andy, you're getting on really well," he said. "There's only one man to beat now — this lad called Davie Jameson. He's about a year older than you. He's never been in the army but he's very, very good."

"I don't think so, Dunky. I don't think I'll manage."

"You can do it, boy. I'm telling you, you're coming on great." He kept telling me that all the time.

One Saturday afternoon, when I had been home for a good six months, I went out for a run along the canal bank up at Maryhill. I was going very slowly and Jameson was with us.

Bob Bell shouted, "Right, half a mile to go, make for home, everybody!"

When he said to make for home, it was a race from then onwards to the finish. I was in a group and away we went. Jameson had always won during the war while I was away. He was about 20 yards in front when one of my mates urged me on: "Go on, Andy, you can catch him."

I was only interested in finishing, but I caught up with him and he was quite shocked when I overtook him — so was I!

"I told you," Dunky said. "I told you that you would beat him."

It was great to be back.

One day, Jackie Campbell, the lad from upstairs, came down to see me. He was waiting to be demobbed from the RAF.

"Andy, c'mon, let's go dancing this afternoon."

Tuesday afternoon was a half-day in Glasgow and the dance halls were packed out with workers enjoying their time off.

"Naw, I don't feel like it. I'm not sure."

Mum chipped in, "Away ye go, it'll be the best thing for you. It'll get you out the hoose."

So I agreed to go. I went to the wardrobe and borrowed Eddie's sports jacket and a shirt and tie. I got as well dressed as I could. Jackie was in his RAF uniform and looked like one of the Brylcreem boys. We went to the Plaza ballroom, which had one of the best afternoon dances. It was a beautiful place and we stood for a while waiting for a table. Then we got one with two girls sitting at it. Jackie gave them all the patter; he was full of confidence.

One of the girls was called Bessie, and she asked if I had been in the army. I said that I had, but I didn't tell her about being a prisoner. I didn't want to mention it. Her friend caught my eye and I asked her name. She told me that she was called Myra but she didn't seem able to hear me very well. It transpired that she had a hearing problem and was waiting to go in for an operation. She had been this way since she was young.

I sat to one side of her so she could hear me. I got a wee bit more confidence then and we got up to dance.

Myra came from Kilbarchan outside Glasgow. I was able to talk to her about the place, because I had happy memories of going there with the Harriers to run against a well-known athletics club. They took me through all these ploughed fields, and I never forgot it. That got me talking and it helped me to come out of my shell a wee bit. It was her first time at the Plaza and, just like me, her friend had brought her along. She worked as a children's nurse in a nursery. When it came time to go home, we made a loose arrangement to maybe meet again. I was not very forward and a bit shy.

The following week, Jackie asked if I wanted to go back to the Plaza. I said I would and wondered if Myra would be there. Sure enough, the girls were there and we started dancing. I was coming out of my shell a little more and my hair had started to grow in a bit. I was embarrassed, though. I still had to get my eye fixed too and I wore glasses; there were a lot of things I was embarrassed about. It was a cold day, so I had put on my Canadian uniform, which made me look smart. I was thinner too, as the bloating effect of the pills wore off. We talked and talked and got on fine. Eventually, I asked her if she would like to go to the pictures with me. I was thrilled when she said she would. We arranged to meet the next night at Paisley Cross.

On the way there on the tram, I nervously wondered if Myra would turn up, but she was standing waiting there for me. We went to a little place called the Royal Oak for a cup of tea because she had been standing for a while. Then we went to the pictures to see *Gone with the Wind*.

We enjoyed it and we got speaking a wee bit more. I got her on the bus to Kilbarchan and took her home. We said goodnight on the doorstep of her family's cottage, which was on a smallholding. Before I made my way back home to Glasgow, I asked her when we would see each other again. Myra said that she wasn't sure, as she was waiting to go into hospital. So we didn't have a firm arrangement, but I said that I hoped that we would meet up again at the dancing and we exchanged addresses.

I was still in the army and had to have a medical before being discharged. The army doctor told me he had made arrangements for me to have my squint fixed at Cowglen Military Hospital.

I was in there a week before I got my operation. During that period, they didn't let me out of the hospital, but I enjoyed being there. I was kept busy, cleaning the floors and the toilets of the huts, which were full of wounded and injured men from the war. The nurses were good fun and I had a good laugh with them — it made me feel better. They kept me for a good fortnight, and one evening my brothers Frank and Pat came up with a letter for me from Myra, asking why I had never written to her. I lost her address and all I knew was that she lived in Kilbarchan. Myra was a Presbyterian and I was a Catholic, so I had wondered if that was why she hadn't written to me. Now here she was asking how I was getting on and telling me that she was in Victoria Hospital, having an operation on her

310

ear. The hospital was only about 20 minutes from where I was.

"Great, it's from Myra," I told Frank and Pat. "She's not forgotten me."

"Well, you'd better go and see her," they said.

I didn't know what to do and told a young nurse.

"Why don't you go and see her, Andy?" she said, then joked, "If she doesn't want you, I'll take you."

She was a great character and offered to help me. She showed me the room where my uniform was kept, and the next day she organised a lift in the van that went between the two hospitals twice a day. I got up to Victoria Hospital and went into the ward. There was Myra lying in bed all bandaged up and kind of dazed.

"Hello, Myra, how are you feeling?"

She had to take her time to recognise me because my eyes were bloodshot from my operation. She was very weak and tired after her operation, but she seemed more interested in how I was. I said how pleased I was to see her again and sat a good hour with her. When a nurse came up and said that my lift had arrived, I just held her hand and said, "I will come back and see you, Myra."

It was the real start of our relationship, and after that I went up to see her every second night; on the other nights, Frank and Pat visited her. They were always full of fun and she looked forward to seeing them.

On my regular visits to Myra's bedside, I met her mother, a tall, well-dressed lady who wore a hat and had her hair in a bun at the back. She thanked me for coming to see Myra and encouraged me to keep coming.

We started courting properly when Myra got out of hospital. I would go to Kilbarchan on a Sunday night for a sing-song. Myra's brother-in-law was a fiddler and her sister was a pianist. Myra was good on the piano too and we were all soon singing. They always wanted me to sing "Rowan Tree". I hadn't sung it since those dark days in Changi prison camp, when instead of a warm family singing along, it was hundreds of ill and homesick Scottish soldiers. The family were really good to me and made me feel welcome. We would walk into the hills above Kilbarchan. Up at the top, there was a wee cottage with a restaurant in one of the rooms where we could get a boiled egg and toast. We used to go over to a stone well where there was a wee image of a hare. They were really nice walks.

We spent a lot of our courting at the pictures or the theatre. I would meet Myra off the bus and we would go to the pictures in Paisley or to the Glasgow Empire or Metropole. We saw a lot of comedians like Danny Kaye, Tommy Morgan and Jack Radcliffe, whose sketches we had re-created in the camps. It was great; you got a laugh at these guys and there was no vulgarity. They were really good comedians. As soon as Jack Radcliffe came onto the stage, he would say, "Is Dunky Wright here tonight? You tell him I'll take him on any time he likes for two miles — any time."

Jack Radcliffe was a skinny wee crater! He would come out dressed as a boxer and it made you laugh right away. Then they started singing and before you knew it you were all singing along with them.

There was a big religious divide at the time, but we were too keen on each other to let religion get between us; in the prison camps, we were all the same. It was a bit of a worry because the priests were dead against marrying outside the Catholic faith. I went to tell my mother that we wanted to get engaged.

She was pleased for me and said, "That's great, Andrew. Myra is a really nice girl."

"Are you not worried that she's not a Catholic?"

"It doesn't worry me at all. She's a lovely girl. You're not marrying a priest or a minister."

By this time, all of us brothers had a trade. Eddie's time was up as a bricklayer and he decided to start a new life in Australia. Pat was a plasterer and tiler, and young Frank was serving his time as a plumber. My sister Betty had married my friend Alex Weir, a marathon runner with the Maryhill Harriers, and they had two children. Alex had been in the navy and was just demobbed too.

Everything was going fine for my mother. We wanted to build her a house, but she wouldn't have it, as she wanted to stay in the Gorbals near all her pals.

Myra and I set a date to get married and we tied the knot on 31 March 1947 at the Co-operative Halls in Paisley, where Myra's minister performed the ceremony. Things were still on ration and most of the guests who came gave extra to get stuff for the wedding. We had a wonderful night. We had a band playing, and I forgot I was married — I was dancing all the time with everybody. Myra's friend Bessie, who was our bridesmaid, came up and said, "It's time you were away. Myra's ready to go."

We finished up in the Ivanhoe Hotel in Buchanan Street. The next day, we went to Largs on the Ayrshire coast, where we stayed in a boarding house run by two old spinsters who were forever trying to sell us things they made. We hired bicycles to tour around and had a wonderful honeymoon.

I was beginning to feel better; my spell at Cowglen Hospital helping out with the cleaning and larking about with the nurses had been beneficial. Meeting Myra and her family and getting married had been good for me too. More than anything, though, it was getting back to the running with the Maryhill Harriers that helped me start to feel normal.

When I was demobbed from the army, I received my back pay — and all thoughts of pig farms and new beginnings were shelved. I was paid 75 pounds for my years of jungle fighting and slavery as a prisoner. Deductions were made for our "keep" — we had to pay for all those maggoty bowls of rice! To add insult to injury, apparently when we joined up with the 11th Indian Division, we were put on lower Indian army wages — but were still subject to British taxes! I didn't dwell on the injustice of it and simply wanted to get on with rebuilding my life.

On the other side of the world, other accounts were being settled. The majority of Japanese war criminals were never prosecuted, but a few notables were. Strangely enough, they had not died the warrior's death of the so-called bushido code or committed suicide as required. They had surrendered and been taken prisoner — just as we had been. General Fukuye, who had ordered the execution of the four prisoners at Selarang, was given a trial and then taken to the same spot where he had executed the young Australian and English escapees and was shot. Tamaki and Suzuki had been lucky to survive their capture by Chinese prisoners who beat them almost to death. They were tried in the Hong Kong war-crimes trial of 1946. Tamaki was sentenced to fifteen years and Suzuki got off very lightly with ten years.

Luckily, I got a job with Glasgow Council and they started me right away. They sent me to a big housing scheme called Knightswood to do maintenance on the houses. The windows and doors had been neglected during the war and badly needed painting. There were about five or six painters and I was one of the youngest blokes there. I enjoyed working with the lads; it was good for me.

One day, when I was working on a house, I said to the lady who lived there, "Missus, that's a beautiful garden. I don't want to put my ladder among your bonny flowers. If you don't mind, I'll take my shoes off and I'll come up and paint your window from the inside."

She said that would be fine. So I went in the front door and took my shoes off. I was wearing a pair of white overalls, which were very clean. I went up the stairs and she said, "This is the bedroom and my son is in his bed, if you don't mind."

I went in and saw the lad lying in his bed. "Sorry to bother you," I said.

"No bother," he murmured.

"I'm gonna paint your window but I won't keep it open too long."

I put a sheet down and sat on the window to paint it. I told him I would be back the next day to give it a second coat.

"Thank you very much," he said.

"I won't bother you tomorrow much."

Then I went downstairs and I said to his mother, "I'm sorry I had to bother you. What's wrong with the lad?"

"He's not been right since he came back. He was a prisoner of the Japanese."

"So was I. Where was he?"

"He was in Singapore and Formosa."

"Do you mind if I go up and see him?"

I nipped back up the stairs and went into the bedroom. "Excuse me, your mother has just told me you were a prisoner of the Japanese. I was too. Which regiment were you with?"

"The Lanarkshire Yeomanry."

"Christ, so was I."

He sat up and completely brightened up. We talked and talked, and I forgot I was meant to be painting. His mum brought up a tray with cups of tea and sandwiches.

As his mum showed me out, I told her that we had enjoyed a good blether and got on fine together.

"That's marvellous," she said. "He's never been really right since he got back and he takes terrible nightmares."

"I hope he gets better. Thanks for the tea and sandwiches. What did your son work at?"

"He worked for a variety agent in West Nile Street. It was Harry Collins. He booked all the turns for the Empire. He was a good athlete too and was a runner."

"Wait a minute, missus."

I went upstairs to see the lad again. "Did you work for Harry Collins? Were ye with the Garscube Harriers?"

"Aye."

"Do you remember the painter who was painting the room when a wee man came in with a bowler hat and a navy-blue suit. I said, 'Who's that man?' and you said, 'That's Harry Lauder.' Do you remember the painter?"

"Jesus, it cannae be. That's amazing. Are you the lad from Maryhill that ran against Wooderson?"

"Aye, that's me."

We laughed, and his mum was smiling. "Honest to God," she said. "That's the brightest he's been since he came back."

After that, I called in regularly to see him and brought a couple of pals from the Harriers too. I think it helped him.

After the war, I made an effort to keep up with some of the lads; some of them were pleased to see me and one or two others didn't want to speak about our time in the camps. Gradually, we all went our separate ways and got on with our lives.

I had a job in Glasgow but no house. There was a terrible housing problem in the city after the war, and it was very difficult for young couples. We managed to get a wee furnished room in a house in Paisley, but the owner needed the room back for his son. Myra's sister came to the rescue. She had a big house in Bournemouth and we took the top flat. There was plenty of work in Bournemouth and we enjoyed ourselves there. I worked in a lot of hotels and we were able to get cheese and eggs, things that were normally rationed.

However, while I was in Bournemouth, I missed an important visitor to the Gorbals. One day, my mother heard a knock at the door in Hospital Street and opened it to find an Irish priest on the doorstep: Father Kennedy. He was sorry to have missed me but left an envelope for me with ten pounds in it. He said to my mother, "Tell Andy this is his unpaid wages."

I was very disappointed not to see Father Kennedy. He didn't leave an address but I wrote to him via the Jesuits in Dublin and returned the ten pounds. He was very generous but I wanted the money to go to the Jesuits. I heard later that Father Kennedy had gone round to all of us after the war before returning to the Far East. He used an inheritance to set up a school for poor children and died as the Bishop of Hong Kong in 1983.

After about six months in Bournemouth, Myra became pregnant with our son Andy and wanted to return to Scotland. She had two elderly aunts, who were both very religious, in Monifieth on the east coast in Angus. Myra was fond of her aunties and we went up there to stay with them for a bit until we got settled. Myra was booked into the Westbay Nursing Home in Monifieth to give birth. I was lucky; Myra's sister Laura worked on the railway in Bournemouth and got me free passes in the name of Sergeant Smith. I got the train from Bournemouth to Monifieth, changing at London, but was worried the whole time in case I got found out.

I found it quite easy to find a job back in Scotland. At Broughty Ferry, a seaside suburb of Dundee, I got a job through a paint shop run by a Mr Low.

For my first job, Mr Low took me to a big house in West Ferry and introduced me to Mrs Goodfellow, whose family owned a well-known bakery. She made me feel very welcome and even gave me a wee dram to welcome me to the area. I ended up doing a lot of painting and papering at their house. They were pleased with the work, and I got on well with Mrs Goodfellow, who was a kindly person. I was working in her house when Myra was taken into Westbay Nursing Home to have our first child. Mrs Goodfellow had a phone in the house, and, as she watched me painting, she would say, "No word yet, painter, no word yet." Then at last she announced, "Right, you'd better get cleaned up and away along to see your son."

She gave me a beautiful bouquet of flowers for Myra and a big box of every kind of cake you could mention for the ward. She also gave me a big parcel of baby clothes. It was so good of her.

We were looking for a place of our own when I spotted an advert in the local paper for a furnished

319

cottage in Carnoustie. I went along to see the solicitor who was renting out the property. It was expensive and the rent would be a struggle, but we were desperate for a place, so I signed the agreement.

As I got up to go, I thought the lawyer looked familiar. "Excuse me, sir, were you ever in Malaya?" I asked.

He looked surprised. "Yes, I was — during the war."

"Were you with the Gurkhas?"

"Yes."

"Do you remember the signaller who dished out the biscuits and cigarettes to your troops?"

"My God! Sit down, sit down."

We had a great chat and he tore up the rental agreement and issued a new one at half the price! When I told him I was a self-employed painter, he got me loads of work on estate cottages and the like. It was a great start, and if people were too slow in paying me, he would write them a stern lawyer's letter!

Carnoustie had another amazing coincidence to offer me. One day, I was walking along the main street of the town when I spotted a familiar figure. I could not believe my eyes and did a double take at the man standing in the doorway of the YMCA.

"Is that you, Jack?" I asked in disbelief.

"Jackie Coogan! What the hell are you doing here?" Jack Scott was as incredulous as I was.

"I live here."

"So do I! I work here in the YMCA as the caretaker and I coach some of the youngsters in boxing."

There was no more work that day. Jack got out his scrapbook and we talked about the Gorbals. We spoke for hours about boxing, running, people we knew and people he had chased. Jack invited me to his house, and that night I went up to see him. He apologised for the state of the place, as he was just doing it up. I told him not to do any more. Every evening, I went round to Jack's house and stripped all the walls for him and painted and papered the house. He was delighted with the job. When I finished, I told him, "This is something I've owed you for many years, Jack. I'll never forget the time you put the ten bob on the table to take me up to Maryhill Harriers. Well, there you go."

I was back on the right track in Carnoustie. My daughters Christine and Jean followed Andy into the world. Dunky Wright had advised me to keep up the running and to pass on my love for the sport by coaching others.

In 1948, soon after arriving in Carnoustie, I started up Tayside Amateur Athletics Club (TAAC). I put up notices, let local headteachers and the council know about it, and cycled round local businesses asking them for support. There was plenty of interest and just about all of them supported me by donating money and trophies. The council gave us the use of a park with a track near the seaside and a clubroom for changing and storing our apparatus. Our colours were a royal-blue vest with a black T on the front and black shorts. TAAC was soon thriving and membership grew very quickly. We got properly constituted and registered with the Scottish Amateur Athletic Association. We found a

321

secretary and a happy bunch of parents who all joined in. I remembered what I had been taught by Bob Bell and Dunky Wright, their training routines and their constant talk about "using your head and your physical assets". I passed on Dunky's great advice to me: "Run on your toes, always run on your toes." I put what I had learned from them into practice, having fun and keeping the athletes keen and interested. Athletes joined from all over Angus and Dundee, some travelling quite a distance for our training on Tuesday and Thursday evenings and Sunday afternoons.

When we first started, the existing track in Monifieth was overgrown and dangerous for running, and we needed to get a proper running track if we were going to get serious. So I approached a local factory and asked them if they could dump a lorry full of cinders, and then asked all members to turn up with their garden rakes and spades. They soon set to, shovelling out the cinders round the track. Then we got a couple of old bedsprings, tied them together, attached ropes and the lads hauled the springs over the cinders to sift out bigger stones and level out the cinders. At the end of the week, everyone had helped out and we had a track — the only athletics track between Glasgow and Aberdeen. Next, I got an old council building that had been set aside as a morgue for civilian casualties in the war. We painted it up and now we had a clubhouse.

At the time, many people didn't approve of sport on the Sabbath, and so I went round the local ministers to ask if they had any objection to my organising meetings on a Sunday. None of them did and so we set up the

North Eastern League. It was a great success. Clubs from all over Scotland started to compete and we were travelling in buses to competitions nearly every weekend.

TAAC had some first-class runners, some of whom ran for Scotland in the Commonwealth Games (in 1958, Doris Tyndall ran in the 100 yards and 220 yards in Cardiff, and, in 1966, Barbara Lyall ran the 220 yards in Jamaica). Over the years, there were dozens of very good runners competing at all levels and in all age groups. The club ran for well over 40 years and became my main interest in life. In later years, I was training youngsters who'd been brought along by their mums and dads, and I'd trained them too! I won a gold medal in the Commonwealth seniors for the 800 metres at the age of 75 and kept running well into my eighties, competing in the veterans' meetings, which were always great fun, although deadly serious.

In the wonderful surroundings of Carnoustie links, I also took up golf and enjoyed playing on one of the world's best courses. I also caddied for many years, and it was as a caddy that I had one of my most memorable golfing moments.

One day, I was asked to caddy for some VIPs that were to be brought over from the Royal and Ancient Golf Club of St Andrews. Naturally, I was delighted. I was a wee bit surprised when the party that turned up consisted of R&A bigwigs and the Japanese ambassador to Britain, along with the Japanese consul to Scotland. I was to caddy for the ambassador, but I quickly pointed out that he had one club too many in his bag.

As I counted out his clubs in Japanese, I glanced at the R&A officials. Their eyes were widening. They knew that there was only one way that a Scotsman of my generation could speak Japanese. They guessed that I had been a prisoner and were obviously concerned. The treatment we had received as prisoners was well known in Scotland. They looked at each other in mounting panic, expecting the most undiplomatic of incidents as I carried on in Japanese.

When I finished, the ambassador piped up, "You speak Japanese very well. Where did you learn Japanese?"

I looked at him for a moment and thought of "Doc" Sweeney, Charlie Farmer, Tammy Donnelly, Willie "Tubby" Daly and all the other young men murdered by the starvation, slavery and suffering imposed on us by the Japanese Imperial Army.

Then I replied quietly, "I was in Japan — on my holidays."

As we walked onto the course, one of the gentlemen from the R&A whispered, "Thank you, Mr Coogan. Thank you."

He had no need to thank me. I have always believed that bitterness and hatred are self-destructive emotions. I forgive the Japanese people but I cannot forget the awful cruelty of the Japanese army.

Most of all, I do not forget the amazing self-sacrifice and comradeship of a group of ordinary lads who found themselves in extraordinary circumstances and who got each other through it — the men of the Lanarkshire Yeomanry.

EPILOGUE

Thanks to the Reverend Paul Grant for the following words.

War is not a word
But a smell, a fear in the gut,
A bloodstain on a shirt,
A shovel digging a friend's grave,
A wound that stampedes through dreams

I lived through war but will never understand its
    nature,
Taken fresh from my trade and running track, our
family table,
From a Saturday night's carefree dancing
And suddenly asked to kill strangers
And risk being killed by them

How many birthdays passed
Not among those who raised me,
Running the street and kicking a ball,
How many birthdays passed
Laying cables and screaming warnings

Getting through the hell of another day
In Japanese captivity

I left my kin behind and found another family:
The men I served with.
That comradeship was the last candle left
In the dark and brutal night in Japanese captivity.
But it brought enough light to know that
We were decent human beings

The light came from sharing the little there was to
    live on,
The light risked bearing the burden of a sick friend,
The light fed our spirit to go on living,
To never give up

So for every kindness planted in the camp's barren
    ground,
For every seed of gentleness sown in brutal soil,
Whenever the miracle of a smile could still be found
A true victory was won
That no jackboot, or roar or bullet could defeat

Those years live deep within us;
They rise up like ghosts in the lawlessness of dreams
The thirst, the smell, the humidity and hunger,
The fear and shadow of death
My pals that never made it back
But who came home in my heart

We were told never to name those terrible years;
It was a continued brutality
To send us lads to war
And then not allow us to speak of it.
But then, how do you describe hell to someone who
has never been?

I salute my comrades, I honour the lives of those who
brought back
Broken pieces of who they were,
And slowly tried hard to see themselves once
more

As son, father, husband, brother,
Yet always there on the mirror
Was the deep scar of being a survivor

I honour my friends in sport and the people of the
Gorbals
Who will never know how they sustained me;
I honour my mother and father and my brothers and
sister
And the affection of my family

Please God, we shall all find a final healing
Where not one of the lambs
Who were left behind
Shall ever be lost again.

This epilogue is taken from a fuller address given by
the Reverend Paul Grant of St Ninian's Church,

Stonehouse, Lanarkshire on 12 February 2012, in a poignant remembrance service held to honour the men of the Lanarkshire Yeomanry.

Also available in ISIS Large Print:

Wings

Patrick Bishop

The Royal Air Force is synonymous with its heroic achievements in the summer of 1940, when Winston Churchill's "famous few" held Göering's Luftwaffe at bay in the Battle of Britain, thereby changing the course of the war. For much of the 20th century, warplanes were fixed in the world's imagination, a symbol of the modern era. But within the space of a hundred years, military aviation has morphed from the exotic to the mundane. An activity which was charged with danger is now carried out by computers and unpiloted drones.

Aviators have always seemed different from soldiers and sailors — more adventurous, questing and imaginative. In both world wars air aces dominated each side's propaganda, capturing hearts and dreams. Writing with verve, passion and sheer narrative aplomb, Patrick Bishop brings us a rich and compelling account of military flying from its heroic early days to the present.

ISBN 978-0-7531-5326-0 (hb)
ISBN 978-0-7531-5327-7 (pb)

Behind Enemy Lines

Sir Tommy Macpherson with Richard Bath

With three Military Crosses, three Croix de Guerre, a Légion d'honneur and a papal knighthood for his heroics during the Second World War, Sir Tommy Macpherson is the most decorated soldier in the history of the British Army.

Yet for 65 years, the Highlander's story has remained untold. Few know how, aged 21, he persuaded 23,000 SS soldiers of the feared SS Das Reich tank column to surrender, or how Tommy almost single-handedly stopped Tito's Yugoslavia annexing the whole of north-east Italy.

Still a schoolboy when war broke out, Tommy quickly matured into a legendary commando. Twice captured, he escaped both times, marching through hundreds of miles of German-held territory to get home. With a dizzyingly diverse cast of characters, *Behind Enemy Lines* is an astonishing story of how an ordinary boy came to achieve truly extraordinary feats.

ISBN 978-0-7531-5283-6 (hb)
ISBN 978-0-7531-5284-3 (pb)

Hero of the Fleet

William Stone

William Stone died on Saturday 10th January 2009 aged 108. He received a hero's funeral. Born in rural Devon, he joined the navy during the First World War, travelled the globe just before the British Empire's light began to fade and saw action in some of the most significant sea battles of the Second World War. Afterwards, he returned to Devon to run a barber's shop, an altogether more peaceable existence.

Through his years of retirement, he tended his garden, unaware that celebrity was stalking him. As time passed, he became one of a dwindling number of men who served in the Great War. This meant that for some of the most momentous anniversaries clocked up recently — including the 90th anniversary of the end of the First World War — William was a guest of honour. This is his astonishing story.

ISBN 978-0-7531-5247-8 (hb)
ISBN 978-0-7531-5248-5 (pb)

Kitchener's Last Volunteer

Henry Allingham with Dennis Goodwin

[Allingham's] recollections are more striking for being so understated and unburnished **The Times**

Allingham tells his story simply, fluently and modestly **Telegraph**

Henry Allingham is the last British serviceman alive to have volunteered for active duty in the First World War. He vividly recaptures life in the Edwardian era and how it was altered irrevocably by the Great War, and the subsequent coming of the modern age. Henry is unique in that he saw action on land, sea and in the air with the British Naval Air Service. He was present at the Battle of Jutland in 1916 and went on to serve on the Western Front. In recent years, Henry was given the opportunity to tell his remarkable story to a wider audience through a BBC documentary, and he has since become a hero to many, meeting royalty and receiving many honours such as the Legion d'honneur — France's highest accolade.

ISBN 978-0-7531-8290-1 (hb)
ISBN 978-0-7531-8291-8 (pb)

World War One

Norman Stone

In 1914, dynamic, prosperous countries across Europe at last mobilised the vast armies they had spent years preparing. Each nation was confident of victory. Instead Europe destroyed itself.

The First World War remains the fundamental tragedy that still haunts us all nearly a century after its outbreak. It was a war that baffled those who fought it: what was meant to be a grab for imperial loot or a settling of scores turned into a nightmare with millions of men killed by hideous technologies.

Ultimately, almost all the principal states engaged in the war were ruined, with even the notional winners irreparably damaged: the loot proved worthless and the world was doomed to an even more terrible settling of scores only 20 years later.

World War One: A Short History is a brilliantly written, often very witty account, which makes a familiar story fresh and surprising.

ISBN 978-0-7531-5681-0 (hb)
ISBN 978-0-7531-5682-7 (pb)

Isis publish a wide range of books in large print, from fiction to biography. Any suggestions for books you would like to see in large print or audio are always welcome. Please send to the Editorial Department at:

Isis Publishing Limited
7 Centremead
Osney Mead
Oxford OX2 0ES

A full list of titles is available free of charge from:

Ulverscroft Large Print Books Limited

(UK)
The Green
Bradgate Road, Anstey
Leicester LE7 7FU
Tel: (0116) 236 4325

(Australia)
P.O. Box 314
St Leonards
NSW 1590
Tel: (02) 9436 2622

(USA)
P.O. Box 1230
West Seneca
N.Y. 14224-1230
Tel: (716) 674 4270

(Canada)
P.O. Box 80038
Burlington
Ontario L7L 6B1
Tel: (905) 637 8734

(New Zealand)
P.O. Box 456
Feilding
Tel: (06) 323 6828

Details of **Isis** complete and unabridged audio books are also available from these offices. Alternatively, contact your local library for details of their collection of **Isis** large print and unabridged audio books.